GLENCOE

The AMERICAN VISION

Reading Essentials and Note-Taking Guide

STUDENT WORKBOOK

McGraw Hill Glencoe

New York, New York Columbus, Ohio Chicago, Illinois Woodland Hills, California

To the Student

The *American Vision* **Reading Essentials and Note-Taking Guide** is designed to help you use recognized reading strategies to improve your reading-for-information skills. For each section of the student textbook, you are alerted to key content. Then, you are asked to draw from prior knowledge, organize your thoughts with a graphic organizer, and follow a process to read and understand the text. The **Reading Essentials and Note-Taking Guide** was prepared to help you get more from your textbook by reading with a purpose.

The McGraw·Hill Companies

Glencoe

Send all inquiries to:
Glencoe/McGraw-Hill
8787 Orion Place
Columbus, OH 43240

ISBN: 978-0-07-878438-5
MHID: 0-07-878438-7

Printed in the United States of America.
7 8 9 10 11 HES 14 13 12 11

Table of Contents

Chapter 1: Colonizing America: Prehistory to 1754
Section 1: North America Before Columbus....1
Section 2: Europe Begins to Explore....4
Section 3: Founding the Thirteen Colonies....8
Section 4: Economics, Trade, and Rebellion....11
Section 5: A Diverse Society....14

Chapter 2: The American Revolution, 1754–1783
Section 1: The Colonies Fight for Their Rights....17
Section 2: The Revolution Begins....20
Section 3: The War for Independence....23
Section 4: The War Changes American Society....26

Chapter 3: Creating a Constitution, 1781–1789
Section 1: The Confederation....29
Section 2: A New Constitution....32
Section 3: Ratifying the Constitution....35

Chapter 4: Federalists and Republicans, 1789–1816
Section 1: Washington and Congress....38
Section 2: Partisan Politics....41
Section 3: Jefferson in Office....44
Section 4: The War of 1812....47

Chapter 5: Growth and Division, 1816–1832
Section 1: American Nationalism....50
Section 2: Early Industry....53
Section 3: The Land of Cotton....56
Section 4: Growing Sectionalism....59

Chapter 6: The Spirit of Reform, 1828–1845
Section 1: Jacksonian America....62
Section 2: A Changing Culture....66
Section 3: Reforming Society....69
Section 4: The Abolitionist Movement....72

Chapter 7: Manifest Destiny, 1820–1848
Section 1: The Western Pioneers....75
Section 2: The Hispanic Southwest....78
Section 3: Independence for Texas....80
Section 4: The War With Mexico....83

Chapter 8: Sectional Conflict Intensifies, 1848–1860
Section 1: Slavery and Western Expansion....87
Section 2: The Crisis Deepens....90
Section 3: The Union Dissolves....93

Chapter 9: The Civil War, 1861–1865
Section 1: The Opposing Sides 96
Section 2: The Early Stages 99
Section 3: Life During the War 102
Section 4: The Turning Point 105
Section 5: The War Ends 108

Chapter 10: Reconstruction, 1865–1877
Section 1: The Debate Over Reconstruction 111
Section 2: Republican Rule 113
Section 3: Reconstruction Collapses 117

Chapter 11: Settling the West, 1865–1890
Section 1: Miners and Ranchers 120
Section 2: Farming the Plains 123
Section 3: Native Americans 126

Chapter 12: Industrialization, 1865–1901
Section 1: The Rise of Industry 129
Section 2: The Railroads 132
Section 3: Big Business 135
Section 4: Unions 138

Chapter 13: Urban America, 1865–1896
Section 1: Immigration 141
Section 2: Urbanization 144
Section 3: The Gilded Age 147
Section 4: Populism 150
Section 5: The Rise of Segregation 153

Chapter 14: Becoming a World Power, 1872–1917
Section 1: The Imperialist Vision 156
Section 2: The Spanish-American War 159
Section 3: New American Diplomacy 162

Chapter 15: The Progressive Movement, 1890–1920
Section 1: The Roots of Progressivism 165
Section 2: Roosevelt and Taft 168
Section 3: The Wilson Years 171

Chapter 16: World War I and Its Aftermath, 1914–1920
Section 1: The United States Enters World War I 174
Section 2: The Home Front 177
Section 3: A Bloody Conflict 180
Section 4: The War's Impact 183

Chapter 17: The Jazz Age, 1921–1929
Section 1: The Politics of the 1920s 186
Section 2: A Growing Economy 189
Section 3: A Clash of Values 192
Section 4: Cultural Innovations 195
Section 5: African American Culture 198

Chapter 18: The Great Depression Begins, 1929–1932
Section 1: The Causes of the Great Depression 201
Section 2: Life During the Depression 204
Section 3: Hoover Responds to the Depression 207

Chapter 19: Roosevelt and the New Deal, 1933–1941
Section 1: The First New Deal 210
Section 2: The Second New Deal 214
Section 3: The New Deal Coalition 217

Chapter 20: A World in Flames, 1931–1941
Section 1: America and the World 220
Section 2: World War II Begins 223
Section 3: The Holocaust 226
Section 4: America Enters the War 229

Chapter 21: America and World War II, 1941–1945
Section 1: Mobilizing for War 232
Section 2: The Early Battles 235
Section 3: Life on the Home Front 238
Section 4: Pushing Back the Axis 241
Section 5: The War Ends 244

Chapter 22: The Cold War Begins, 1945–1960
Section 1: The Origins of the Cold War 247
Section 2: The Early Cold War Years 250
Section 3: The Cold War and American Society 253
Section 4: Eisenhower's Cold War Policies 256

Chapter 23: Postwar America, 1945–1960
Section 1: Truman and Eisenhower 259
Section 2: The Affluent Society 262
Section 3: The Other Side of American Life 265

Chapter 24: The New Frontier and the Great Society, 1961–1968
Section 1: The New Frontier 268
Section 2: JFK and the Cold War 271
Section 3: The Great Society 274

Chapter 25: The Civil Rights Movement, 1954–1968
Section 1: The Movement Begins 277
Section 2: Challenging Segregation 280
Section 3: New Civil Rights Issues 283

Chapter 26: The Vietnam War, 1954–1975
Section 1: Going to War in Vietnam 284
Section 2: Vietnam Divides the Nation 289
Section 3: The War Winds Down 292

Chapter 27: The Politics of Protest, 1960–1980
Section 1: Students and the Counterculture 295
Section 2: The Feminist Movement 298
Section 3: Latino Americans Organize 301

Chapter 28: Politics and Economics, 1968–1980
Section 1: The Nixon Administration....304
Section 2: The Watergate Scandal....307
Section 3: Ford and Carter....310
Section 4: New Approaches to Civil Rights....313
Section 5: Environmentalism....316

Chapter 29: Resurgence of Conservatism, 1980–1992
Section 1: The New Conservatism....319
Section 2: The Reagan Years....322
Section 3: Life in the 1980s....325
Section 4: The End of the Cold War....328

Chapter 30: A Time of Change, 1980–2000
Section 1: The Technological Revolution....331
Section 2: The Clinton Years....334
Section 3: A New Wave of Immigration....337
Section 4: An Interdependent World....340

Chapter 31: A New Century Begins, 2001–Present
Section 1: America Enters a New Century....343
Section 2: The War on Terrorism Begins....346
Section 3: The Invasion of Iraq....349
Section 4: A Time of Challenges....352

North America Before Columbus

Big Idea

As you read pages 4–11 in your textbook, complete the graphic organizer by filling in the names of Native American groups who settled in various regions.

Region	Native American Groups
Mesoamerica	1.
North America Southwest	2.
North America Midwest	3.
North America Northeast	4.

Notes | Read to Learn

Mesoamerican Cultures *(page 4)*

Comparing and Contrasting

List one detail about the Olmec and one about the Aztec. Then list one trait they shared.

Olmec: ____________

____

Aztec: ____________

____

Both: ____________

____

____

Scientists think the first humans arrived in the Americas between 15,000 and 30,000 years ago. The last Ice Age created a land bridge between Alaska and Asia, known as Beringia. Scientists think that people from Asia may have crossed this land bridge as they hunted large animals. Their descendents learned to plant and raise crops in Mesoamerica. This **agricultural revolution** made possible the rise of America's first civilizations.

Anthropologists think that the Olmec people created America's first civilization between 1500 and 1200 B.C. The Olmec built large villages and pyramids. Olmec ideas spread throughout Mesoamerica. The Maya culture emerged around A.D. 200. The Maya had a talent for engineering and mathematics. By the 1500s, the last Mayan cities were in decline. Further north, the Toltec people built a large city called Tula. These master builders were invaded by the Chichimec around the year 1200. One group of Chichimec began calling themselves the Aztec. This group expanded into a great empire by conquering neighboring cities. They controlled trade in the region. They also demanded payment, or **tribute,** from the cities they conquered.

Notes

Read to Learn

Western Cultures *(page 6)*

Identifying the Main Idea

Write the main idea of the passage.

Many anthropologists think that farming technology spread north into the American Southwest. The Hohokam people lived in what is now Arizona from about A.D. 300 to the 1300s. The intricate system of irrigation canals they built enabled them to farm corn, beans, and squash.

The Anasazi lived in the Four Corners area of the American Southwest. Some Anasazi living in Chaco Canyon built large multi-storied buildings of adobe and cut stone. They contained ceremonial rooms called **kivas.** Early Spanish explorers called these large buildings **pueblos.** By the 1300s, the pueblos had been abandoned. The Zuni, Hopi, and other Pueblo peoples also lived in the Southwest and were descendents of the Anasazi and Hohokam. Corn was a major part of their diet, and they also farmed squash and beans. Between 1200 and 1500, the Apache and Navajo moved into this region.

Many groups of peoples lived along the Pacific coast. In the north, the Tlingit, Haida, and others relied on the forests and the coastal waters rich in fish for survival. The Pomo and other peoples lived in what is today central California. They hunted wildlife and enjoyed mild weather. When meat was scarce, the Pomo picked acorns, which they made into flour.

Mississippian Culture and Its Descendants *(page 8)*

Making Inferences

Make an inference about why some western plains people became nomads.

Between A.D. 700 and 900, farming technology and better strains of maize and beans spread north from Mexico and up the Mississippi River. The Mississippian culture emerged around this time. The Mississippians were great builders. Cahokia, one of their largest cities, was home to 16,000 people and more than 100 flat-topped pyramids and mounds.

Almost all the peoples in the American Southeast lived in towns. The Cherokee were the largest group in the Southeast, living in what is today North Carolina and Tennessee. Other peoples living in the Southeast included the Choctaw, Chickasaw, Natchez, and Creek.

Around 1500, the peoples of the western plains abandoned their villages and farm fields and became nomads. Peoples in the East, including the Pawnee, Kansas, and Iowa, continued to farm as well as hunt. Life for the Sioux and other Great Plains peoples changed after they began taming horses. The Spanish brought horses to North America, and the animals eventually reached the Great Plains. The Sioux soon became some of the world's greatest mounted hunters and warriors.

Notes | Read to Learn

Northeastern Peoples *(page 10)*

Determining Cause and Effect

List the cause.

Cause:

____

____

____

Effect: Five nations formed the Iroquois Confederacy.

Almost all Native Americans in the Eastern Woodlands hunted, fished, and farmed. Most peoples in the Northeast spoke Algonquian or Iroquoian languages. Algonquian-speaking peoples included the Wampanoag, Narragansett, and Pequot. The peoples of the Northeast practiced slash-and-burn farming. They lived in several kinds of houses. These included long-houses and wigwams.

The Iroquoian-speaking peoples lived in what is today New York and parts of Canada. Among them were the Huron, Neutral, Erie, Wenro, Seneca, Cayuga, Onondaga, Oneida, and Mohawk. All these peoples shared a similar way of life. In the late 1500s, five nations formed what is now called the Iroquois Confederacy to maintain peace and provide defense against their common enemy, the Huron.

Section Wrap-up

Answer these questions to check your understanding of the entire section.

1. How do scientists think the earliest Americans migrated from Asia to North America?

____

____

2. What factors led to the emergence of civilizations along the Mississippi River?

____

____

Descriptive Writing

In the space provided write a short description of Cahokia from the viewpoint of a person visiting it for the first time.

____

____

____

____

____

____

____

____

____

Chapter 1, Section 2 (Pages 14–23)

Europe Begins to Explore

Big Idea

As you read pages 14–23 in your textbook, complete the chart by filling in the outcome of each exploration.

Exploration	Outcome
Columbus	1.
Vespucci	2.
Balboa	3.

Notes

Read to Learn

European Explorations *(page 14)*

Making Generalizations

Complete the generalization.

The Middle Ages

____

____

____

______________________.

For centuries the Roman Empire had controlled much of Europe with a stable social and political order. By A.D. 500, however, the empire had ended. Western Europe became isolated. Its trade declined, and law and order ended. This period, from about A.D. 500 to 1400, is called the Middle Ages.

The Crusades greatly changed Western Europe as western Europeans came into contact with the Muslim civilizations of the Middle East. Trade also increased in the eastern Mediterranean area. Italian city-states especially profited.

By the mid-1400s Portugal, Spain, England, and France sought to expand trade and find routes to Asia. The period known as the Renaissance lasted from about 1350 to 1600. It marked an artistic flowering as well as a scientific revolution. Studying Arab texts, Europeans learned about better sail designs and the **astrolabe,** a navigational device that helped sailors determine their position. Shipbuilders in Portugal designed the **caravel** in the 1400s. It embodied new sailing advances. Henry the Navigator founded a center for astronomy and geography in 1419. In the 1490s Vasco da Gama found a water route to Asia by sailing around the southern coast of Africa.

Notes

Read to Learn

African Cultures (page 16)

Drawing Conclusions

Draw a conclusion based on the following facts from the passage:

Fact: Ghana grew wealthy by taxing the salt and gold trade.

Fact: Mali prospered by controlling the salt and gold trade.

Conclusion:

____

____

____

____

The empire of Ghana emerged during the A.D. 400s. It sat between the salt mines of the Sahara and the gold mines to the south. Ghana grew wealthy by taxing trade. Eventually, trade routes to new gold mines in the east bypassed Ghana, and the empire collapsed by the early 1200s.

By the mid-1300s, the empire of Mali extended eastward along the Niger River and westward to the Atlantic Ocean. Mali also prospered by controlling the salt and gold trade. Mali reached its peak in the 1300s under the rule of Mansa Musa. During this time, Timbuktu became a great center of trade and Muslim learning. The ruler of Songhai, Sonni Ali, captured Timbuktu in 1468. He expanded the Songhai empire into the Sahara and southward along the Niger River. Songhai remained a powerful empire until 1591.

Slavery existed in Africa as it did in other parts of the world. West African slavery changed with the arrival of Arab traders. In the 1400s Spain and Portugal established sugarcane plantations on the Canary and Madeira Islands. Producing sugar required heavy manual labor. Enslaved Africans were brought to the islands to work on the plantations.

Exploring America (page 18)

Problems and Solutions

List two problems you think the Treaty of Tordesillas may have created among Western European countries.

1. ______________________

____

2. ______________________

____

By the 1400s, most educated Europeans knew that the world was round. Around this time, the works of Claudius Ptolemy were rediscovered. Ptolemy developed the system of latitude and longitude that is used by navigators today.

In August 1492, Columbus sailed from Spain. He reached the Bahamas in October. Columbus called the Taino people whom he met "Indians" because he thought he had reached the Indies. In 1494 the Treaty of Tordesillas gave Portugal the right to control the route around Africa to India. It also gave Spain most of the lands of America.

In 1499 Amerigo Vespucci tried to sail west to Asia but ended up exploring the coast of South America. A German mapmaker in 1507 suggested that the continent be named for him. Spanish explorers continued to search for a passage to China and India. In 1513 Juan Ponce de Leon discovered Florida. In 1513 Vasco de Balboa became the first European to reach America's Pacific coast. Ferdinand Magellan's crew became the first people to **circumnavigate,** or circle, the globe in 1522.

Notes | Read to Learn

New Spain (page 20)

Synthesizing Information

Reread paragraphs one and two. Describe the Spanish explorations into South and North America.

____

____

____

____

____

____

In 1519 the Spaniard Hernán Cortés and 550 men explored the Yucatán Peninsula. The local Tlaxcalan people agreed to join the Spanish against the Aztec. Believing the Spanish unstoppable, the Aztec ruler Montezuma allowed them to enter Tenochtitlán, the Aztec capital. Eventually Cortés conquered the Aztecs and destroyed Tenochtitlán. On its ruins, the Spanish built Mexico City. This city became the capital of the colony New Spain. Cortés then sent expeditions to conquer the rest of Central America. The leaders of these expeditions became known as *conquistadors.*

Spanish priests and missionaries spread out across what is now the American Southwest. The priest Junípero Serra took control of California by establishing a chain of missions. In New Mexico, some native Pueblo people did not welcome the Spanish priests. Popé, a Pueblo leader, led a revolt in 1680 that destroyed most of New Mexico's Spanish missions.

A major feature of Spanish colonial society was the *encomienda.* This system gave control of towns to Spanish leaders. Many of the Spanish leaders abused their power and mistreated the Native Americans.

New France (page 23)

Formulating Questions

Place an X next to the question best answered by the passage.

____ ***Why did France establish settlements in North America?***

____ ***What problems did France face in establishing New France?***

In 1524 King Francis I of France sent Giovanni da Verrazano to find the Northwest Passage through North America. He never found such a passage. In 1534 Jacques Cartier set off for the same purpose. Although he explored the St. Lawrence River, he found no passage, either.

In 1602 King Henry IV of France authorized a group of French merchants to found a colony in North America. The merchants hired Samuel de Champlain to help them. In 1608 he established the city of Quebec, which became the capital of the colony of New France. New France grew slowly because most settlers were fur traders who lived among the Native Americans with whom they traded.

The French continued to explore North America. They eventually reached the mouth of the Mississippi River at the Gulf of Mexico, a territory they named "Louisiana" in honor of Louis XIV. Settlement here was slowed because of the oppressive heat and an unhealthy climate.

To counter French expansion in North America, the Spanish founded St. Augustine, Florida. They also built their first mission in Texas in 1690 to block French expansion to the west.

Section Wrap-up

Answer these questions to check your understanding of the entire section.

1. In what way did Muslim civilizations impact European explorations?

2. Why did New France grow slowly?

Informative Writing

Suppose you are contributing to a Web site about early American history. Write a short entry about the establishment of New Spain. Be sure to include important dates, figures, and events.

Chapter 1, Section 3 (Pages 24–33)

Founding the Thirteen Colonies

Big Idea

As you read pages 24–33 in your textbook, complete the graphic organizer by listing the problems that faced the colonists at Jamestown.

Jamestown's Troubles

1. ____________________
2. ____________________
3. ____________________

Notes

Read to Learn

England's First Colonies *(page 24)*

Making Generalizations

Complete the generalization below.

The 1600s in Europe was a period of time marked by

____

____

____

____

John Cabot led the first English expedition to arrive in North America. In 1497 Cabot's team sailed to present-day Nova Scotia. England did not try to establish colonies there for another 80 years. Economic changes caused evicted English tenant farmers to move to America. Many merchants organized **joint-stock companies** to find new markets. These companies raised money and founded colonies throughout the world. Political battles among the powers of Europe forced England to establish outposts in America. From these outposts, English **privateers** could attack Spanish ships. Privateers are pirate ships a country licenses to attack ships of other countries.

In 1606 investors of the Virginia Company sent a group of English settlers to Virginia. The settlers founded Jamestown in 1607. It struggled to survive for years. Colonist named John Rolfe developed a new variety of tobacco. Settlers grew lots of it to ship to England. The leaders of the Jamestown colony introduced the system of **headrights.** This system gave land to new settlers in exchange for moving to the colony.

Persecution of his fellow English Catholics led Lord Baltimore to found the colony of Maryland in 1632. Maryland was England's first **proprietary colony.** The proprietor, or owner, could govern the colony as he saw fit.

Notes

Read to Learn

Pilgrims and Puritans *(page 28)*

Formulating Questions

Place an X next to the question best answered by the passage.

___ ***Why did many English people seek new lives in America?***

___ ***What crop offered English investors the best profit?***

Some Puritans, called Separatists or Pilgrims, left England to escape persecution. They eventually sailed on the *Mayflower* to America. In 1620 they settled at Plymouth, Massachusetts. A Native American named Squanto helped the Pilgrims survive. A harvest celebration in 1621 was the beginning of the Thanksgiving holiday.

In 1630 John Winthrop and about 900 Puritans sailed to America. They founded the Massachusetts Bay Colony, which grew quickly. The colony's leaders did not tolerate differences in religious beliefs. People who disagreed with established religious beliefs, or **heretics** were considered a threat to the colony.

Religious dissenters founded new colonies. Roger Williams was a strict Separatist who bought land from the Native Americans. He founded Providence. A devout Puritan named Anne Hutchinson was banished from Boston for criticizing the teachings of several ministers. She founded the town of Portsmouth.

By 1700 the New England colonies had expanded to include Connecticut and New Hampshire. English colonists and Native Americans fought King Phillip's War in the 1670s. The settlers won. After the war, few Native Americans were left in New England.

Restoration Colonies *(page 31)*

Drawing Conclusions

Draw two conclusions based on the passage.

1. ______________________

____

2. ______________________

____

In 1642 England fell into a civil war. Puritans in Parliament fought supporters of King Charles I. After years of battles, the Parliament's army won, and they beheaded the king. Commander Oliver Cromwell ruled as a dictator until he died in 1658 and England's leaders restored King Charles's son, Charles II, to the throne in 1660. The American colonies founded at this time are called Restoration colonies.

Charles II took New Netherland from the Dutch in 1664. Charles's brother James, the Duke of York, renamed the colony New York. James later granted some land between Delaware Bay and the Connecticut River to two of the king's advisers. This area became New Jersey.

William Penn, a Quaker, founded Pennsylvania, another Restoration colony. Quakers believed in religious toleration and opposed war. Penn received a large tract of land between New York and Maryland from Charles II. This land settled a debt Charles II had owed to Penn's late father. In 1682 Penn bought three counties from the Duke of York. These later became the colony of Delaware. Farther south, Charles II also established Carolina colony which was later split in two. Settlers arrived in the new colony of Georgia in 1733.

Section Wrap-up

Answer these questions to check your understanding of the entire section.

1. How was Jamestown founded, and why did it eventually succeed?

2. What were some of the main factors that caused settlers to move to America?

Persuasive Writing

Write a letter from the perspective of a settler in New England in the 1600s. Persuade a relative to join you in America. Include several reasons to support your argument.

Chapter 1, Section 4 (Pages 34–41)

Economics, Trade, and Rebellion

Big Idea

As you read pages 34–41 in your textbook, complete the graphic organizer by describing the social order in the South.

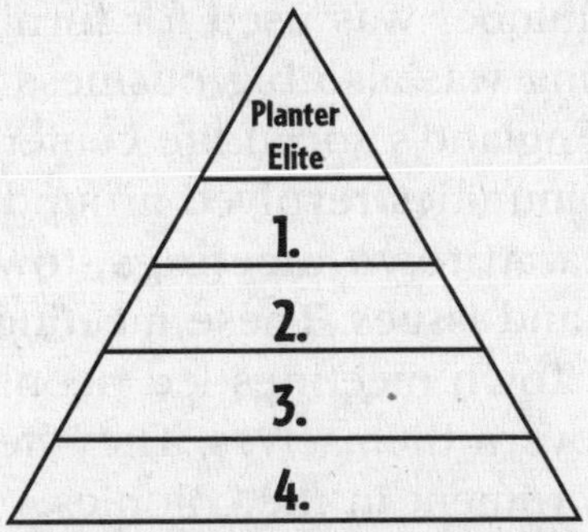

Notes

Read to Learn

Southern Society *(page 34)*

Problems and Solutions

Identify the tobacco farmers' solution.

Problem: Tobacco farmers needed a large workforce to work their fields.

Solution:

____

____

____

Tobacco became the South's first successful cash crop. To be profitable, tobacco farmers needed a large workforce. Poor English tenant farmers agreed to become **indentured servants** in America. These servants worked for their owners for a certain number of years. In exchange, they received the cost of passage and food, shelter, and clothes. Few Southern planters became wealthy. Those who did enjoyed great political and economic power. Most landowners in the South were "backcountry" farmers who grew only enough crops to feed their own families.

In 1675 war broke out between backcountry farmers and the local Native Americans. Nathaniel Bacon led the backcountry farmers. He organized a militia and attacked the Native Americans. Unfair policies enacted by Virginia's leaders also upset backcountry farmers. Bacon's militia tried to take control of Virginia's government. A civil war erupted. Bacon's Rebellion ended with his death in 1676. The rebellion helped to increase both western expansion of the colony and the use of enslaved Africans for labor. New English government policies made it easier to acquire enslaved people.

Notes

Read to Learn

New England Society *(page 37)*

Analyzing Information

Why did New England farms not require large labor forces?

____

____

____

____

New England's climate and soil were unsuitable for large plantations. New England farmers practiced subsistence farming. Their main crop was wheat, though farmers also grew other grains, vegetables, and fruits, and raised livestock.

Fishing and whaling brought the greatest prosperity to New England. In addition to rich fishing regions, New England had large timber supplies for building boats and good harbors. Colonists sold their fish in the colonies, southern Europe, and the Caribbean. New England also developed a healthy timber trade. Its lumber was used for furniture, buildings, and barrels. Shipbuilding was also big business in New England.

New England's social life centered on the town. Life in these small communities revolved around a "town common," or open public area. At **town meetings,** townspeople discussed local problems and issues. These meetings developed into local governments. Town meetings led people to believe that they had a right to govern themselves. They helped set the stage for democratic government in the colonies.

Trade and the Rise of Cities *(page 38)*

Determining Cause and Effect

List one cause of and one effect of the emergence of colonial cities.

Cause:

____

____

Effect:

____

____

Colonial merchants developed a system of **triangular trade** to get the products that they needed from England. They traded goods in the Caribbean and received either products or bills of exchange in return. These were then traded with English merchants for manufactured goods.

Trade caused the growth of the colonies' first cities, in which distinct social classes developed. Wealthy merchants were at the top of the social structure. Skilled workers, made up half the population. Next were people without skills or property. Below them were indentured servants and enslaved Africans.

Mercantilism is an economic theory about the world economy. Mercantilists believed a country should sell more goods than it buys from other countries in order to get more gold and silver. They also believed a country should be self-sufficient in raw materials. Therefore, a country should establish colonies to provide raw materials.

Political troubles in England impacted the American colonies greatly in the late 1600s. King Charles II enacted laws that regulated colonial trade. James II merged several colonies into a royal province. The English Bill of Rights was enforced. Its ideas would later influence colonial demands leading to the American Revolution and shape the American Bill of Rights.

Section Wrap-up

Answer these questions to check your understanding of the entire section.

1. What were the majority of farms like in the early English colonies?

2. How did American colonists get the manufactured items from England that they needed?

Expository Writing

In the space provided describe the Southern and New England colonial societies. How were they alike or different?

Chapter 1, Section 5 (Pages 42–47)

A Diverse Society

Big Idea

As you read pages 42–47 in your textbook, complete the graphic organizer by identifying why immigrants settled in the colonies.

Group	Where They Settled	Reasons for Immigrating
Germans	1.	2.
Scotch-Irish	3.	4.
Jews	5.	6.

Notes

Read to Learn

Colonial America Grows *(page 42)*

Predicting

Predict what the future holds for enslaved Africans in America.

____

____

____

____

____

____

____

The American colonies population grew quickly during the eighteenth century. Colonists were having large families. Some 300,000 European immigrants arrived between 1700 and 1775.

Women in the American colonies had few legal rights. Married women could not own property or make a contract or will. Single women had more rights. They could own property, file lawsuits, and run businesses. By the 1700s the status of married women improved.

Roughly 10 to 12 million enslaved Africans were sent to America between 1450 and 1870. The first enslaved Africans in the American colonies could gain their freedom by converting to Christianity. By 1660 slavery became a hereditary system based on race. Virginia created a **slave code** in 1705. These laws defined the relationship between enslaved people and free people. Enslaved Africans endured lower status and more hardship than any group in the colonies. Family and religion helped the enslaved Africans deal with their hard lives. Some escaped to the North, while others refused to work and even rebelled.

Notes

Read to Learn

New Ideas *(page 45)*

Distinguishing Fact from Opinion

Read the second paragraph.

Circle two sentences that explain opinions.

Underline two sentences that tell facts.

Identifying the Main Idea

Write the main idea of the passage.

____

____

____

____

____

____

Two European cultural movements influenced the American colonists during the 1700s. One movement was called the Enlightenment. Enlightenment thinkers challenged the authority of the church in science and philosophy. They also emphasized logic and reasoning. This was known as **rationalism.**

John Locke was an influential Enlightenment writer. His contract theory of government and natural rights influenced American political leaders. Locke argued that people were not born sinful as the Church claimed. He believed that society and education could make people better. Locke's idea that all people have rights became a core belief in American society.

French thinker Jean-Jacques Rousseau argued that people should form a government and make their own laws. Baron Montesquieu was an Enlightenment thinker who suggested that the powers of government should be separated into three branches. This would help protect people's freedom. These ideas influenced the writers of the American Constitution.

Many Americans followed a religious movement called **pietism.** This movement stressed an individual's devoutness and union with God. Ministers spread pietism through **revivals.** These were large public meetings for preaching and prayer. This rebirth of religious feeling became known as the Great Awakening. Two preachers of the Great Awakening were Jonathan Edwards and George Whitefield. Both men led religious revivals throughout the colonies. Edwards preached in a very emotional, rather than rational, style.

The Great Awakening peaked around 1740. It split many churches into factions. Religious groups that embraced new ideas won many converts. The Great Awakening had a great impact in the South. Baptists gained a strong following among backcountry farmers. Baptists also welcomed Africans at their revivals and condemned slavery.

Both the Enlightenment and the Great Awakening changed colonial society. The Enlightenment provided arguments against British rule. The Great Awakening caused people to question traditional authority.

Section Wrap-up

Answer these questions to check your understanding of the entire section.

1. What challenges did married women face in colonial America?

2. What effect did the Enlightenment and the Great Awakening have on colonists?

Informative Writing

In the space provided write a short, first-person account of a Great Awakening revival.

Chapter 2, Section 1 (Pages 54–61)

The Colonies Fight for Their Rights

Big Idea

As you read pages 54–61 in your textbook, complete the graphic organizer by listing the causes of the French and Indian War.

Causes

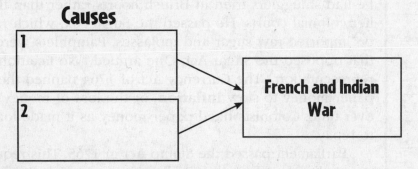

1 → French and Indian War

2 → French and Indian War

Notes | Read to Learn

The French and Indian War *(page 54)*

Making Inferences

Read the passage. Answer the question.

Why was the Albany Conference important?

____

____

____

____

____

____

____

In the 1740s, the British and French were interested in the Ohio River valley. Both nations tried to build forts in order to claim the region. George Washington and the Virginia militia fought the French in 1754, but were forced to retreat.

To prepare for war, colonies tried to form an alliance with the Iroquois, who controlled western New York. Leaders from seven colonies met with the Iroquois at the Albany Conference in June 1754. The Iroquois refused to ally with the British. However, at the conference the colonial leaders agreed to that all British troops in the colonies should have one leader.

In 1755 George Braddock took command of almost 2,000 British troops. The French and their Native American allies later ambushed these troops, killing Braddock. George Washington took command. Fighting took place along the frontier. Spain entered the war, but lost Cuba and the Philippines to the British. The Treaty of Paris ended the war in 1763. The French lost New France and part of Louisiana to the British, and Spain gave up Florida to regain Cuba and the Philippines. Spain also gained control of New Orleans and part of Louisiana from France.

Notes

Read to Learn

Growing Discontent *(page 56)*

Determining Cause and Effect

List two effects.

Cause: The Stamp Act went into effect in November 1765.

1. ______________________

____

____

____

____

2. ______________________

____

____

____

____

The French and Indian War left Britain in debt, so it decided that the colonies should help to pay for their own defense. Then, in 1763, Pontiac—the chief of the Ottawa people—decided to go to war to stop colonists from moving into western Pennsylvania. The British defeated Pontiac. They passed the Proclamation of 1763, which tried to stop all settlement west of the Appalachians.

Prime Minister George Grenville learned that smugglers were bringing goods into and out of the colonies without paying **customs duties**—taxes on imports and exports. To stop this, he had smugglers tried in British courts rather than the friendlier colonial courts. He passed the Sugar Act, which raised taxes on imported raw sugar and molasses. Pamphlets were written that opposed the Sugar Act. One argued, "No taxation without representation." The Currency Act of 1764 banned the use of paper money to slow **inflation,** or the loss of money's value over time. Colonists liked paper money as it made loans easier to repay.

Parliament passed the Stamp Act in 1765. This required that stamps be placed on almost all printed materials. It was a direct tax. Colonists protested the Stamp Act and ignored it when it went into effect. They also boycotted all British goods. Many merchants signed **nonimportation agreements,** agreeing not to buy British goods until the Stamp Act was repealed. The British repealed the Stamp Act. Parliament then passed the Declaratory Act. It said Parliament could make laws for the colonies.

The Townshend Acts *(page 60)*

Drawing Conclusions

Circle the conclusion that best fits the passage.

1. The colonists fiercely resisted British taxes.

2. The British were more violent than the colonists.

In 1767 Parliament passed the Townshend Acts, which placed taxes on glass, lead, paper, and tea imported into the colonies. The acts also legalized **writs of assistance,** or search warrants used to arrest smugglers.

The colonists were angry. The Massachusetts Assembly began to resist these laws. Samuel Adams and James Otis wrote a letter that urged the other colonies to oppose the laws. The British dissolved the assembly. Then merchants and leaders in New York, Boston, Philadelphia, and Virginia stopped the sale of British goods. In 1768 British troops arrived in Boston to stop violence against customs officers. The move led to violence between the colonists and the troops. In March of 1770, British troops fired into a crowd of angry colonists. Five people died and six others were wounded. This event was called the Boston Massacre. News of the killing ended the Townshend Acts, but the taxes on tea remained.

Section Wrap-up

Answer these questions to check your understanding of the entire section.

1. How did the map of North America change after the Treaty of Paris?

2. How was the colonists' reaction to the Townshend Acts different from their reaction to the Sugar Act?

Persuasive Writing

In the space provided write a short article for a pamphlet arguing against British taxation of the colonies. Write your article from a colonial merchant's perspective.

Chapter 2, Section 2 (Pages 64–73)

The Revolution Begins

Big Idea

As you read pages 64–73 in your textbook, complete the outline using the major headings of the section.

The Revolution Begins

I. Massachusetts Defies Britain
   A. ______
   B. ______
   C. ______
   D. ______

II. ______
   A. ______
   B. ______
   C. ______

III. ______
   A. ______
   B. ______
   C. ______

Notes

Read to Learn

Massachusetts Defies Britain *(page 64)*

Identifying the Main Idea

Put an X by the main idea of the passage.

1. ___ The colonies began to break away because of the* Gaspee *affair.

2. ___ The colonists began organizing in response to the British policies.

In 1772 the British started sending customs ships to the colonies to put a stop to smuggling. Rhode Island colonists burned one of the ships called the *Gaspee*. The British wanted to send the responsible colonists to Britain for trial. The colonists believed this violated their right to a trial by their peers. The Rhode Island Assembly asked for help. Thomas Jefferson suggested that each colony create a **committee of correspondence** to share information with the other colonies.

The Tea Act of 1773 allowed the British East India Company to sell low-priced tea directly to colonial shopkeepers, angering American merchants. In Boston 150 men boarded tea ships and threw the boxes of tea overboard, an event called the Boston Tea Party. The British then passed the Coercive Acts. They closed Boston's port, banned town meetings, prevented colonists from trying British officials in court, and housed troops in private homes. The colonists held the First Continental Congress in September 1774. It formed the Continental Association, which set up committees in towns and counties that boycotted British goods.

Notes | Read to Learn

The Revolution Begins *(page 68)*

Making Generalizations

What do you think the British expected to happen in Concord? Why?

____

____

____

____

____

____

____

____

When the British suspended the Massachusetts Assembly, its members founded the Massachusetts Provincial Congress. It in turn formed the Committee of Safety, which could call up the colonial militias. These militias began to drill and practice shooting. The town of Concord even created the **minutemen,** a unit trained to be ready at a minute's notice. Colonists who were still loyal to Britain and British laws were called Loyalists, or Tories. Colonists who rebelled against the British were called Patriots, or Whigs. The Patriots had support in New England and Virginia. Many Loyalists lived in Georgia, the Carolinas, and New York. Many Americans did not support either group.

On April 18, 1775, British troops in Boston set out to seize the militia supply depot at Concord. Paul Revere and William Dawes were sent to warn the colonists in Lexington and Concord. On April 19, the British arrived in Lexington, where they defeated about 70 minutemen. They went on to fight another 400 minutemen at Concord, but were forced to retreat to Boston. The militia surrounded the city. Then the Second Continental Congress met. They formed the Continental Army and appointed General George Washington to lead it. Meanwhile, the British in Boston received reinforcements. They tried to retake the area around the city but were defeated in the Battle of Bunker Hill.

The Decision to Declare Independence *(page 71)*

Synthesizing Information

Reread the passage. Circle sentences that show that the colonists struggled with the idea of independence.

In July 1775, the Continental Congress sent the Olive Branch Petition to King George III. In it, the colonists swore loyalty to the king and offered peace. However, before the king saw it, the Continental Army attacked Quebec and seized the city of Montreal. The king refused to read the petition. Instead, he stated that the colonists were enemies. The Continental Congress began to act like a government. It negotiated with the Native Americans and set up a postal system, navy, and marine corps.

The Continental Army defeated Loyalist armies in Virginia and North Carolina. It also forced the British to leave Boston. In December 1775, the king stopped all trade with the colonies. He also ordered a naval blockade of the colonies. He then hired German soldiers to fight the colonists. Soon, more Patriots began to think the colonies should declare independence. In January 1776, a pamphlet called *Common Sense* became popular. It claimed that both the king and Parliament were the enemies. On July 4, 1776, the Continental Congress issued the Declaration of Independence.

Section Wrap-up

Answer these questions to check your understanding of the entire section.

1. Who were the Loyalists and the Patriots?

2. Why did the Olive Branch Petition fail?

Expository Writing

In the space provided describe how the Patriots might have viewed the advantages of independence. Then explain what the Loyalists might have thought.

The War for Independence

Big Idea

As you read pages 78–85 in your textbook, complete the time line by recording some major battles and their outcomes.

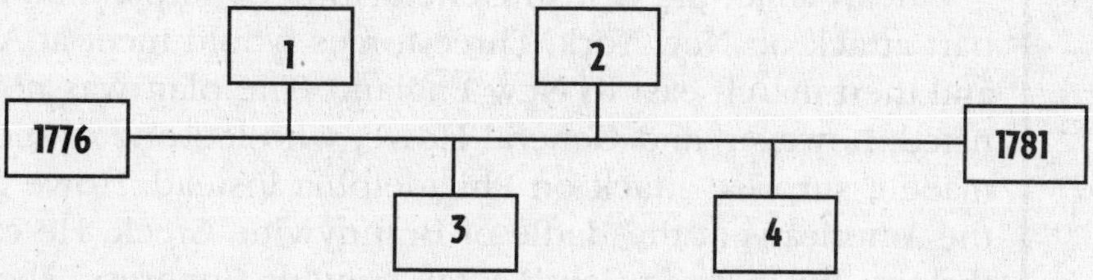

Notes | Read to Learn

The Opposing Sides *(page 78)*

Formulating Questions

Circle the question that might help you learn more about the opposing armies.

1. What advantages did the British army and the Continental Army have?

2. How did the militias help the Continental Army?

The British amassed an army of 32,000 men under General Howe. The British troops were well trained and well equipped, but the Continental Army was not. Many American soldiers deserted and refused to reenlist. American troops did not typically number more than 20,000 at any one time.

The Continental Congress had trouble paying for the war. It issued paper money called "Continentals" that quickly became worthless. A merchant named Robert Morris helped fund the war. He gave money, arranged foreign loans, and pushed Congress to create a bank.

American militias used **guerrilla warfare** and hid behind trees and walls. The British military strategy was not effective against this type of fighting. At home, many British merchants and others were against the war. The British had to defeat the Americans quickly. They decided to capture New York to separate the colonies and show the Americans that they could not win. Then the British invited colonial leaders to a peace conference and promised pardons for loyalty to the king. The conference failed.

Notes

Read to Learn

Battles in the North *(page 80)*

Making Generalizations

Reread the passage. Make a generalization about the Continental Army at this time.

At New York City, Washington's inexperienced army was forced to retreat. The British captured New York. Washington moved his troops to White Plains, New York but again was forced to retreat. The British then headed south to Philadelphia to capture the Continental Congress, but the Americans beat them there. Instead of attacking, the British made winter camps in New Jersey. In December, Washington decided to cross the Delaware River and attack them. He defeated the British at Trenton and Princeton.

Meanwhile, the British General Burgoyne planned a three-part attack on New York. Three forces would meet at Albany and then march east to New England. The plan was not coordinated, however, and General Howe, who led one of the forces, made a surprise attack on Philadelphia instead. Howe defeated the Americans at the Battle of Brandywine Creek. He captured the city, but not the Continental Army or Congress. The Continental Army took up winter quarters at Valley Forge and received training. In New York, Burgoyne and the British forces surrendered at Saratoga. Soon the French recognized the United States as an independent nation and sent troops.

In the west, Patriot George Rogers Clark seized control of the Ohio River region. The Iroquois and the Cherokee joined the British, but were eventually defeated by American troops and militias. Americans also fought the British at sea to hurt British trade. The Congress issued **letters of marque** to ship owners that allowed them to attack British merchant ships.

Battles in the South *(page 83)*

Predicting

Based on the passage, predict what might happen to the southern Loyalists who supported the British.

The British shifted focus to the southern states. They had more support from the Loyalists there. In 1778 they captured Savannah and, later, Charles Town. The Continental Congress sent troops to protect the South Carolina backcountry. Many Loyalists fought for the British and seized much of the backcountry. However, the British did not take the Appalachian Mountain region. Its people defeated the British at the Battle of Kings Mountain. Soon, the British lost control of the South.

The British then focused on capturing Virginia, but American troops forced them to retreat to Yorktown. They planned to escape by sea, but a French fleet stopped them. The British surrendered on October 19, 1781. The Treaty of Paris was signed on September 3, 1783. It recognized the United States as a new nation with the Mississippi River as its border.

Section Wrap-up

Answer these questions to check your understanding of the entire section.

1. What were the differences between the British army and the Continental Army?

2. Why did the colonial militias pose a problem for the British?

Descriptive Writing

Describe General Washington's efforts to stop the British from taking Philadelphia. Tell about the scene in New York and how it led to the battles at Trenton and Princeton from the point of view of a soldier who was there.

Chapter 2, Section 4 (Pages 86–91)

The War Changes American Society

Big Idea

As you read pages 86–91 in your textbook, complete the graphic organizer by listing the features of the U.S. political system set up after the war.

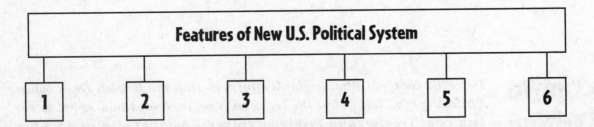

Features of New U.S. Political System

1	2	3	4	5	6

Notes

Read to Learn

New Political Ideas *(page 86)*

Detecting Bias

Circle the sentence below that best agrees with John Adams' ideas.

1. The lower classes demanded a greater role in choosing leaders.

2. Massachusetts had an elected governor, a senate, and an assembly.

After the war, Americans created a **republic**—a form of government in which the power resides with the voting citizens. The citizens elect representatives who are responsible to them. This was different than traditional ideas of government.

American leaders believed that the best form of government was a constitutional republic. Many states drafted new constitutions during the Revolution. Leaders such as John Adams believed that the best government had three branches: executive, legislative, and judicial. He pushed to divide the legislature into two houses. Many states adopted his ideas. They also attached lists of rights to their constitutions, including freedom of religion and speech.

The Revolution led to greater voting rights. Farmers and artisans decided they were the equals of the rich planters and merchants, and demanded a greater role in choosing leaders. Many new state constitutions gave voting rights to all taxpaying men, not just property owners. The war also changed the relationship between churches and states. Virginia was one state that ended its official church.

Notes | Read to Learn

The War and American Society *(page 88)*

Comparing and Contrasting

Complete the sentence below based on the passage.

Neither ____________ nor ____________ benefited from ideas about ____________ after the Revolution.

Problems and Solutions

Review the passage. Fill in the problem.

Problem:

____

____

____

____

____

____

____

Solution: The Loyalists fled to Britain, Canada, and the British West Indies.

After the Revolution, ideas about freedom mainly aplied to white men only. Most women and African Americans did not benefit from them. Women did, however, play an important role in the war. Some took over family farms, while others served on the front lines. They traveled with the army, cooking, washing, and nursing the wounded. One such woman, Magaret Corbin, even manned a cannon during a battle. Women made some advances after the Revolution. They could more easily get a divorce and had better access to education.

Thousands of enslaved African Americans were carried away by the British, while some were freed in exchange for military service. Washington allowed African Americans to serve in the Continental Army and state militias. Thousands of enslaved people were given their freedom in exchange for this service. After the war, **emancipation**—or freedom from enslavement—became a major issue. Many northern states took steps to end slavery. Slavery ended slowly over several decades in the North. Many freed African Americans began moving to the cities, but they had difficulty finding work and faced voting restrictions and segregation. They even feared being kidnapped and enslaved in the South. Despite all the difficulties, African Americans began creating their own culture.

The South continued to rely on enslaved labor. As a result, many Southerners had no interest in ending slavery. Virginia was the only state to attempt to do so. In 1782 the state passed a law that encouraged **manumission,** or voluntary freeing of enslaved persons. However, only about 10,000 people received their freedom this way.

The end of the war changed life for the Loyalists also. They were often shunned by others. Some had their property seized by state governments. About 100,000 Loyalists fled the United States. Some went to Britain or the British West Indies, but the majority fled to Canada.

The Revolutionary War led to a growing nationalism and a new culture for Americans. The war had brought all types of Americans together to fight a common enemy and produced patriotic symbols and heroic stories. American artists such as John Trumbull and Charles Willson Peale painted these heroic deeds and leaders.

Education also became important to American leaders. They knew that they needed an educated public for a republic to succeed, so states began to create universities. Elementary schools began teaching republican ideas and stopped using British textbooks.

Section Wrap-up

Answer these questions to check your understanding of the entire section.

1. How did women participate in the Revolutionary War?

2. What was one cause of the new American culture?

Informative Writing

In the space provided write a pamphlet that reports about the struggle to end slavery. Provide details about the different efforts that freed some enslaved Americans. Describe some steps that states took to free more people.

Chapter 3, Section 1 (Pages 98–103)

The Confederation

Big Idea

As you read pages 98–103 in your textbook, complete the graphic organizer by listing the achievements of the Congress.

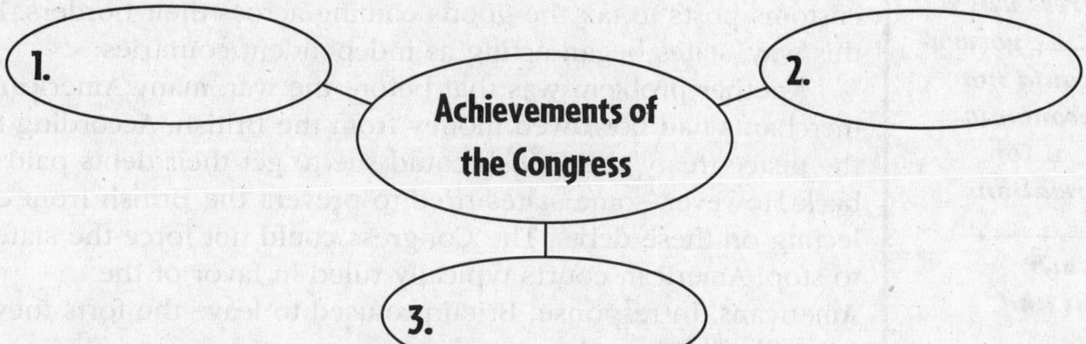

Notes | Read to Learn

Congress Under the Articles of Confederation *(page 98)*

Making Inferences

Read the passage. Make an inference about why the states did not want a strong government.

The Continental Congress adopted the Articles of Confederation and Perpetual Union in November 1777. The Articles created a loose union of the states under the authority of the Congress. Every year, each state would send a delegation to the Congress. It was a weak national government. It could declare war, raise armies, and sign treaties, but could not set taxes or regulate trade. To raise money, the Congress decided to sell the land west of the Appalachian Mountains. In 1785 it set up a system for surveying these lands.

Congress passed the Northwest Ordinance in 1787. It created a new territory called the Northwest Territory, which could later be divided into three to five states. When 5,000 adult male citizens settled there, they could elect a territorial lawmaking body. When 60,000 people lived there, the territory could apply for statehood. The ordinance also protected freedom of religion and property rights and prohibited slavery.

The Congress also negotiated trade treaties with other countries. By 1790, the trade of the United States was greater than it was before the Revolution.

Notes

Read to Learn

The Congress Falters *(page 100)*

Drawing Conclusions

Fill in the missing words to complete the conclusion.

The Congress was a ____________ government. It could not stop the economic ____________ or improve relations with ____________ nations such as Britain and ____________.

Predicting

Based on the passage, predict what the Americans will do about the weaknesses of the Congress.

____

____

____

____

____

____

____

____

The Articles of Confederation had many problems. After the war, British merchants flooded the United States with low-cost goods, which drove many American artisans out of business. The states fought back by restricting British imports. However, the states did not all charge the same **duties,** or taxes, on imported goods. The British sent their goods to states that had the lowest taxes or fewest restrictions. Then the states set up customs posts to tax the goods coming across their borders. In this way, states began acting as independent countries.

Another problem was that before the war, many American merchants had borrowed money from the British. According to the peace treaty, the British could sue to get their debts paid back However, some states tried to prevent the British from collecting on these debts. The Congress could not force the states to stop. American courts typically ruled in favor of the Americans. In response, Britain refused to leave the forts they controlled in the west.

The United States also had problems with Spain. The two countries disagreed about the boundary between Georgia and Spanish territory. To pressure the United States, Spain closed off access to the Mississippi and would not allow Americans to ship goods down river.

The Congress could not help the nation's economic problems. After the war, the nation experienced a **recession,** or economic slowdown. The war left many states in debt. Many had issued bonds to wealthy citizens to borrow money for the war. When the war ended, these citizens wanted their money back. The states began to issue paper money to pay off the debts, but it was worth less than its face value. Debtors were able to pay off their debts more easily, but people who lent the money would not receive the full amount owed. Some merchants refused to accept the money. Rhode Island even passed a law that forced people to accept paper money. Some Americans feared that the government was being used to steal from the wealthy.

Shays's Rebellion broke out in Massachusetts in 1786. Massachusetts had raised taxes to help pay off its debt. The state's farmers were forced to pay most of these taxes. Many farmers could not afford to pay the taxes and began to lose their farms. A bankrupt farmer named Daniel Shays led a rebellion, seizing courthouses to stop them from foreclosing on farms. Then the rebels headed to a state arsenal for weapons. They wanted to march on Boston. The governor sent the militia to protect the arsenal, and Shays and the rebels attacked. Four farmers were killed and the rebellion ended.

Section Wrap-up

Answer these questions to check your understanding of the entire section.

1. What problems did the United States have with Britain after the war?

2. What was the cause of Shays's Rebellion?

Persuasive Writing

Write a speech to the Congress. Explain why the United States needs a stronger government. Include specific events from the post-war period that support your argument.

Chapter 3, Section 2 (Pages 104–109)

A New Constitution

Big Idea

As you read pages 104–109 in your textbook, complete the outline using the major headings of the section.

A New Constitution

I. The Constitutional Convention
   A. ____________________
   B. ____________________
II. ____________________
   A. ____________________
   B. ____________________
III. ____________________
   A. ____________________
   B. ____________________

Notes

Read to Learn

The Constitutional Convention *(page 104)*

Distinguishing Fact from Opinion

Read the passage. Circle a sentence that gives the nationalists' opinion of the Articles of Confederation. Underline a sentence that gives a fact about the nationalists.

Many leaders called "nationalists" believed that the United States needed a strong national government. They included George Washington, Benjamin Franklin, and James Madison. In 1786 Virginia's assembly called a convention to discuss the problems with trade and taxation. Only delegates from five states came to the convention. This was not enough.

In 1787 Alexander Hamilton urged Congress to call a constitutional convention. He wanted to change the Articles of Confederation. Fifty-five delegates came and included important national leaders. Washington presided. Madison kept records. The Virginia delegation brought a plan for a new national government with branches. Its legislature would have two houses. The number of representatives in both houses would be based on state population. This helped the larger states, but the smaller states opposed the plan. A New Jersey Plan called for changing the Articles of Confederation to make the central government stronger. Delegates decided to use the Virginia Plan. Then they began working on a new constitution.

Notes | Read to Learn

A Union Built on Compromise (page 106)

Problems and Solutions

Read the problem. Write the solution.

Problem: Small states did not want representation based on population.

Solution:

The delegates disagreed on the Virginia Plan. Those from smaller states wanted each state to have an equal vote in Congress. Those from larger states wanted representation based on population. The convention formed a committee to solve the problem. The Great Compromise called for two houses of Congress, one based on state population and the other with an equal number of representatives from each state. The committee proposed that each state elect one representative to the House of Representatives for every 40,000 people in the state. Southern delegates wanted to count enslaved people, too. Northern states disagreed because enslaved people could not vote. The committee proposed the Three-Fifths Compromise. It stated that every five enslaved people would count as three free people.

Southern delegates did not want the new Constitution to restrict any trade, including the slave trade. Northern delegates wanted a new government to control imports. Another compromise stopped Congress from taxing exports or banning the slave trade until 1808.

A Framework for Limited Government (page 108)

Synthesizing Information

List one duty of each branch of government.

1. Executive:

2. Judicial:

3. Legislative:

The new constitution was based on the idea of **popular sovereignty,** or rule by the people. It set up a representative system of government with elected officials. It also created a system called **federalism** in which the power was divided between the federal and state governments. The Constitution provided for a **separation of powers** among the three branches of the federal government. Congress was the legislative branch, which made laws. The executive branch enforced the laws. The judicial branch interpreted the laws. The Constitution also created **checks and balances** to stop any branch from becoming too powerful. The president could **veto** or reject acts of Congress, but Congress could override a veto with a two-thirds vote. Congress could impeach, or accuse of misconduct, the president or other officials. Members of the judicial branch were to be nominated by the executive branch and approved by the legislature.

Congress also wanted a way to change the Constitution, so they set up a system of making **amendments,** or changes. An amendment is proposed by two-thirds of the members of both houses of Congress. Two-thirds of the states may also propose an amendment. The proposed amendment would have to be ratified by three-fourths of the states.

Section Wrap-up

Answer these questions to check your understanding of the entire section.

1. What concerns did the Southern states have with the Virginia Plan?

2. How did the Constitutional Convention compromise on the issues of slavery and trade?

Expository Writing

In the space provided write an encyclopedia entry explaining how the United States government is organized. Include details about how the branches of the government work together.

Ratifying the Constitution

Big Idea

As you read pages 110–115 in your textbook, complete the graphic organizer by listing the supporters and goals of the Federalists and the Antifederalists.

	Federalists	Anti-Federalists
Source of Support	1.	3.
Goals	2.	4.

Notes

Read to Learn

A Great Debate (page 110)

Comparing and Contrasting

Write F or A to tell that the phrase describes the Federalists or the Antifederalists.

1. ___ believed a strong national government would help interstate trade

2. ___ felt the Constitution did not protect people's rights

Each state had to elect a convention to vote on the new Constitution. Its supporters were called Federalists. They supported the federal system of government but wanted the states to keep many of their powers. Their supporters were large landowners, merchants, artisans, and farmers along waterways who shipped goods across state borders.

Americans who opposed the Constitution were called Antifederalists. They also supported the idea of a strong national government. However, they did not think that the national government should be dominant over the states. Some Antifederalists did not support it because it did not protect the people's rights with a **bill of rights.** Western farmers suspected a strong national government might benefit the wealthy.

The Federalists were well organized. They presented their program in speeches, pamphlets, and debates. The Federalists explained why the Constitution should be ratified in a collection of essays called *The Federalist.* The Antifederalists did not present any programs for solving the nation's problems or protecting people's rights.

Notes

Read to Learn

Battle for Ratification *(page 112)*

Detecting Bias

Place a check mark next to Samuel Adams's ideas about the new Constitution.

1. ____ The Constitution needed a bill of rights.

2. ____ The Constitution should not interfere with the slave trade.

3. ____ The Constitution will end the independence of the states.

Determining Cause and Effect

Identify the effect.

Cause: The New York delegates learned that Virginia and New Hampshire ratified the Constitution.

Effect:

____

____

____

____

____

The states began to ratify the Constitution in December 1787. Delaware, Pennsylvania, New Jersey, Georgia, and Connecticut quickly ratified the Constitution. A great debate began in Massachusetts. Antifederalists were in the majority in that state's convention. They included Samuel Adams, who thought that the Constitution should have a bill of rights. He also thought that it took away the independence of the states. The Federalists worked quickly to change his opinions. They promised to attach a bill of rights once the Constitution was passed. They also agreed to an amendment that would give the states all of the powers not given to the federal government. This changed Samuel Adams's opinion. Massachusetts approved the new Constitution. Maryland, South Carolina, and New Hampshire also voted for the Constitution by June 1788. However, Virginia and New York had not voted to ratify it yet. Federalists needed the support of these two large states. They believed the new government would fail without these states.

In Virginia, George Washington, James Madison, and other Federalists pushed the convention to accept the new Constitution. Finally, Virginia voted to support it once Madison promised to add a bill of rights. In New York, the Federalists did not vote until they heard that New Hampshire and Virginia accepted the new Constitution. The New York delegates did not want New York to be governed differently than its neighbors, so New York ratified the Constitution after a very close vote. All the states except Rhode Island and North Carolina ratified the Constitution by July 1788. Only nine states were needed to approve the Constitution. So, the new government could start without those two states. However, both Rhode Island and North Carolina ratified the Constitution by 1790.

Americans were nervous and excited about their new government. No one knew if the Constitution would work any better than the Articles of Confederation. However, many people had confidence in George Washington, who was chosen to be the first president.

Section Wrap-up

Answer these questions to check your understanding of the entire section.

1. What groups of people supported the Antifederalists? Why did they do so?

2. What was needed to convince the Massachusetts and Virginia conventions to ratify the Constitution?

Descriptive Writing

In the space provided write a short journal entry from the perspective of a person attending Virginia's ratification convention. Describe the Federalist and Antifederalist views and include the speakers that argued on each side.

Chapter 4, Section 1 (Pages 154–159)

Washington and Congress

Big Idea

As you read pages 154–159 in your textbook, complete the graphic organizer by indicating the tasks completed by Congress.

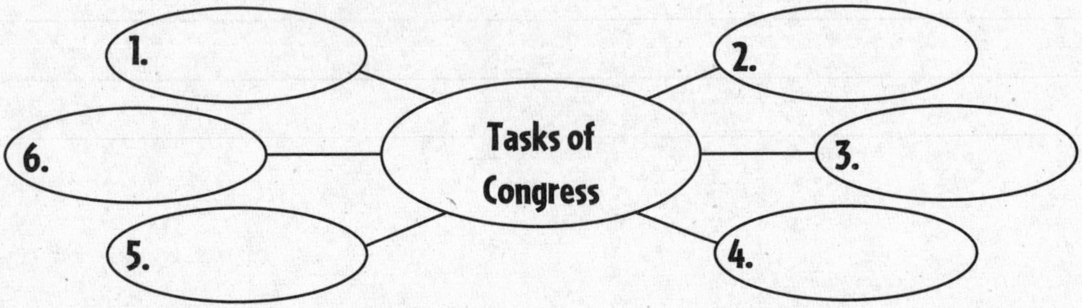

Notes

Read to Learn

Creating a New Government *(page 154)*

Problems and Solutions

Identify the solution.

Problem: Creation of a national bank was not an enumerated power.

Solution:

____

____

____

____

____

____

The new Congress set up government departments, and Washington chose people to head them. These department heads were called the **cabinet,** a group of advisers to the president. Congress also quickly passed the Bill of Rights and the Tariff Act of 1789.

Congress under the Articles of Confederation had issued bonds to pay for the Revolutionary War. **Bonds** are paper notes that promise to repay money later with interest. Hamilton believed the government should pay these debts. Critics thought this was unfair to the people who first bought the bonds. Many had sold their bonds at a discount to **speculators**—people willing to take a risk in hopes of future financial gain. Hamilton's plan eventually passed.

Hamilton also asked Congress to create a national bank. Madison argued that Congress could not establish a bank because it was not among the federal government's **enumerated powers**—powers specifically mentioned in the Constitution. Hamilton argued that the Constitution gave the federal government **implied powers**—powers not explicitly listed in the Constitution, but necessary for the government to do its job. President Washington agreed to sign the bill.

Notes

Read to Learn

The Rise of Political Parties *(page 158)*

Comparing and Contrasting

Write J by Jefferson's beliefs. Write H by Hamilton's beliefs.

1. ____ A healthy economy depends on manufacturing and trade.

2. ____ Agrarianism is the key to the strength of the United States.

3. ____ States' rights come before the power of the federal government.

4. ____ Democracy is a threat to liberty.

Distinguishing Fact from Opinion

Reread the passage. Place an X next to statements that show Jefferson's opinion of agrarianism.

The debate over Hamilton's financial plan split Congress into two sides. These sides became the nation's first political parties. Hamilton's supporters called themselves Federalists. Hamilton's opponents were led by Madison and Jefferson. They took the name Democratic-Republicans. Most people called them Republicans.

Hamilton supported a strong national government. He believed that democracy was a threat to liberty. He wanted to put the government into the hands of the rich. Hamilton believed that manufacturing and trade were important for the health of the nation's economy. His policies supported these areas of the economy. Merchants, manufacturers, and bankers supported the Federalist Party. Urban workers and farmers who benefited from trade were also Federalists.

Thomas Jefferson opposed Hamilton. Jefferson was the leader of the Democratic-Republicans. He believed that the strength of the United States was its independent farmers. This belief is known as **agrarianism.** Jefferson feared an economy led by business. He thought this would lead to a society divided between rich and poor. Democratic-Republicans supported agriculture. They thought agriculture was more important than manufacturing and trade and that it was best for a healthy national economy. They also felt that Hamilton's plan favored the North over the South. The Democratic-Republican Party also stood for the rights of the states over the federal government.

The different opinions of the two political parties divided the country. The more rural South and West tended to support the Republicans. The urban Northeast supported the Federalists. Future events would further divide the new nation.

Section Wrap-up

Answer these questions to check your understanding of the entire section.

1. Why did critics argue that Hamilton's economic plan was unfair to the original bond purchasers?

2. What influenced the growing tension between the nation's political parties?

Expository Writing

In the space provided write a speech for Hamilton to deliver to Congress explaining the difference between enumerated and implied powers and why the latter are important to the federal government.

Chapter 4, Section 2 (Pages 162–167)

Partisan Politics

Big Idea

As you read pages 162–167 in your textbook, complete the graphic organizer by filling in the provisions of treaties made by the United States.

Treaty	Provisions
Jay's Treaty	1.
Pinckney's Treaty	2.
Convention of 1800	3.

Notes

Read to Learn

Trade and Western Expansion *(page 162)*

Determining Cause and Effect

List two causes of the Battle of Fallen Timbers.

1. ______________________

2. ______________________

The French Revolution began in 1789. When France declared war on Britain, the United States was in a difficult position. President Washington declared the United States neutral. However, the British navy seized American ships carrying goods to France. Britain also occupied forts on U.S. land. To avoid war, Washington sent John Jay to Britain to negotiate. Britain agreed to sign Jay's Treaty. It said Britain could seize goods bound for France. In return, Britain gave the United States **most-favored nation** status. This protected U.S. merchants from discrimination when they traded with Britain. The treaty prevented war with Britain and protected the U.S. economy.

In the 1780s, white settlement between the Appalachian Mountains and the Mississippi River had grown rapidly. In the Northwest Territory, a confederacy of several Native American groups defended their lands against settlers. President Washington sent troops to put down the resistance. They killed many Native Americans in the Battle of Fallen Timbers. As a result, the Native American nations signed the Treaty of Greenville. They gave up part of present-day southern Ohio and Indiana.

Notes | Read to Learn

The War Between the Parties *(page 164)*

Making Generalizations

Reread the passage. Underline two sentences that support the generalization below.
The Alien and Sedition Acts were controversial laws.

Detecting Bias

Reread the passage. Write a statement from the passage that shows how Hamilton may have felt about Jefferson.

____
____
____
____
____
____
____
____

Angered by Jay's Treaty, France began seizing goods from American ships going to Britain. In June 1798, Congress stopped trade with France and directed the navy to capture armed French ships. The United States and France were soon fighting an undeclared war at sea. Both countries agreed to end the fighting in 1800. The United States gave up all claims against France for damages to U.S. shipping. France agreed to release the United States from the treaty of 1778.

This war affected U.S. domestic policies. In 1798, the Federalists pushed four laws through Congress that became known as the Alien and Sedition Acts. Three were aimed at **aliens**—people living in the country who are not citizens. Many recent immigrants were French and Irish. They usually voted for the Republican Party. One law required immigrants to wait 14 years before becoming citizens. The next two laws gave the president the power to deport any alien believed to be dangerous to the United States. The fourth law was aimed at stopping **sedition,** or incitement to rebellion. The law made it a crime to say or print anything against the federal government.

In 1798 and 1799, Republicans controlled the legislatures of Kentucky and Virginia. They passed resolutions criticizing the Alien and Sedition Acts. The Virginia Resolutions introduced the theory of **interposition.** This said that if the federal government did something unconstitutional, the states could step in to stop the illegal action. The Kentucky Resolutions introduced the theory of **nullification**—that states could declare federal law invalid if it was unconstitutional.

Many people were upset with the Alien and Sedition Acts. The Republican nominees in the election of 1800 were Thomas Jefferson for president and Aaron Burr for vice president. They campaigned against the Federalists and their laws. The election outcome was unexpected. The Constitution called for each state to choose the same number of electors as it had senators plus representatives. The group of electors, know as the Electoral College, then voted for the president. Each elector was to vote for two people. The candidate with the most votes became president. The one in second place became vice president.

In the election of 1800, Jefferson and Burr had the same number of votes. The Federalist-controlled House of Representatives had to choose a president. Hamilton urged the Federalists to support Jefferson. One Federalist cast a blank vote and broke the tie. Jefferson became the new president. The election of 1800 showed that power in the United States could be transferred peacefully.

Section Wrap-up

Answer these questions to check your understanding of the entire section.

1. In what ways did Jay's Treaty most likely affect the U.S. economy?

2. How did the Federalists work with the Republicans to resolve the election of 1800?

Descriptive Writing

Suppose you are an immigrant from France who has just arrived in the United States in 1798 and has seen an article about the Alien and Sedition Acts. Describe how you feel about them and how you think they might affect your life.

Chapter 4, Section 3 (Pages 168–173)

Jefferson in Office

Big Idea

As you read pages 168–173 in your textbook, complete the time line by recording some major events of Jefferson's presidency.

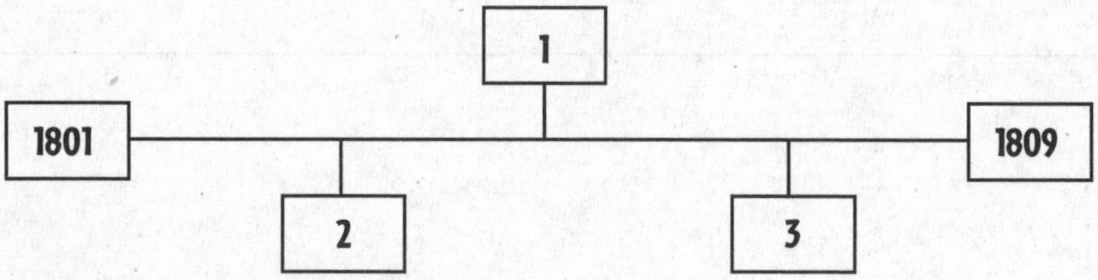

Notes

Read to Learn

Jefferson's Administration *(page 168)*

Formulating Questions

Write A by the question answered in the passage. Write S by the question that needs further study.

1. ___ What were Jefferson's goals during his presidency?

2. ___ What were the terms of the Louisiana Purchase?

Thomas Jefferson tried to bring Republican ideas and Federalist policies together. He hoped to limit the federal government's power. He began to pay off the federal debt and limit federal spending. Instead of having a standing army, he wanted to rely on local militias. Federalists worried that Jefferson would get rid of the national bank. However, Jefferson appointed a supporter of Hamilton's as secretary of the treasury.

In 1801 Jefferson sent Robert Livingston to make a deal with France about the Louisiana Territory, which it purchased in 1803. As a result, the country more than doubled in size and gained control of the Mississippi River. Some Federalists worried that New England would lose its say in the nation's affairs. One group even made a plan to take New England out of the Union.

The role of the Supreme Court grew in the early 1800s. In 1803 the Supreme Court ruled the Judiciary Act of 1789 unconstitutional. This was the first time it had asserted the power of **judicial review**—the power to decide whether laws passed by Congress were constitutional or not. The Supreme Court could strike down unconstitutional laws.

Notes

Read to Learn

Rising International Tensions *(page 172)*

Identifying the Main Idea

Write the main idea of the passage.

____

____

____

____

____

____

Synthesizing Information

Number the events below in the order in which they occurred.

____ ***The Embargo Act hurt the U.S. economy.***

____ ***Britain and France stopped ships going to Europe.***

____ ***The British fired on the American ship* Chesapeake.**

In 1803 war between Britain and France began again. The war helped the United States at first. Because the British seized French ships, U.S. merchants began trading with French colonies. The British left the American ships alone because the United States was neutral. But in 1806 both Britain and France stopped merchant ships going to Europe. Americans were caught in the middle.

The British stopped American ships in order to seize sailors. This upset Americans even more. The British navy was short of sailors. Britain tried to solve the problem by impressment, a legalized form of kidnapping. They stopped American ships to search for British deserters, but sometimes the British forced American citizens into service.

In 1807 the British warship *Leopard* stopped the American warship *Chesapeake.* The British wanted to search the *Chesapeake* for British deserters. When the American ship refused, the British ship opened fire. The British killed three Americans and seized four sailors.

Americans were outraged. President Jefferson did not want the United States to go to war. He asked Congress to pass the Embargo Act of 1807, which stopped all trade between the United States and Europe. The **embargo,** a government ban on trade with other countries, hurt the U. S. economy more than Britain or France. Congress repealed the act in 1809.

President Jefferson left office shortly after the act was repealed. The embargo had made Jefferson unpopular. However, his administration had been successful in limiting the power of the federal government.

Section Wrap-up

Answer these questions to check your understanding of the entire section.

1. Why did the Federalists oppose the Louisiana Purchase?

2. How did the British try to expand their navy?

Informative Writing

In the space provided write a newspaper article on the conflict between the* Leopard *and the* Chesapeake. *Be sure to tell who, what, why, when, and how.

Chapter 4, Section 4 (Pages 176–181)

The War of 1812

Big Idea

As you read pages 176–181 in your textbook, complete the graphic organizer by listing the causes of the War of 1812.

Causes

1.
2.
3.
4.
5.

War of 1812

Notes

Read to Learn

The Decision for War *(page 176)*

Predicting

Make a prediction about how the war will progress.

Republican James Madison won the presidency in 1808. Like Jefferson, he wanted to avoid war with Britain. Madison asked Congress to pass the Non-Intercourse Act, which banned trade with Britain and France. The president could resume trade with the country that removed its trade restrictions first. France did so first. Madison hoped Britain would follow suit. The British refused, so Congress passed a bill to stop imports from Britain. This hurt the British economy. In June of 1812 Britain agreed to end restrictions on trade, but this decision came too late. Congress had declared war on Great Britain.

Most members who voted for war came from the South and the West. Southern planters and Western farmers lost money due to British trade restrictions. Eastern merchants still made a profit, because they passed the cost of losing ships and goods on to the farmers. Western farmers also blamed the British for their conflicts with Native Americans. Many Americans believed that war with Britain would help the United States gain Canada and end Native American attacks. President Madison gave in to pressure and asked Congress to declare war.

Notes

Read to Learn

The Invasion of Canada *(page 178)*

Drawing Conclusions

Underline statements in the passage that support this conclusion:

A military force that is not prepared or well equipped is unlikely to be successful.

Although the United States had declared war, it was not ready to fight. The country did not have enough troops or equipment. It also did not have the money necessary to fight a war. President Madison ordered the military to invade Canada despite these problems. American military leaders attacked Canada from three directions. All three attacks failed.

The United States had more success at sea. The U.S. fleet attacked the British fleet on Lake Erie in September 1813. The British surrendered after a four-hour battle. The victory gave the United States control of Lake Erie. However, by the end of 1813, the United States had not conquered any territory in Canada.

The War Ends *(page 180)*

Analyzing Information

Circle the statements that show the successes of Britain's three-part strategy. Underline the statements that show its failures.

In 1814 the war between Britain and France ended. Britain now turned its attention on the United States. Britain planned a three-part attack strategy. The first part involved attacking cities along the coast. The second involved cutting New England off from the rest of the country. The third involved seizing New Orleans and cutting off the Mississippi River from Western farmers. The British attacked Washington, D.C., and set fire to the White House and the Capitol. They prepared to attack Baltimore, but the militia in Baltimore was ready for them. The British abandoned their attack on the city.

The British offensive made New England even more opposed to the war. Some New Englanders met in Hartford, Connecticut, to talk about what the region could do. The Hartford Convention called for several constitutional amendments to increase the region's political power.

Then in January 1815 American troops under General Andrew Jackson defeated the British in the Battle of New Orleans. The victory made Jackson a national hero and strengthened **nationalism,** or feelings of strong patriotism. The Federalists lost popularity, and in a few years the Federalist Party dissolved. In 1814 the Treaty of Ghent ended the War of 1812. The treaty restored prewar boundaries, but no territory changed hands. However, the War of 1812 increased U.S. prestige overseas and started a wave of patriotism and national unity.

Section Wrap-up

Answer these questions to check your understanding of the entire section.

1. Why did the United States declare war on Britain in 1812?

2. What were the results of the Treaty of Ghent?

Persuasive Writing

In the space provided write a persuasive letter to a merchant in the Eastern United States explaining how war will help the U. S. economy. Include reasons that support your opinion.

Chapter 5, Section 1 (Pages 188–193)

American Nationalism

Big Idea

As you read pages 188–193 in your textbook, complete the graphic organizer by listing actions that strengthened the federal government after the War of 1812.

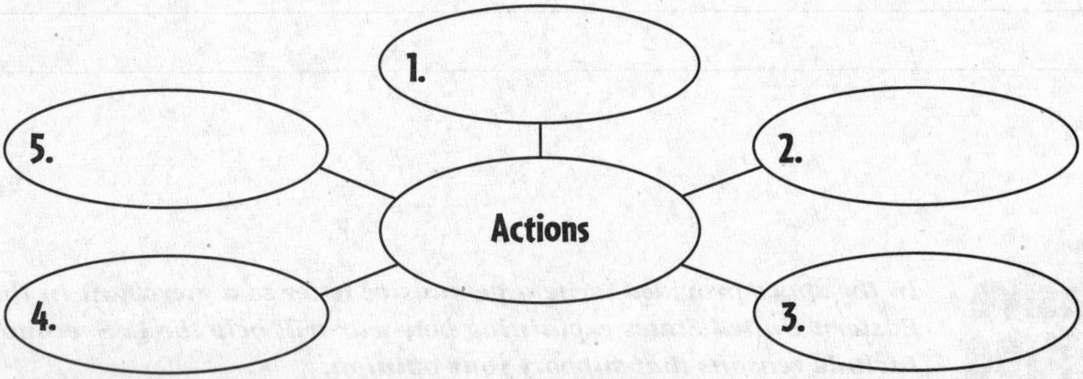

Notes

Read to Learn

Economic Nationalism *(page 188)*

Formulating Questions

Place an X next to the question best answered by the passage.

___ ***What were the results of the War of 1812?***

___ ***How did Congress help bring the nation together?***

In 1811 Republicans had blocked the rechartering of the First Bank of the United States. As a result, state banks and private banks made loans with bank notes that were used as money. During the War of 1812, prices rose rapidly. The U.S. government had to pay high interest on money it borrowed to pay for the war. In 1816 Congressman John C. Calhoun proposed a bill to create the Second Bank of the United States. Congress passed it that year.

During the War of 1812, an embargo stopped Americans from buying British goods. When the war ended, low-priced British goods flooded American markets. Congress passed the Tariff of 1816 to protect domestic manufacturers from foreign competition. Earlier **revenue tariffs** provided income for the federal government. The Tariff of 1816 was a **protective tariff.** It helped American manufacturers by taxing imports from foreign countries to drive up the prices.

In 1816 Calhoun sponsored a federal plan to improve the U.S. transportation system. President Madison vetoed it. Private businesses and state and local governments paid for improvements.

Notes | Read to Learn

Judicial Nationalism *(page 190)*

Making Generalizations

Complete the statement below based on the passage.

The rulings in the three cases helped establish ____________

____

____

____

____

____

____________________.

Between 1816 and 1824, Chief Justice John Marshall helped bring the nation together. He ruled in three cases that established the U.S. government's power over the states.

In 1816 the Supreme Court decided the *Martin* v. *Hunter's Lessee* case. It ruled that it could hear all appeals of state court decisions that involved federal laws and treaties. This established the Supreme Court as the nation's court of final appeal.

In 1819 the Court ruled on *McCulloch* v. *Maryland*. This case decided that the formation of the Second Bank of the United States was constitutional. The ruling said that the federal government could use any method to carry out its powers, as long as the method was not forbidden in the Constitution.

In 1824 the Court decided *Gibbons* v. *Ogden*. The Court ruled that the Constitution gave the federal government control over interstate commerce. States could regulate commerce only within their borders. This ruling made it clear that federal law had priority over state law in interstate transportation.

Nationalist Diplomacy *(page 192)*

Making Inferences

How might Spain and Russia have reacted to the Monroe Doctrine?

____

____

____

____

____

____

____

____

Nationalism in Congress and among voters changed the country's foreign affairs. The United States expanded its borders and became involved in world affairs.

In the early 1800s, many Southerners were angry with Spanish Florida. Enslaved people fled there. Seminoles in Florida and Americans in Georgia attacked each other. In 1818 General Andrew Jackson disobeyed orders and captured Spanish settlements in Florida. He then removed the governor of Florida from power. In 1819 Spain gave all of Florida to the United States in the Adams-Onís Treaty. The countries also set the western border of the Louisiana Purchase.

By 1824 all of Spain's colonies on the American mainland had declared independence. Great Britain, Austria, Prussia, and Russia formed the Quadruple Alliance. France later joined them. These countries wanted to protect their governments in Europe. The group, excluding Great Britain, discussed helping Spain reclaim its colonies. American leaders were also concerned about Russia, which claimed Alaska and announced that it would extend the Russian Empire south into the Oregon Territory country.

President Monroe soon announced what became known as the Monroe Doctrine. He stated that European countries could no longer colonize parts of the American continents.

Section Wrap-up

Answer these questions to check your understanding of the entire section.

1. How did nationalism affect the nation's foreign policy after the War of 1812?

2. What is the difference between a protective tariff and a revenue tariff? Which was the Tariff of 1816?

Informative Writing

Suppose you are writing an essay about the history of the Supreme Court. Write a paragraph about the major cases from 1816 to 1824. Explain why they were significant.

Chapter 5, Section 2 (Pages 194–201)

Early Industry

Big Idea

As you read pages 194–201 in your textbook, complete the graphic organizer by filling in some milestones in transportation and industrialization.

Transportation	Industrialization
1.	4.
2.	5.
3.	6.

Notes | Read to Learn

A Revolution in Transportation *(page 194)*

Problems and Solutions

Write one problem with river travel before 1807. Then write the solution.

Problem:

___

___

___

Solution:

___

___

___

In 1806 Congress funded the building of the National Road, a major east–west highway that started in Cumberland, Maryland, and ended in Wheeling, Virginia (now West Virginia). Conestoga wagons carried pioneers west on this road. Farmers traveled the opposite way to bring their farm products to markets in the East. The National Road was the only federally funded transportation project of its time.

Rivers were a faster, easier, and cheaper way than roads to move goods during this time. However, boats and barges could only travel downstream or with the current. That changed in 1807 when the *Clermont,* a steamboat, chugged upstream on the Hudson River. This transportation advance made river travel more reliable and easier. Steamboats spurred an increase in river travel and canal building. This increased trade between regions, which created economic growth.

Railroads also began in America in the early 1800s. Trains were faster than stagecoaches or wagons, and they could go more places than steamboats. Railroads helped settle the West and expand trade among the nation's regions.

Notes

Read to Learn

A New System of Production *(page 197)*

Determining Cause and Effect

Why did industrialization begin in the Northeast? List two causes.

1. ______________________

____

____

2. ______________________

____

____

The Industrial Revolution began in Britain in the 1700s. It included several developments in business and industry. Manufacturing went from hand tools to large, complex machines. Unskilled workers replaced skilled artisans. Factories replaced home workshops. Goods were sold all over instead of just locally. Industry developed quickly in the United States in the early 1800s. One factor was the **free enterprise system,** which let people make money and choose how to use it. Free enterprise encouraged industry because it allowed companies to compete with one another.

Industrialization began in the Northeast. Streams provided waterpower for factories. Citizens in the Northeast also had money to invest in industry. Inventions and technological advances helped industry grow. Eli Whitney made the idea of **interchangeable parts** popular in the gun industry. In this system, machines made large amounts of identical pieces. Unskilled workers then assembled the identical parts into finished goods at a cheaper price. In 1832 Samuel F. B. Morse began work on the telegraph. He created the Morse code for sending messages. Newspapers used the telegraph to quickly collect and share news stories.

Industrialization encouraged the growth of large cities. Thousands of people moved from farms and villages to towns and cities in search of factory jobs and better pay. By 1860 there were 1.3 million factory workers in the United States. During the late 1820s and early 1830s, many workers joined **labor unions** to improve working conditions. The unions, however, had little power. They could not support **strikes,** or work stoppages. Courts often ruled against these early unions.

Life in the North *(page 200)*

Identifying the Main Idea

Write the main idea of the passage.

____

____

____

____

____

As Northern cities grew, so did there problems. Some cities started police departments to combat crime, and some formalized their fire departments. Because of unsanitary conditions and unsafe water, diseases such as cholera and typhoid raged in cities. Most cities did not have public schools until the 1850s, and those that did generally did not require students to attend. Cities became havens for often-poor runaway slaves and free African Americans.

Farming was still important in the North. Northern farmers produced enough to sell their surplus in eastern cities and towns. They not only helped feed the people of the region, but also nourished the region's economy.

Section Wrap-up

Answer these questions to check your understanding of the entire section.

1. What changes took place in transportation in the early 1800s?

2. How did the Industrial Revolution change methods of production?

Expository Writing

Describe the advantages and disadvantages of the new methods of production brought about by the Industrial Revolution. Describe possible effects on businesses and people.

Chapter 5, Section 3 (Pages 202–209)

The Land of Cotton

Big Idea

As you read pages 202–209 in your textbook, complete the graphic organizer by listing the main categories of Southern society.

Southern Society

Hightest 1. ______________________

2. ______________________

3. ______________________

Lowest 4. ______________________

Notes | Read to Learn

The Southern Economy *(page 202)*

Determining Cause and Effect

List two causes.

1. Cause:

____

____

____

2. Cause:

____

____

____

Effect: Cotton became the chief cash crop in the South.

The South's economy was based on farming several major cash crops, such as tobacco, rice, and sugarcane. Cotton, the chief cash crop, was grown in many states, including South Carolina, Georgia, Alabama, Mississippi, and Texas.

In 1793 Eli Whitney invented the **cotton gin,** which removed the seeds from cotton bolls. This technological advancement greatly increased cotton production in the South. In Europe textile mills were expanding and wanted large amounts of cotton for cloth production. In 1860 Southern cotton made up almost two-thirds of total U.S. exports. This demand for cotton also created a huge demand for slave labor. Between 1820 and 1850, the number of enslaved people in the South rose from 1.5 million to nearly 4 million.

With its focus on agriculture, the South did not industrialize as quickly as the North. The South remained a region of rural villages and plantations. It had only three large cities. The South did have some industry, including coal, iron, salt, and copper mines as well as ironworks and textile mills. However, the South had to import most of its manufactured goods.

Notes

Read to Learn

Society in the South *(page 204)*

Identifying the Main Idea

Write the main idea of the passage.

The South developed a rigid and clearly defined class structure. At the top of Southern society were the planters, or owners of the larger plantations. This group made up less than one percent of the white population, but they ran the region's economy and political system. Next were the **yeoman farmers,** or common farmers, who may have had four or fewer enslaved people. Most of the white population of the South were yeoman farmers.

Near the bottom of Southern society were the rural poor. These people mostly hunted, fished, gardened, and raised a few hogs and chickens. African Americans, most of whom were enslaved, made up the very bottom of Southern society. A small urban class of professionals also made up part of Southern society. Many of these professionals invested in or owned farms.

Slavery *(page 206)*

Drawing Conclusions

Write one conclusion you can draw based on the passage.

Rice and cotton plantations depended on enslaved labor to exist. Most enslaved African Americans worked in the fields, but some worked as skilled workers or house servants. There were two basic labor systems for enslaved African Americans who worked in the fields. The **task system** was used on farms and small plantations. Under this system, workers had certain jobs to finish every day. They worked until their tasks were done, and then they were allowed to do other things. Some enslaved people earned money as artisans, and others gardened for extra food. Large plantations used the gang system. Under this system, enslaved people were put in work gangs that worked in the fields the entire day.

Enslaved people had few legal rights. In many states, enslaved people could not own property or leave their owners' land without permission. They were not allowed to learn to read and write. Songs were important to many enslaved people. Field workers often sang to help pass the long workday and express a continuing hope for freedom. Songs also played a key role in the religion of African Americans. Many were Christians.

Many enslaved people resisted slavery by quietly staging work slowdowns. Others broke farm tools, set houses and barns on fire, or even ran away. On occasion, enslaved people plotted uprisings. Nat Turner led a revolt in Virginia in 1831 in which he and his followers killed more than 50 white people.

Section Wrap-up

Answer these questions to check your understanding of the entire section.

1. Why did cotton dominate the Southern economy?

2. How did farming affect all the different classes of Southern society in the 1800s?

Descriptive Writing

In the space provided write a short, descriptive poem about Southern society prior to the Civil War. You might write your poem from an enslaved person's perspective.

Chapter 5, Section 4 (Pages 212–215)

Growing Sectionalism

Big Idea

As you read pages 212–215 in your textbook, complete the graphic organizer by filling in some of the divisive issues of the 1820s.

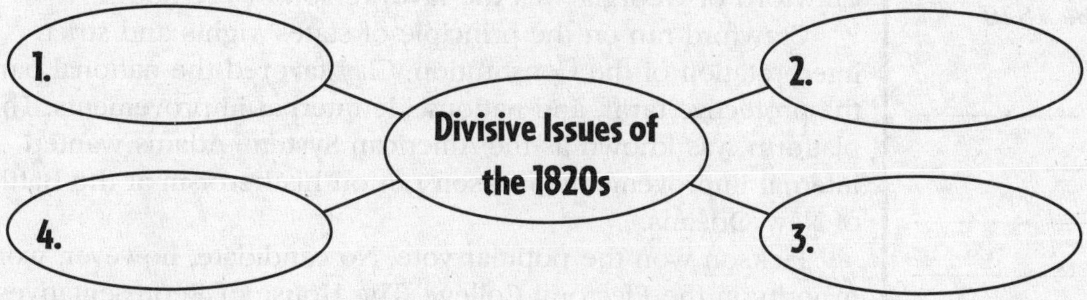

Notes

Read to Learn

The Missouri Compromise *(page 212)*

Predicting

Read the first paragraph. Predict what might happen next.

____

____

____

____

____

____

In 1819 Missouri applied for statehood as a slave state, stirring up the divisive issue of whether slavery should expand westward. At that time the Union had 11 free states and 11 slave states. Admitting any new state, either slave or free, would upset the balance in the Senate and start a struggle for political power.

When Maine applied for statehood, the Senate decided to address the admission of both states at the same time. The result was the Missouri Compromise. It called for Maine to enter the Union as a free state while Missouri entered as a slave state. The compromise included an amendment prohibiting slavery in the Louisiana Purchase territory north of Missouri's southern border. The House members accepted the compromise.

A new problem soon threatened the compromise. The Missouri constitutional convention added a clause to the proposed state constitution. It prohibited free African Americans from entering the state. This threatened the final approval of Missouri's admission to the Union. Henry Clay solved the problem by getting the state legislature to agree that they would not honor the spirit of the clause's wording.

Notes

Read to Learn

The Elections of 1824 and 1828 *(page 214)*

Comparing and Contrasting

How did Andrew Jackson contrast himself with John Quincy Adams during the 1828 election?

____

____

____

____

____

____

____

____

Distinguishing Fact from Opinion

Read the last paragraph. Circle two sentences that state opinions.

Sectional differences over beliefs and policies were part of the election of 1824. All four candidates in the presidential election were from the Republican Party. They all were **favorite sons,** or men who had the support of leaders from their own state and region. Henry Clay of Kentucky and Andrew Jackson of Tennessee represented the West. John Quincy Adams of Massachusetts was the favorite son of New England. William Crawford of Georgia was the favorite son of the South.

Crawford ran on the principle of states' rights and strict interpretation of the Constitution. Clay favored the national bank, the protective tariff, and nationwide internal improvements. This platform was known as the American System. Adams wanted internal improvements. Jackson ran on his heroism at the Battle of New Orleans.

Jackson won the popular vote. No candidate, however, won a majority in the Electoral College. The House of Representatives had to vote to select the president from the three candidates with the highest number of electoral votes. Clay had the least votes, so he was eliminated. Clay, who was Speaker of the House, had great influence. He threw his support to John Quincy Adams, who won the House vote.

Jackson's supporters accused Clay of winning votes for Adams in return for a cabinet post. Adams and Clay were accused of making a **"corrupt bargain."** Although Adams and Clay said they had done nothing wrong, the incident split the party. Jackson's supporters began calling themselves Democrats.

In his first message to Congress, Adams proposed a program of nationalist legislation. It included internal improvements, a national university, astronomical observatories, and funding for scientific research. His opponents argued that his proposals were a waste of taxpayers' money. Congress granted money only to improve rivers and harbors and to extend the National Road westward.

John Quincy Adams ran against Andrew Jackson in the presidential election of 1828. Both candidates engaged in **mudslinging,** or criticizing each other's personalities and morals. Adams claimed that Jackson was incompetent. Jackson said he was the candidate of the common man and called Adams an out-of-touch aristocrat. Jackson reminded voters of the alleged "corrupt bargain" between Adams and Clay in the election of 1824. He claimed that this proved Adams was untrustworthy. Jackson won the popular vote and the electoral vote, with much support from the West and South. Many of his supporters were rural and small-town men who thought Jackson would represent their interests.

Section Wrap-up

Answer these questions to check your understanding of the entire section.

1. What were the major parts of the Missouri Compromise?

2. Why was the election of 1824 controversial?

Persuasive Writing

Write a letter to a newspaper defending your choice for president in the 1828 presidential election. Include several reasons why you think that either President John Quincy Adams or Andrew Jackson should be elected.

Chapter 6, Section 1 (Pages 222–229)

Jacksonian America

Big Idea

As you read pages 222–229 in your textbook, complete the graphic organizer by listing the positions of Jackson and Calhoun during the nullification crisis.

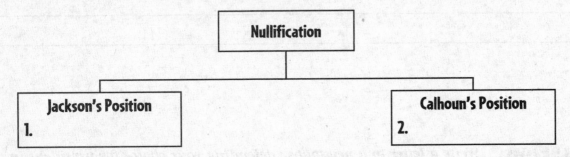

Nullification

Jackson's Position	**Calhoun's Position**
1.	2.

Notes

Read to Learn

A New Era in Politics *(page 222)*

Identifying the Main Idea

Complete the sentence to tell the passage's main idea.

During this era, ordinary citizens

____

____

____

____

____

____

____

In the early 1800s, the United States saw a growth of democracy. Many states got rid of property ownership as a voting qualification. As a result, hundreds of thousands of men gained **suffrage,** or the right to vote. Urban workers who did not own property but did pay taxes also wanted to vote. Many of these new voters cast their ballots for Andrew Jackson in the 1828 election.

President Jackson believed that ordinary citizens should play an active role in government. Jackson supported the **spoils system,** the practice of giving government jobs to people who supported the party. He believed that opening government offices to ordinary citizens increased democracy.

Jackson also wanted to make the process of choosing presidential candidates more democratic. Members of Congress chose presidential nominees at that time. This method was called the **caucus system.** Jackson believed it gave only the well connected the chance to hold office. Jackson created the national nominating convention. In this system, delegates from the states decided on the party's presidential nominee. Jackson was nominated for president by this method in 1832.

Notes

Read to Learn

The Nullification Crisis *(page 225)*

Problems and Solutions

Reread the passage. Then do the following:

Circle Calhoun's solution to South Carolina's problem with tariffs.

Underline Clay's solution for South Carolina's problem with tariffs.

South Carolina's economy weakened in the early 1800s. Many people blamed the nation's tariffs for this situation. South Carolina bought many goods from Europe, and tariffs on these imported goods made them very expensive. In 1828 Congress placed a new tariff on imports. In response, many South Carolinians wanted to **secede,** or withdraw, from the Union.

Vice President John C. Calhoun was torn between following the country's policies and helping his fellow South Carolinians. He came up with the idea of nullification, which said that the states had the right to declare a federal law null, or not valid.

President Jackson asked Congress to cut tariffs, which they did with a new law in 1832. South Carolina was still upset and declared the tariffs null. Jackson saw this as an act of treason. He sent a warship to Charleston, South Carolina. Congress passed the Force Bill in 1833, which allowed the president to use the military to enforce acts of Congress. Senator Henry Clay pushed through a bill to lower tariffs within two years. South Carolina repealed its nullification of the tariff law.

Policies Toward Native Americans *(page 226)*

Making Inferences

Based on the passage, how did Native Americans most likely feel about being relocated?

____

____

____

____

____

____

____

____

____

Like many other people, President Jackson believed that conflicts with Native Americans would end if Native Americans were moved to the Great Plains. In 1830 Jackson pushed through Congress the Indian Removal Act, which provided money to relocate Native Americans.

Most Native Americans gave in and moved to the West. However, the Cherokee of Georgia refused. They sued the state of Georgia, and their case reached the Supreme Court. Chief Justice John Marshall sided with the Cherokee. He ordered the state to honor the Cherokee's property rights. President Jackson did not honor or enforce the Court's decision.

President Martin Van Buren eventually sent the army to settle the problem with the Cherokee. The army forced them out of their homes and marched them west to what is now Oklahoma. Thousands of Cherokee died on the journey, which became known as the Trail of Tears. By 1838 the government had moved the majority of Native Americans still living east of the Mississippi to reservations. Although most Americans supported this removal policy, some, such as a few National Republicans and some religious groups, opposed this action.

Notes

Read to Learn

Jackson Battles the National Bank *(page 227)*

Determining Cause and Effect

Circle the sentence that tells the cause.

Effect: William Henry Harrison won the presidency.

President Jackson thought the Second Bank of the United States helped only the wealthy. After being reelected in 1832, he closed the bank. The Whig Party formed in the mid-1830s to oppose Jackson. Whigs wanted a stronger federal government and supported industry and trade.

In 1836 Democrat Martin Van Buren was elected president. Shortly after he became president, an economic crisis hit the United States. The Whigs hoped this crisis would help them weaken the Democrats' political power. In 1840 the Whig candidate William Henry Harrison won the presidency, but he died 32 days after entering office. Vice President John Tyler became president and actually opposed many Whig policies and sided with the Democrats while in office.

Section Wrap-up

Answer these questions to check your understanding of the entire section.

1. How did Jackson support the role of the ordinary citizen in U.S. government?

2. Explain why South Carolina wanted to secede from the Union and how the conflict between South Carolina and the federal government was resolved.

Descriptive Writing

Write a paragraph describing the Trail of Tears from the point of view of a Cherokee person. Use descriptive language, vivid images, and active verbs to make your writing realistic.

Chapter 6, Section 2 (Pages 230–235)

A Changing Culture

Big Idea

As you read pages 230–235 in your textbook, complete the graphic organizer by listing beliefs of various religious groups of the Second Great Awakening.

Religious Groups	Beliefs
1.	2.
3.	4.
5.	6.
7.	8.

Notes

Read to Learn

The New Wave of Immigrants *(page 230)*

Determining Cause and Effect

Write the cause.

Cause:

____

____

____

____

____

____

Effect: Many Irish immigrants arrive in the United States after 1845.

Between 1815 and 1860, more than 5 million immigrants arrived in the United States. Almost 2 million came from Ireland. The Irish came because in 1845 a fungus destroyed much of the nation's potato crop, causing a great famine. The Irish generally settled in the cities of the Northeast. They worked as unskilled laborers. More than 1.5 million Germans came to the United States. Most settled Ohio and Pennsylvania where they farmed or started businesses.

Some immigrants faced discrimination in America. The presence of people with different languages and religions produced a feeling of **nativism,** or hostility toward foreigners. Many Americans were anti-Catholic, and the arrival of millions of Irish and German Catholic immigrants led to the start of nativist groups. These groups promised never to vote for a Catholic. They supported laws that stopped immigrants from holding public office. In 1854 members from these natavist groups formed the American Party. Membership in the party was secret. Members were told to answer, "I know nothing," when questioned, so the party earned the nickname "the Know-Nothings." It had many followers in the 1850s.

Notes | Read to Learn

A Religious Revival *(page 232)*

Synthesizing Information

Based on the passage, what are some characteristics of a utopian society?

1. ______________

____

____

2. ______________

____

____

In the 1800s religious leaders wanted to restore Americans' commitment to religion. They started a movement called the Second Great Awakening. Thousands of followers came to revival meetings held by Protestant leaders. During these revivals, people were urged to bring God back into their lives.

Some new religions grew during the mid-1800s. Among these were the Unitarians and Universalists. Joseph Smith founded the Church of Jesus Christ of Latter-day Saints. The followers of this religion are called Mormons. After facing persecution by other Americans, the Mormons moved west in search of a secluded place to practice their beliefs.

Some people believed that society corrupted human nature. They separated from society and formed their own **utopias,** or ideal societies. In these communities, they lived cooperatively without private property. Brook Farm in Massachusetts was one such community. A religious group called the Shakers also started several utopian communities.

Cultural Renaissance *(page 234)*

Comparing and Contrasting

Reread the passage. Circle the characteristics of romanticism. Underline the characteristics of transcendentalism.

In the 1800s **romanticism** influenced culture in the United States. Romanticism was a movement or way of thinking that started in Europe. It advocated feeling over reason. It also favored nature over environments created by humans. Some New England thinkers adopted the philosophy of **transcendentalism.** It was a type of romanticism. It urged people to transcend, or overcome, the limits of their minds so their souls could take in the beauty of the universe.

The most important transcendentalist was Ralph Waldo Emerson. He wrote that people who wanted fulfillment should work for union with nature. Another transcendentalist writer, Henry David Thoreau, wrote that people should fight the pressure to conform. Other writers created uniquely American works. These writers included Washington Irving, James Fenimore Cooper, Nathaniel Hawthorne, Herman Melville, and Edgar Allan Poe. Walt Whitman and Emily Dickinson were among the most important poets of the era.

During the early 1800s more Americans learned to read and more men gained voting rights. Publishers began producing inexpensive newspapers that reported on crime, gossip, politics, and local news. These newspapers were very popular. Magazines such as *The Atlantic Monthly* and *Harper's Weekly* also started around this time.

Section Wrap-up

Answer these questions to check your understanding of the entire section.

1. Explain the rise of nativism and give an example of a nativist group from the 1800s.

2. What was the goal of the Second Great Awakening?

Expository Writing

In the space provided compare and contrast two ways that Americans revived or restored a commitment to religion during the 1800s.

Chapter 6, Section 3 (Pages 236–241)

Reforming Society

Big Idea

As you read pages 236–241 in your textbook, complete the outline using the major headings of the section.

Reforming Society

I. The Reform Spirit
   A. ______
   B. ______
   C. ______
   D. ______

II. ______
   A. ______
   B. ______

Notes

Read to Learn

The Reform Spirit *(page 236)*

Predicting

List one possible result of opening up more educational opportunities to women.

______

______

______

Many people in the mid-1800s worked to reform American society. Dorothea Dix worked to improve conditions for the mentally ill. Lyman Beecher, a revivalist minister, started **benevolent societies.** These organizations worked to spread God's word and solve social problems. Many people believed that alcohol caused social problems. Some reformers supported **temperance,** or moderation in the consumption of alcohol.

Some reformers supported programs to help rehabilitate prisoners rather than simply to lock them up. The new prisons, called **penitentiaries,** tried to teach prisoners remorse. Many reformers also worked for public education, with government-funded schools were open to all. Horace Mann, a Massachusetts legislator, helped create a state board of education. Tax-supported schools soon spread all over the country.

Some women worked to create educational opportunities for women. Emma Willard opened a girls' school that taught subjects such as math and literature, unusual for that time. Mary Lyon opened the first institution of higher education for women only. Elizabeth Blackwell became the first woman to earn a medical degree.

Notes

Read to Learn

The Early Women's Movement *(page 240)*

Detecting Bias

Reread the passage. Underline sentences that show biases toward women as brought forth by the ideas of "true womanhood."

Formulating Questions

Write two questions that occur to you as you read the passage.

1. ______________________

____

____

____

2. ______________________

____

____

____

In the 1800s the Industrial Revolution began to change the roles of men and women. The development of factories and other places of work separated the home and the workplace. Men often left home to go to work, and women took care of the house and children. Many people believed that the home was the proper place for women. The idea that women should be homemakers and be responsible for the development of their children came to be known as "true womanhood." Women were often seen as more moral and charitable than men. They were expected to be models of virtue to their children and husbands.

Many women did not feel limited by the ideas of true womanhood. They felt that that as wives they were partners with their husbands and in some ways, morally superior to them. The idea that women played an important role in building a virtuous home soon extended to building a more virtuous society. Women became more involved in the social reforms of the day. Some women argued that they need greater political rights to promote their ideas.

Margaret Fuller argued that many injustices in society would end if men and women were treated equally. In 1848 Lucretia Mott and Elizabeth Cady Stanton organized the Seneca Falls Convention. This was a gathering of women and the start of an organized women's movement. The convention declared that all men and women are created equal. Stanton also proposed that women focus on gaining the right to vote, which shocked many people. Women continued to meet throughout the 1850s to work toward greater rights. By 1860 fifteen states had passed laws that let married women keep their property if their husbands died.

Section Wrap-up

Answer these questions to check your understanding of the entire section.

1. What were the major issues and areas of society that reformers set out to improve?

2. What was the Seneca Falls Convention? Why was it significant?

Persuasive Writing

In the space provided write an editorial to appear in a newspaper in 1845. Tell readers what "true womanhood" is and tell why they should support its ideas.

Chapter 6, Section 4 (Pages 242–247)

The Abolitionist Movement

Big Idea

As you read pages 242–247 in your textbook, complete the time line to record some early events of the abolitionist movement.

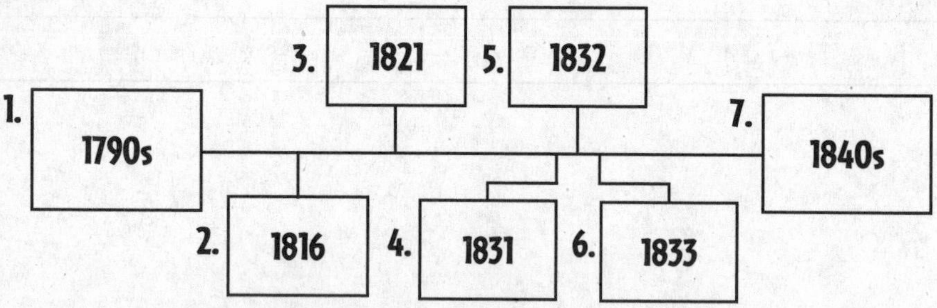

Notes

Read to Learn

The New Abolitionists *(page 242)*

Formulating Questions

Reread the passage. Write a question that would help you learn more about the topic.

Early antislavery societies supported an idea called **gradualism**—that slavery should end slowly. They also believed slaveholders should be compensated for their losses. Supporters thought this would give the economy of the South time to adjust to the loss of enslaved labor. Some antislavery societies also believed that ending slavery would not end racism. They thought the best solution was to send African Americans back to Africa. Most African Americans saw the United States as their home and did not want to move.

In the 1830s the idea of **abolition** took hold. Abolitionists argued that enslaved African Americans should be freed at once without compensation for slave holders. Abolitionists believed slavery was an evil for which the country needed to be sorry. William Lloyd Garrison helped start a national abolitionist movement in the 1830s. He published a newspaper that called for complete **emancipation,** or the freeing of all enslaved people. Many people supported Garrison's goal. Frederick Douglass was one of the most famous African American abolitionists. He published his own antislavery newspaper, the *North Star.*

Notes

Read to Learn

The Response to Abolitionism *(page 246)*

Distinguishing Fact from Opinion

Read the second paragraph. Write an opinion some Southerners had about slavery. Then write one fact about slavery in the South.

Opinion:

____

____

____

____

Fact:

____

____

____

____

Evaluating Information

Look at the opinion you wrote above. Do you think it is accurate? Why or why not?

____

____

____

____

____

____

Many Northerners disapproved of slavery. However, some Northerners opposed abolition even more because they feared that the abolitionist movement was a threat to society. Some believed that it would create conflict between the North and the South. Others were afraid that it would cause many freed African Americans to move to the North. They feared this would cause a shortage of houses and jobs. Mobs in Northern cities attacked abolitionists. But some Northerners also disliked Southern slave-catchers, who caught African American runaways in the North and brought them back to the South. Some Northern states passed laws against slave recapture.

Most Southerners viewed slavery as necessary to the Southern way of life. These Southerners argued that the labor of enslaved people was essential to the South's agriculture-based economy. They also claimed that most enslaved people did not want freedom because of their close relationship with the slave-holders.

William Lloyd Garrison first published his abolitionist newspaper in 1831. Less than eight months later, an enslaved preacher named Nat Turner led a revolt of enslaved workers. More than 50 Virginians died as a result. Southerners furiously demanded that abolitionist material not be circulated in the South. Postal workers there refused to deliver abolitionist newspapers. In response to pressure from the South, the House of Representatives refused to debate any abolitionist petitions.

Despite widespread conflict over abolitionism, the movement remained small. Few people before the Civil War accepted the idea that slavery should end immediately.

Section Wrap-up

Answer these questions to check your understanding of the entire section.

1. What groups were involved in the early antislavery movement?

2. How did Northerners and Southerners view abolitionism?

Informative Writing

In the space provided write a short history of the early antislavery movement. Write for someone unfamiliar with U.S. history during this period. Discuss what happened, when it happened, why it happened, how it happened, and who was involved.

Chapter 7, Section 1 (Pages 254–257)

The Western Pioneers

Big Idea

As you read pages 254–257 in your textbook, complete the graphic organizer by filling in the names of some of the main trails used by westward emigrants in the 1840s.

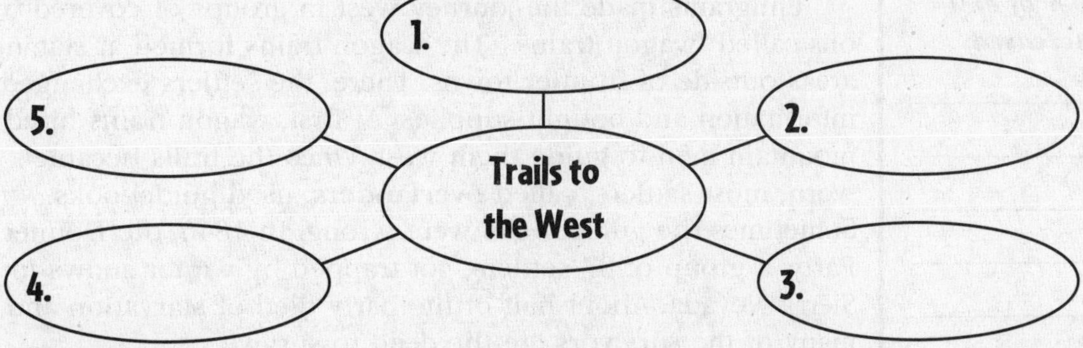

Notes

Read to Learn

Settling New Lands *(page 254)*

Problems and Solutions

Read the passage. List two problems faced by early settlers.

1. ____________________

____

____

2. ____________________

____

____

____

In 1800 about 387,000 settlers lived west of the Appalachian Mountains. By 1820 there were about 2.4 million settlers. Some settlers moved west for religious freedom and others wanted to own their own farms. Many believed in Manifest Destiny, the idea that God had given the American people the entire continent to settle.

The first people settling west were called **squatters.** They settled on land that they did not own. The government planned to sell this land to real estate companies. The squatters, however, wanted to buy the land directly from the government. In 1830 the Preemption Act was passed. It stated that squatters could buy up to 160 acres for $1.25 per acre.

Midwestern settlers took advantage of several new farming inventions. The iron-blade plow, steel-blade plow, and a mechanical reaper helped to create farms from the thick Midwestern sod. Many settlers, however, continued west to the Pacific Coast. In the 1830s, American missionaries arrived in Oregon Country, a land claimed by both the United States and Britain. They spread news of the lush Willamette Valley and present-day Oregon.

Notes

Predicting

Reread the passage. Think about Native Americans' worries about the emigrants. Predict what may have happened as the number of emigrants increased.

____

____

____

____

____

____

____

____

Making Inferences

Underline examples in the passage that support the following inference.

Life on the trails was difficult.

Read to Learn

Westward Migration *(page 256)*

Much of the land that the emigrants had to cross was difficult terrain. Mountain men such as Kit Carson and Jim Bridger were trailblazers. They made their living by trapping beaver and selling the furs to traders. They learned about the land and the Native Americans who lived there. By the 1840s, the mountain men had made several east–west trails, such as the Oregon Trail, the California Trail, and the Santa Fe Trail. These trails helped emigrants to move west.

Emigrants made the journey west in groups of covered wagons called "wagon trains." The wagon trains formed at staging areas outside of frontier towns. There, the settlers exchanged information and bought supplies. At first, wagon trains hired the mountain men to guide them west. Once the trails became worn, most settlers, called **overlanders,** used guidebooks. Sometimes the guidebooks were wrong. In 1846, the Donner Party, a group of 87 settlers, got trapped by winter snows in the Sierra Nevada. About half of the party died of starvation and many of the survivors ate the dead to survive.

A typical trip to the Pacific coast could take up to six months. Wagon trains traveled about 15 miles per day. Along the trail, the men of the group would drive the wagons, hunt, and bed down the animals at night. The women looked after children, cooked, cleaned, and washed clothes.

Many travelers feared Native American attacks. However, these attacks were rare. Only 362 emigrants died in Native American attacks between 1840 and 1860. The emigrants killed 426 Native Americans. Native Americans often gave the emigrants food and information about routes and water sources. As overland traffic increased, the Native Americans became afraid and angry that the immigration might change their way of life. The Native Americans in this region relied on buffalo for food, shelter, and clothing. They feared that the settlers might disrupt the buffalo herds. The U.S. government and eight Native American groups negotiated the Treaty of Fort Laramie in 1851. It made territories for each group and gave them ownership of these territories forever.

The Mormons traveled west to find religious freedom. In 1844 a mob murdered the Mormon founder Joseph Smith. As a result, the new leader Brigham Young decided to take his people west to escape religious persecution. Thousands of Mormons emigrated west on the Mormon Trail. This trail became an important route to the western United States. In 1847 the Mormons stopped at the Great Salt Lake. Brigham Young decided to build a new settlement there.

Section Wrap-up

Answer these questions to check your understanding of the entire section.

1. Why did the United States and the Native Americans negotiate the Treaty of Fort Laramie?

2. What is Manifest Destiny and how did it help Americans to settle the West?

Descriptive Writing

Suppose it is 1850, and you have just arrived in the Willamette Valley with your family. Write a letter to a friend back in New York describing your journey westward. Include many details about the trip and daily life on the trail.

Chapter 7, Section 2 (Pages 260–263)

The Hispanic Southwest

Big Idea

As you read pages 260–263 in your textbook, complete the chart by listing features of the California, New Mexico, and Texas territories at this time.

Territory	Features
California	1.
New Mexico	2.
Texas	3.

Notes

Read to Learn

Mexican Independence and the Borderlands *(page 260)*

Determining Cause and Effect

Complete the items.

1. Cause: Mexico won its independence from Spain in 1821.

Effect:

____

____

2. Cause:

____

____

Effect: Missions were taken over by Rancheros.

After Mexico won its independence from Spain in 1821 it struggled to create a stable government. California, New Mexico, and Texas were part of Mexico. They were mostly independent and had small Hispanic populations, but faced Native American attacks and American and Russian expansion.

Spain had settled the northern frontier of New Spain with missions. The missions spread Christianity and Spanish culture to Native Americans, who worked on the missions under harsh conditions. In 1834 the Mexican government **secularized** the missions, transferring them to civil control. Most of the missions were taken over by cattle ranchers called Rancheros. They relied on the work of Native Americans.

In California, Rancheros and their families were less than 10 percent of the population. They owned much of the land and controlled society. The middle class, the ***mestizos,*** were of mixed European and Native American ancestry. Many were skilled craftsmen or cowboys called **vaqueros.** Most of the population was Native American. In New Mexico, Native American attacks led to a revolt in 1837.

Notes

Making Inferences

Reread the passage. What can you infer about Spanish rule in California? Complete the sentences below.

1. The Spanish did not allow ____________ from outside their empire.

2. Soon after Mexican independence, ____________ flocked to the borderlands with their trade goods.

Identifying the Main Idea

Write the main idea below.

____

____

____

____

____

____

Read to Learn

Americans Arrive in the Borderlands *(page 263)*

Americans began moving to California before Mexico won its independence. After Mexican independence, the number of Americans in California grew. Traders from the United States, Russia, and other countries began coming to California. They traded their manufactured goods for animal skins and tallow.

In 1839 the governor of California gave an immigrant named John Sutter 50,000 acres of land. Sutter built a trading post and a cattle ranch. The post was called Sutter's Fort. It was the first stop for many Americans traveling to California. The increase in the American population and American products caused changes. Differences grew between the people of California and southern Mexico.

Changes occurred in New Mexico too. Before 1821 the people of New Mexico bought most of their manufactured goods from southern Mexico. An American named Will Becknell opened up the Santa Fe Trail in 1821. The trail connected Independence, Missouri, with Santa Fe, New Mexico. Wagons brought American goods to New Mexico along this trail. The Americans traded their goods for silver, mules, and furs. Trade grew and Americans began to settle in Santa Fe.

East of New Mexico was Texas. This region was a buffer between southern Mexico and the United States. It had only about 2,500 Spanish-speaking settlers. They were called *Tejanos.* The *Tejanos* faced constant attacks by Native Americans. Most of the settlers lived in the towns of San Antonio and Goliad. Just before Mexico won its independence, Spain allowed foreigners to settle in Texas. Mexico continued this policy. Soon Americans flooded into Texas and they outnumbered the Tejanos.

The decision to allow Americans into Texas led to a revolt. Texas won its independence fifteen years after Mexican independence. California and New Mexico broke away from Mexico after twenty-five years.

Section Wrap-up

Answer these questions to check your understanding of the entire section.

1. Who were the *Tejanos* and how did Mexican independence affect them?

2. What impact did the Americans have on the borderlands?

Expository Writing

In the space provided compare the different types of people in California society. Include as many details about each class as you can.

Chapter 7, Section 3 (Pages 264–269)

Independence for Texas

Big Idea

As you read pages 264–269 in your textbook, complete the graphic organizer by filling in the major battles of the Texas revolution and the outcome of each.

Major Battle	Outcome
1.	2.
3.	4.
5.	6.

Notes

Read to Learn

Opening Texas to Americans *(page 264)*

Formulating Questions

Read the passage. Think about why the American settlers had problems living under Mexican rule. Write one question you might ask about the settlers' struggle.

Mexico could not widely settle Texas. So it continued the Spanish policy of immigration. Between 1823 and 1825, Mexico passed three colonization laws offering cheap land to settlers in Texas. However, they had to become Mexican citizens, convert to Catholicism, and follow Mexican law. Most Americans came to Texas at the encouragement of ***empresarios,*** or agents. Under the National Colonization Act, Mexico gave large pieces of land to 26 *empresarios* who promised to bring settlers to their land. They also governed their colonies. Stephen Austin was the most successful agent. He moved 1,500 people to his colony.

At first, many Americans agreed to Mexican citizenship. However, they did not adopt Mexican customs or convert to Catholicism. Few learned Spanish. The Mexicans distrusted the new settlers. In 1826 Benjamin Edwards led a rebellion to free the settlers from Mexico. Stephen Austin and his troops ended the Edwards revolt. Mexico feared that the revolt was an American plot to steal Texas. In 1830, Mexico closed its border to immigration and taxed trade with the United States. The Texans resented the new Mexican laws.

Notes

Read to Learn

Texas Goes to War *(page 266)*

Drawing Conclusions

Read the first paragraph. Put an X by the conclusion it best supports.

___ ***1. Separating Texas from Coahuila was the American settlers' most important need.***

___ ***2. Austin's efforts were shaped by his desire to open the border and allow further immigration.***

___ ***3. The need for continued immigration, self rule, and open trade shaped the settlers' relations with Mexico.***

Making Generalizations

Read the second paragraph. What did Austin and the Texan leaders think of Santa Anna's leadership?

____

____

____

____

____

____

Starting in 1832, the American settlers in Texas held two conventions. The members asked Mexico to allow American immigration again, to lower taxes on imported goods, and to make Texas a separate state. Then they sent Stephen Austin to Mexico City to talk with the government. The talks did not go far. Austin wrote a letter to the Texan leaders. He suggested that Texas organize its own state government. However, Mexican officials got the letter before it went to Texas.

Soon after, Austin met with the Mexican president Antonio López de Santa Anna. Austin convinced him to reopen Texas to American settlers and to grant other Texan demands. Then he was arrested by Mexican officials and jailed for treason because of his letter. In April 1834, Santa Anna made himself dictator. When Austin was released from prison in 1835, he pushed Texans to organize an army, which they did.

The Texan army's first victories were at Gonzales and San Antonio. However, the Texan army faced many difficulties. Few men had military training. They also could not agree who would lead them. Finally, Sam Houston took command. Houston was a former Tennessee governor and an experienced military leader.

In February 1836, 6,000 of Santa Anna's troops came to San Antonio. Over 180 Texan rebels and 32 settlers were at the Alamo, an abandoned mission. Joined by 32 settlers from Gonzales, they held off Santa Anna's army for 13 days, giving the Texan army time to organize. Meanwhile, the new Texas government declared independence. On March 6, 1836, Santa Anna's army defeated the Texans at the Alamo.

Two weeks later, the Mexican army forced the Texan troops to surrender at Goliad, a town southeast of San Antonio. Santa Anna had the Texan troops executed. The losses at the Alamo and Goliad united Texans behind their new country.

At the Battle of San Jacinto on April 21, Sam Houston and his Texas troops launched a surprise attack on the Mexican army. During the attack, Houston's men shouted, "Remember the Alamo" and "Remember Goliad." The battle ended quickly. The Texans captured Santa Anna. He signed a treaty recognizing Texas's independence. However, the Mexican government did not.

In September 1836, Texans elected Sam Houston president of Texas. They also voted for **annexation**—to become part of the United States. However, many in Congress were against admitting another slave state. Also, President Jackson did not want to risk war with Mexico. However, he did officially recognize the Republic of Texas.

Section Wrap-up ***Answer these questions to check your understanding of the entire section.***

1. How did Edwards' revolt against the Mexican government affect Americans in Texas?

2. How did Austin's letter impact the Texas revolution?

Persuasive Writing ***Suppose you are Stephen Austin. Write a letter to the Texan leaders. Encourage them to organize their own state government. Include examples of the Mexicans' actions that you think makes this necessary.***

Chapter 7, Section 4 (Pages 270–275)

The War With Mexico

Big Idea

As you read pages 270–275 in your textbook, use the major headings of the section to complete the outline.

The War With Mexico

I. The Lingering Question of Texas
 A. ______________________
II. ______________________
 A. ______________________
 B. ______________________
 C. ______________________
 D. ______________________

Notes

Read to Learn

The Lingering Question of Texas *(page 270)*

Synthesizing Information

Circle the statement that is true based on the passage.

1. Expansion into Texas and Oregon was important to Polk to balance the number of free and slave states.

2. President Tyler's resolution to annex Texas was a plot to expand slavery and anger Mexico.

Tensions between Texans and antislavery leaders in Congress grew as President John Tyler pushed to bring Texas into the Union. In 1844 Congress voted against the annexation of Texas. James K. Polk, a former Congressman and governor from Tennessee, was the Democratic candidate in the 1844. Polk promised to annex Texas and Oregon and to buy California from Mexico. His platform appealed to all because it expanded the country. It also balanced free and slave states. Polk won the election against Whig candidate Henry Clay.

The United States and Britain negotiated the Oregon Treaty in June of 1846. The United States gained all the territory south of 49° north latitude, but not Vancouver Island.

Before leaving office, President Tyler pushed a resolution through Congress that annexed Texas. This angered Mexico and it broke off diplomatic relations. Mexico and the United States also could not agree on Texas' southwest border. A special **envoy,** or representative, went to Mexico to buy California. Mexico's president refused to meet him.

Notes

Read to Learn

The War With Mexico *(page 272)*

After Mexico's president refused to meet with the U.S. envoy, Polk ordered General Zachary Taylor to move his troops across the Nueces River. Mexico considered this an invasion. Polk wanted Mexico to attack the American soldiers first. He wanted to win popular support for war. Finally, in May 1846, a Mexican force attacked Taylor's men. Polk pushed Congress to declare war. Many in Congress questioned Polk's actions but voted to declare war.

Polk and his advisers created a three-part attack plan. Taylor would continue south. Another group would attack Santa Fe, New Mexico, and then attack California with the navy's help. Finally, U.S. forces would head for Mexico City. The United States needed to expand its army. Polk asked for 50,000 volunteers. Instead, 73,000 volunteered, but they were undisciplined.

Before Polk even signed the declaration of war, Taylor's troops defeated Mexican troops at Palo Alto and at Resaca de la Palma. They then continued south to Matamoros and Monterrey. Further north an American force, led by Stephen Kearny, took Santa Fe after the Mexican troops there fled. They continued on to California. Settlers in northern California led by John Frémont revolted. They defeated the Mexican troops in California. The settlers declared California independent from Mexico. They created the Bear Flag Republic. A few weeks later, the American navy took possession of California for the United States.

Mexico refused to surrender. President Polk sent troops to Veracruz. From that port, they marched west to Mexico City. Polk saw General Taylor as a possible rival in the 1848 election. He feared Taylor's popularity as a war hero. So he replaced General Taylor with Winfield Scott. Polk ordered Scott and his troops to capture Mexico City. The city was captured on September 14, 1847, after hard fighting. Mexico and the United States signed the Treaty of Guadalupe Hidalgo on February 2, 1848. The treaty forced Mexico to **cede**—or give up—more than 500,000 square miles of land. Mexico also agreed to the Rio Grande as the southern border of Texas. The United States agreed to pay Mexico $15 million and take over $3.25 million in debt that the Mexican government owed to Americans.

After the war with Mexico, the American dream of Manifest Destiny was fulfilled. The United States stretched from ocean to ocean. However, whether the new lands would be slave states or free states would soon lead the country into another war.

Detecting Bias

Read the passage. Complete the sentence below.

Polk made the decision to replace Taylor because

____

____

____

____

______________________.

Comparing and Contrasting

How did southern and northern Mexicans respond to the American invasion?

Place an* N *next to the words that describe the northern Mexicans and an* S *next to the words that describe southern Mexicans.

____ *resisted*

____ *fled*

____ *revolted*

____ *surrendered*

Section Wrap-up

Answer these questions to check your understanding of the entire section.

1. How was the annexation of Texas different from that of Oregon?

2. What did the United States gain from the Treaty of Guadalupe Hidalgo?

Informative Writing

In the space provided write a journal entry from an American soldier marching into Mexico with generals Zachary Taylor and Winfield Scott.

Chapter 8, Section 1 (Pages 284–293)

Slavery and Western Expansion

Big Idea

As you read pages 284–293 in your textbook, complete the graphic organizer by pairing the political candidates of 1848 with the positions they took on slavery in the West.

Candidate	Position
1.	2.
3.	4.
5.	6.

Notes

Read to Learn

The Search for Compromise (page 284)

Determining Cause and Effect

List one cause and one effect of the debate about extending slavery.

Cause:

____

____

____

Effect:

____

____

____

The gains from the Mexican War opened vast new lands for settlement and raised the issue of extending slavery westward. In 1846 an amendment to a bill, which became known as the Wilmot Proviso, proposed that slavery not be allowed in any territory gained from Mexico. This proposal angered Southerners.

Senator Lewis Cass proposed an idea known as **popular sovereignty**—that a territory's citizens of each territory should decide whether it permits slavery. This issue split the Whig Party during the 1848 election. The Free-Soil Party emerged from the Whig Party split. Some members opposed slavery on moral grounds, but most believed if slavery were allowed to spread, it would be difficult for free men to find work.

The discovery of gold in California attracted thousands of people hoping to get rich. Soon California applied for statehood as a free state. This would have left the slaveholding states in the minority. Southern leaders began to talk openly about **secession,** or taking their states out of the Union. Congress passed several bills that became known as the Compromise of 1850, which eased tensions over slavery for a time.

Notes

Read to Learn

The Fugitive Slave Act *(page 288)*

Formulating Questions

Write one question you might ask about the Fugitive Slave Act. Then answer it.

Question:

____

____

Answer:

____

____

Congress passed the Fugitive Slave Act of 1850, to help Southerners recover enslaved African Americans who fled north. Under this law, one only needed to point out a person as a runaway slave to take that person into custody. The law required every citizen to help catch the fugitives. Anyone who refused to assist could be jailed. Northerners reacted angrily to this requirement and antislavery activists disobeyed it.

Despite the heavy fines and prison terms, whites and free African Americans helped runaways escape through the Underground Railroad. This was an organized system in which enslaved persons were sheltered transported north. Many people, such as Harriet Tubman, acted as conductors.
In response to the new Fugitive Slave Act, Harriet Beecher Stowe wrote *Uncle Tom's Cabin* to show the horrors of slavery. Her book stirred up people's feelings and changed many Northerners' attitudes about slavery. Southerners tried to have the book banned. They attacked her portrayal of slavery as unjust. The book sold millions of copies.

The Kansas-Nebraska Act *(page 291)*

Problems and Solutions

What problem was Stephen A. Douglas trying to solve with the Kansas-Nebraska Act?

Problem:

____

____

____

____

Solution: Kansas-Nebraska Act

The opening of Oregon and the admission of California to the Union convinced many people of the need for a **transcontinental railroad** to connect the West Coast to the rest of the country. People had to travel weeks overland or by sea around the tip of South America. The railroad would reduce travel time and lead to settlement along its route.

Southerners wanted the railroad to start at New Orleans. This required it to pass through northern Mexico. James Gadsden negotiated the land purchase with the Mexican government. Stephen A. Douglas wanted the railroad to start in Chicago. This northern route required Congress to organize the Nebraska territory. Southern senators insisted he repeal the Missouri Compromise and allow slavery in the new territory.

Douglas first proposed that popular sovereignty be used to determine the issue of slavery. He next proposed to undo the Missouri Compromise as well as divide the region into two territories. Despite opposition, Congress passed the Kansas-Nebraska Act in 1854. Conflict over slavery deepened. Kansas became a battleground. Settlers favoring and opposed to slavery battled to control the writing of the new state's constitution. The conflict spread to the Senate, where abolitionist Charles Sumner was beaten with a cane by a Southerner.

Section Wrap-up

Answer these questions to check your understanding of the entire section.

1. How did the federal government deal with slavery in the territories acquired after the Mexican War?

2. How did the Fugitive Slave Act and the building of the transcontinental railroad heighten sectional tensions?

Descriptive Writing

In the space provided write a description of the dangers experienced on the Underground Railroad from the perspective of a fugitive.

Chapter 8, Section 2 (Pages 294–301)

The Crisis Deepens

Big Idea

As you read pages 294–301 in your textbook, complete the graphic organizer by grouping the major events discussed as executive, legislative, judicial, or nongovernmental.

Executive	**1.**
Legislative	**2.**
Judicial	**3.**
Nongovernmental	**4.**

Notes

Read to Learn

The Birth of the Republican Party *(page 294)*

Predicting

Based on the passage, predict how the* Dred Scott *decision will affect the Union and contribute to sectional tension.

____

____

____

____

____

____

____

____

The Kansas-Nebraska Act's repeal of the Missouri Compromise affected the political party system. The Whig and Know-Nothing parties split. Antislavery forces joined together to form the Republican Party. Although the Republicans did not agree whether slavery should be abolished, the party did agree that slavery should be kept out of the territories. In the 1856 election, the Republicans nominated John Frémont. Democrat James Buchanan won. He believed the Supreme Court should decide the issue of slavery in the territories.

The Court complicated matters with its ruling in the case of *Dred Scott* v. *Sandford.* Dred Scott was an enslaved man whose Missouri slaveholder had taken him to live in free territory before returning to Missouri. Scott sued to end his slavery, arguing his time spent in free territory meant he was free. The Court ruled that African Americans were not citizens and could not sue in the courts. Chief Justice Taney held that the U.S. government could not prohibit slavery in the territories. Many Northerners and African Americans opposed the decision. Southerners insisted that the ruling be obeyed or the South would leave the Union.

Notes | Read to Learn

The Emergence of Abraham Lincoln *(page 298)*

Analyzing Information

How did the Freeport Doctrine affect Douglas's campaign?

Conflict continued between pro- and antislavery forces in Kansas. To end the troubles there, President Buchanan urged the territory to apply for statehood. In 1857 the proslavery legislature drafted a constitution legalizing slavery. The pro-and antislavery sides each held their own **referendum,** or popular vote, to accept or reject this constitution. Antislavery forces voted down the constitution. Proslavery forces approved it. After voting again, Kansas settlers overwhelmingly rejected the proslavery constitution.

In 1858 Illinois Republicans nominated Abraham Lincoln to run against Stephen A. Douglas for the Senate. Lincoln believed slavery was morally wrong. He opposed its spread into the western territories. Challenging Douglas in a series of debates, Lincoln asked Douglas whether a territory could legally exclude slavery. If he said yes, Douglas would appear to oppose the *Dred Scott* ruling. This would lose him support in the South. If he said no, he abandoned popular sovereignty, the concept upon which he had built his Northern support. Douglas dodged the issue by arguing that people could keep slavery out of the territories by refusing to pass laws enforcing it. This became known as the Freeport Doctrine. His response angered the South. Lincoln also attacked Douglas's claim that he did not care whether Kansas voted for or against slavery. Douglas won the election, but Lincoln established a reputation as an insightful man.

John Brown's Raid *(page 301)*

Distinguishing Fact from Opinion

Read the second paragraph. Circle a sentence that tells a fact about John Brown. Underline a sentence that tells an opinion others had about Brown.

John Brown was a dedicated abolitionist. In 1859 he developed a plan to take over the federal arsenal at Harpers Ferry, Virginia. He wanted to free and arm the enslaved people of the area and begin an **insurrection,** or rebellion against slaveholders. Brown and his followers seized the arsenal. Soon a force of U.S. soldiers under the command of Robert E. Lee stopped the attempted insurrection and captured Brown.

A Virginia court tried Brown, convicted him, and sentenced him to death. Brown never repented his violent acts. The day he was executed, Brown claimed "the crimes of this guilty land will never be purged away but with Blood." Many Northerners thought Brown was a hero in a noble cause. Henry David Thoreau predicted the execution would strengthen the abolitionist cause. Most Southerners, however, believed that the raid proved that Northerners were plotting the murder of slaveholders.

Section Wrap-up

Answer these questions to check your understanding of the entire section.

1. Explain the Supreme Court ruling in *Dred Scott* v. *Sandford*. How did it impact the debate about extending slavery?

2. How would you compare the positions of Abraham Lincoln and Stephen Douglas in the 1858 Senate race?

Persuasive Writing

In the space provided write a letter to a local newspaper in 1859. Express your opinion of the events at Harpers Ferry. Write your letter from the point of view of someone who lives in the South or someone who lives in the North.

Chapter 8, Section 3 (Pages 302–307)

The Union Dissolves

Big Idea

As you read pages 302–307 in your textbook, complete the major headings of the section to complete the outline.

The Union Dissolves

I. The Election of 1860
  A. ____________________
  B. ____________________
  C. ____________________
  D. ____________________
II. ____________________
  A. ____________________
  B. ____________________
  C. ____________________

Notes

Read to Learn

The Election of 1860 *(page 302)*

Analyzing Information

Why did the South secede when Lincoln won the 1860 election?

____

____

____

____

____

____

The debate over slavery finally split the Democratic Party. The party met in 1860 to select its presidential nominee. Northern Democrats supported popular sovereignty. Southern Democrats wanted the *Dred Scott* decision upheld and a federal slave code in the territories endorsed. They could not agree on a candidate. They met again in June. Douglas's supporters organized rival delegations to ensure his endorsement. The original delegates walked out and held their own convention, nominating John Breckinridge. The Republicans nominated Lincoln. With the Democratic votes split, Lincoln won the election.

For the South, the election of a Republican president represented a victory for the abolitionists. Survival of Southern society seemed to be at stake. By February 1861, seven southern states seceded. Congress wanted to avoid civil war. Senator John J. Crittenden proposed several amendments, called Crittenden's Compromise. One guaranteed slavery where it existed. Another extended the Missouri Compromise line west to California. It did not pass. In February 1861 the seceding states announced a new nation—the Confederacy—with Jefferson Davis as its president.

Notes

Read to Learn

The Civil War Begins *(page 306)*

Identifying the Main Idea

What message was Lincoln trying to send in his inaugural address?

____

____

____

____

____

____

____

____

Drawing Conclusions

Put an X by the conclusion that is best supported by the passage.

___ ***The Confederate move to occupy Kentucky backfired.***

___ ***The United States thought Fort Sumter was a lost cause.***

In his inaugural address, Lincoln spoke directly to the seceding states. He repeated his promise not to interfere with slavery where it existed. Although he did not threaten them, he announced his intention to hold onto federal property in those states.

In April 1861, Lincoln announced that the federal government would resupply Fort Sumter. Jefferson Davis now faced a dilemma. To let federal troops occupy the South's most important harbor was unacceptable for an independent nation. However, to fire on the supply ship would risk war with the United States. Davis decided to capture Fort Sumter before the supply ship arrived. This might yet preserve the peace. His forces demanded that Major Robert Anderson surrender Fort Sumter. Anderson refused. Confederate forces bombarded the fort until Anderson and his men surrendered. The Civil War had begun.

After Fort Sumter fell, President Lincoln called for volunteers to serve in the military. Many people in the Upper South did not want to secede. Faced with a civil war, however, they felt they had no choice but to leave the Union. Virginia acted first. The capital of the Confederacy was moved to Richmond. Soon three more states left the Union.

Lincoln tried to keep the slaveholding border states of Delaware, Maryland, Kentucky, and Missouri from seceding. Delaware seemed safe, but if Maryland seceded, Washington, D.C., would be surrounded by Confederate territory. To prevent Maryland's secession, Lincoln placed Baltimore under **martial law.** Under this policy, federal military troops in the area replaced civilian authorities. They also suspended certain civil rights. Secessionist leaders were arrested and imprisoned without trial.

Kentucky declared itself neutral until September 1861, when Confederate troops occupied the southwest corner of the state. This prompted Union troops to move in as well. The Confederate occupation angered some Kentucky legislators so much that they voted to fight the Confederacy. Others who supported the Confederacy then created a rival government and seceded. After a struggle between antisecessionist and prosecessionist forces, Missouri stayed with the Union. The stage now shifted to the battlefront.

Section Wrap-up ***Answer these questions to check your understanding of the entire section.***

1. What attempts were made to find a compromise to preserve the Union immediately after the election of 1860?

2. What events led to the outbreak of the Civil War?

Informative Writing ***In the space provided write a brief informative article describing how the election of 1860 led to the founding of the Confederacy.***

Chapter 9, Section 1 (Pages 314–319)

The Opposing Sides

Big Idea

As you read pages 314–319 in your textbook, use the major headings of the section to complete the outline.

The Opposing Sides

I. Choosing Sides
   A. ______________________
   B. ______________________
   C. ______________________
   D. ______________________
   E. ______________________

II. ______________________
   A. ______________________
   B. ______________________
   C. ______________________

Notes | Read to Learn

Choosing Sides *(page 314)*

Comparing and Contrasting

List one advantage and one disadvantage each side had at the war's beginning.

The North:

____

____

____

The South:

____

____

____

The South had a strong military tradition. About one-third of trained officers left the Union army for the Confederacy. The North had a strong naval tradition, more warships, more shipyards, and more people. It also had most of the nation's factories and iron to manufacture weapons and equipment. The Union controlled the treasury and tariff revenues. To pay troops and suppliers, the government printed paper money called **greenbacks.** The South had fewer railroads, which made it easier for the Union to disrupt their supply lines. The Confederacy's finances grew worse and they suffered huge inflation.

Many Republicans were abolitionists, but Lincoln's goal was to preserve the Union. Democrats also challenged his policies, opposing **conscription,** or a military draft. To enforce this law, Lincoln suspended writs of **habeas corpus**—the right of someone to be either charged with a crime or released. Many Southern leaders also opposed a draft, suspension of habeas corpus, or any new taxes. The South tried to get Europeans to recognize its independence, while the North tried to get Europe to respect its blockade of Confederate ports.

Notes | Read to Learn

The First Modern War *(page 318)*

Synthesizing Information

Why did Confederate troops suffer heavier casualties than expected under Davis's strategy of attrition?

____

____

____

____

____

____

Predicting

Based on the information in this passage, list whether the Union or the Confederacy will be successful in the use of attrition as a strategy. Explain why.

1. Union or Confederacy?

____

2. Reason:

____

____

____

____

____

The Civil War was the first modern war. Unlike earlier wars fought in Europe, the Civil War involved huge armies of civilian volunteers that required large amounts of supplies and equipment. Many of the officers who led the Union and Confederate forces had fought in the war with Mexico in the 1840s. They believed the best way to win battles was to organize the troops into columns and then march toward the enemy, while firing. When the troops got close enough, they would charge and attack with bayonets. These tactics were necessary because at the time, soldiers used bullets that were only accurate at close range. By the 1850s, the armies began using a new cone-shaped bullet for rifles. These were far more accurate at longer ranges. Instead of standing in a line, troops defending their positions began to use trenches and barricades to protect themselves. This method led to higher casualties for the attacking forces. Armies had to keep replacing their soldiers. **Attrition,** the wearing down of one side by the other by using up soldiers and resources, played an important role as the war dragged on, since the North had a much larger population than the South to draw upon for replacements.

Early in the war, Jefferson Davis planned a strategy similar to the one used against the British during the Revolutionary War. Confederate generals would pick their battles carefully to avoid large battles with heavy losses. This way, the South could conduct a defensive war of attrition, which Davis hoped would force the Union to spend its resources until it became weary of the war and agreed to negotiate. Many Southerners, believing themselves to be superior fighters, hated this strategy, and Southern troops often went on the offensive. They charged enemy lines, suffering heavy casualties. In six battles, the Confederacy lost 20,000 more soldiers than the North.

Union General Winfield Scott proposed a strategy for defeating the Confederacy early on in the war. Scott suggested blockading Confederate ports and sending gunboats down the Mississippi to divide the Confederacy. Because it was separated, the South would gradually run out of resources and surrender. He thought this strategy would defeat the South with the least amount of bloodshed. Many Northerners disliked the plan, named the Anaconda Plan for the snake that slowly strangles its prey. They argued a massive invasion would bring victory more quickly. Lincoln agreed to try Scott's plan and imposed a blockade of Southern ports. He saw, though, that only a long war that destroyed the South's armies would succeed.

Section Wrap-up

Answer these questions to check your understanding of the entire section.

1. What kind of political problems did Lincoln face? How did he solve these problems?

2. Explain how modern warfare worked against the South's military strategy.

Expository Writing

In the space provided write a brief essay explaining why the North was in a better position to fight the Civil War than the South was.

Chapter 9, Section 2 (Pages 320–327)

The Early Stages

Big Idea

As you read pages 320–327 in your textbook, complete the graphic organizer by filling in the results of each battle listed.

Battle	Results
First Battle of Bull Run	1.
Battle of Shiloh	2.
Battle of Murfreesboro	3.
Seven Days' Battle	4.
Second Battle of Bull Run	5.

Notes

Read to Learn

Mobilizing the Troops *(page 320)*

Identifying the Main Idea

What is the main idea of this passage?

In the early days of the Civil War, Lincoln was under pressure to strike quickly against the South to end the conflict. At Bull Run in northern Virginia, a Union attack on Confederate forces at first seemed to go well. Then, Confederate reinforcements, led by "Stonewall" Jackson, arrived. Union General McDowell decided to fall back. His retreat quickly turned into a panic. The Union defeat at Bull Run made it clear that the North needed a large well-trained army to defeat the South.

Excitement about the war inspired many Northern and Southern men to enlist. However, as the war dragged on and more casualties occurred, fewer men enlisted. This forced both sides to turn to conscription. In 1862 the South began its draft for all white men between the ages of 18 and 35. Exemptions were provided for government workers, teachers, and planters with at least 20 enslaved African Americans. The North tried to enlist men by offering a **bounty,** or a sum of money given as a bonus, to people who signed up for three years. Congress passed the Militia Act in 1862 empowering Lincoln to call up state militias into federal service. Later, in 1863, Congress introduced a national draft.

Notes | Read to Learn

The Naval War *(page 321)*

Drawing Conclusions

Do you think getting supplies became easier or harder for the South during the Union blockades? Why?

President Lincoln wanted to blockade all Confederate ports to hurt the South's economy. By early 1862, the Union navy had blockaded all ports on the Atlantic coast except Charleston, South Carolina, and Wilmington, North Carolina. Union ships, however, found it difficult to stop all the **blockade runners**—or small fast ships—that the South used to smuggle goods past the North's naval blockade. These ships allowed the South to get some of its cotton to market in Europe to exchange for supplies that it needed. The South also attacked Northern merchant ships at sea using warships. Two of these warships had been built in Britain. The damage done by these ships strained relations between the United States and Great Britain.

As its ships closed Southern ports, the Union began to prepare to take over New Orleans to control the southern Mississippi River. In April 1862, David Farragut led Union forces and bombarded Confederate forts on the lower Mississippi River. He then captured New Orleans.

The War in the West *(page 323)*

Evaluating Information

Does this passage help you understand why President Lincoln wanted Buell to capture Chattanooga? Why or why not?

The Union was victorious in several battles in the West. Union General Grant seized Fort Henry and Fort Donelson on the Tennessee and Cumberland rivers. This put Kentucky and most of western Tennessee under Union control.

Grant continued down the Tennessee to attack Corinth, Mississippi. Confederate troops attacked Grant's forces at Shiloh. Grant turned the surprise attack into a Union victory when he mounted an offensive and forced the Confederates to retreat. The battle resulted in heavy casualties.

Confederate General Braxton Bragg and his troops attempted to invade Kentucky. Union General Buell stopped them at Perryville. After the Confederate retreat, Lincoln ordered Buell to capture Chattanooga to cut off the railroad there. This would deprive Confederate forces of vital food supplies. Buell's slow progress caused Lincoln to fire Buell and replace him with General William Rosecrans. Bragg's forces attacked near Murfreesboro. But when reinforcements arrived, Bragg retreated.

Notes

Read to Learn

The War in the East *(page 324)*

Formulating Questions

Write one question about the Emancipation Proclamation that is answered by this passage.

Union General McClellan launched the Peninsula Campaign to take Richmond. McClellan advanced cautiously and allowed his troops to separate, giving General Johnston's Confederate forces the chance to attack and inflict heavy casualties. Robert E. Lee took command, attacking the Union army in the Seven Day's Battle, forcing a Union retreat.

Lee's forces then attacked the Union army defending Washington, leading to a second battle at Bull Run. Lee's army crossed into Maryland. McClellan's troops took positions at Antietam Creek. Antietam was the bloodiest battle of the war. A Confederate defeat convinced Lincoln that it was time to end slavery. Five days later, he announced that the Emancipation Proclamation would free all enslaved persons in states still in rebellion. This changed the Civil War's purpose from a war to preserve the Union to a war of liberation.

Section Wrap-up

Answer these questions to check your understanding of the entire section.

1. How did the first Battle of Bull Run lead Lincoln to change his recruitment strategy?

2. How would you compare the Eastern campaign with the war in the West?

Descriptive Writing

In the space provided write a journal entry describing a Northern observer's response to Lincoln's Emancipation Proclamation.

Chapter 9, Section 3 (Pages 328–333)

Life During the War

Big Idea

As you read pages 328–333 in your textbook, complete the graphic organizer by listing the reasons the North experienced a wartime economic boom.

Reason for North's Economic Boom
1.
2.
3.
4.

Notes

Read to Learn

The Wartime Economies *(page 328)*

Making Generalizations

Make one generalization about the South's economy during the Civil War.

Both the North and South struggled to keep their economies going. The South, with fewer financial resources and little industry, suffered more from wartime inflation and critical shortages. The North, supported by banks and industries, was able to respond quickly to changes caused by the war.

By the end of 1862, Union forces had destroyed the South's transportation system. With Union troops in its several important agricultural regions, the South experienced food shortages. This hurt morale. Many soldiers deserted to help their families. The food shortages led to riots in several Southern communities.

At the same time, the North experienced an economic boom because of the war. Northern factories supplied troops with ammunition, clothes, and other necessities. Northern farmers, many of whom were women, used mechanized reapers and mowers. This made farming possible with fewer workers. Women worked in industries to fill the labor shortages there. Textile factories in the North made clothes for its soldiers. The textile industry profited from government contracts.

Notes | Read to Learn

African Americans in the Military *(page 330)*

Determining Cause and Effect

Circle the cause.

Effect:* New York Tribune *declares African Americans make good soldiers.

The Emancipation Proclamation officially allowed African Americans to enlist in the Union forces. Thousands who believed serving would help end discrimination rushed to join the military. The 54th Massachusetts was among the first African American regiments organized in the North. Its members fought valiantly in the attack on Fort Wagner in July 1863. It lost nearly half of its soldiers in the battle. The regiment's bravery prompted the *New York Tribune* to publicly declare there was proof that African Americans made good soldiers.

Military Life *(page 331)*

Analyzing Information

Why did President Lincoln end all prisoner exchanges?

____

____

____

____

____

____

____

____

____

Both Union and Confederate soldiers suffered hardships. Some Southern soldiers slept without blankets and marched shoeless. Food was scarce. Union soldiers' often ate meals of potatoes, beans, and **hardtack**—a hard biscuit made of wheat flour. Confederate soldiers ate bread made of cornmeal.

The war produced huge numbers of casualties. At the time, doctors did not know about infectious germs. They used unsterilized instruments on their patients. As a result, infection spread quickly in field hospitals. Diseases such as smallpox, dysentery, and pneumonia were grave threats facing Civil War soldiers. Crowded together in army camps, drinking unsanitary water supplies, many became sick.

Women helped the war effort by serving as nurses. Elizabeth Blackwell, the first female physician in the United States, started the nation's first training program for nurses. Her work led to the creation of the United States Sanitary Commission. It provided medical help and supplies to army camps and hospitals. Clara Barton and many other women nursed wounded soldiers.

Prisoners of war, or soldiers captured by the enemy, also suffered. At first, the Union and Confederacy did not hold prisoners captured in battle. Instead they agreed to prisoner exchanges. After Lincoln issued the Emancipation Proclamation, the Confederacy said that it would not recognize African Americans as soldiers and would not exchange them for Southern white prisoners. Instead they would re-enslave them or execute them. Lincoln stopped all prisoner exchanges. As the number of prisoners increased, it became difficult to care for them. The South had a particularly difficult time because of food shortages. The Southern prison in Andersonville had horrible conditions. Prisoners there died of exposure, disease, lack of food, and overcrowding. The head of this prison was the only person executed for war crimes during the Civil War.

Section Wrap-up

Answer these questions to check your understanding of the entire section.

1. Explain why the Northern and Southern economies responded so differently to the stresses of the Civil War.

2. What contributions did women make to the war effort?

Informative Writing

In the space provided write a newspaper editorial that reports what life in the army is like for the soldiers.

Chapter 9, Section 4 (Pages 336–341)

The Turning Point

Big Idea

As you read pages 336–341 in your textbook, complete the graphic organizer by recording the results of the listed battles that shaped the Union victory.

Battle	Results
Vicksburg	1.
Chancellorsville	2.
Gettysburg	3.
Chickamauga Creek	4.
Missionary Ridge	5.

Notes

Read to Learn

Vicksburg Falls *(page 336)*

Distinguishing Fact from Opinion

Read the first paragraph. Circle a statement that is an opinion. Underline a statement that is a fact.

Despite the capture of New Orleans and the earlier successes in the west, there remained one major Confederate stronghold on the Mississippi River—Vicksburg, Mississippi. "Vicksburg is the key," Lincoln wrote. "The war can never be brought to a close until the key is in our pocket."

Capturing Vicksburg would cut the South in two and ensure a victory for the Union. The land to the north of Vicksburg was too swampy, so Grant planned an attack from the south. To distract the Confederates, Grant ordered Benjamin Grierson to conduct a cavalry raid through Mississippi. This allowed Grant and his troops to approach Vicksburg from the south.

As Grant marched toward Vicksburg, his troops lived off the country by **foraging** or searching and raiding for food. Grant's troops fought five battles before driving the defenders back toward Vicksburg. Grant launched two attacks on the city's defenses, but the Confederates stopped both attacks, inflicting heavy casualties. Grant then put Vicksburg under **siege**—cut off its food and supplies and bombard it until the defenders gave up. The Confederates surrendered on July 4, 1863.

Notes | Read to Learn

The Road to Gettysburg *(page 338)*

Analyzing Information

List two reasons why Gettysburg was a turning point in the Civil War.

1. ______________

____

2. ______________

____

General McClellan frustrated President Lincoln by allowing Lee's forces to slip away at Antietam. Lincoln replaced him with General Burnside. Yet Lee scored victories against Burnside at Fredericksburg and also defeated Joseph Hooker at Chancellorsville. Lee again headed north across the Potomac to Pennsylvania.

Lincoln placed General Meade in command of the Union troops. The two armies met at Gettysburg. Lee ordered generals Hill and Pickett to attack the Union forces. This offensive, known as Pickett's Charge, failed to break the Union lines. While both sides suffered huge casualties, the Union defeated the Confederacy at the Battle of Gettysburg, which became a turning point for the war. Politically, it assured that Britain would not recognize the Confederacy. For the rest of war, Lee's forces would stay on the defensive, slowly giving ground to the Union.

Battle for Tennessee *(page 340)*

Determining Cause and Effect

List two Union victories that caused Lincoln to reward General Grant with a promotion.

Causes:

1. ______________

____

2. ______________

____

Effect: Lincoln promoted Grant to lieutenant general.

The Union wanted to capture Chattanooga to control a major railroad that ran to Atlanta. The Union could then advance into Georgia. In September 1863, the Union forced the Confederacy to evacuate Chattanooga. As General Rosecrans advanced, General Bragg attacked his forces at Chickamauga Creek. He forced Rosecrans to retreat to Chattanooga. There Bragg's troops completely surrounded his forces. Lincoln sent some of Meade's forces to help.

Lincoln placed General Grant in overall command of the Union forces in the West. Grant's troops took charge of the Battle of Chattanooga, defeating the Confederates at Lookout Mountain. The retreating Confederates then joined the Southern forces at Missionary Ridge east of Chattanooga. Grant ordered Sherman to attack Confederate troops north of the ridge. When Sherman's troops failed to break through, Grant ordered General George Thomas to attack from the front as a diversion. Thomas's troops overran the Confederate trenches and took Missionary Ridge itself. This caused the surprised Confederates to retreat and leave Chattanooga to the Union forces. Lincoln rewarded Grant for his victories in Chattanooga and Vicksburg by appointing him general in chief of the Union forces. He also promoted Grant to lieutenant general.

Section Wrap-up

Answer these questions to check your understanding of the entire section.

1. What was important about the events at Vicksburg and Gettysburg?

2. How did the battles in Tennessee help the Union in the Civil War?

Persuasive Writing

In the space provided write a report to the president of either the Union or the Confederacy concerning the events at Gettysburg and their impact on war plans.

Chapter 9, Section 5 (Pages 344–349)

The War Ends

Big Idea

As you read pages 344–349 in your textbook, complete the time line below by recording the final battles of the Civil War and their results.

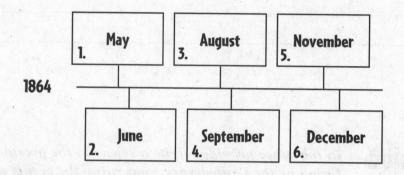

1864

1. May	3. August	5. November
2. June	4. September	6. December

Notes

Read to Learn

Grant vs. Lee *(page 344)*

Making Inferences

Why did Grant want to attack Petersburg?

In the spring of 1864, General Grant placed Union forces in the west under the command of General Sherman. Grant headed to Washington, D.C., to lead the Union troops against General Lee. He was determined to continue fighting until the Confederates surrendered. He fought the Confederates at Wilderness, near Fredericksburg, and at Spotsylvania. The campaign was relentless, consisting of savage combat, advances, retreats, and digging of defensive trenches. Unable to break the Confederate lines, Grant headed to Cold Harbor. This was an important crossroads northeast of Richmond. Grant's all-out attack on Lee's forces resulted in heavy Union losses.

Grant ordered General Philip Sheridan to lead a cavalry raid north and west of Richmond. Grant wanted to distract Lee's troops while he headed south past Richmond and crossed the James River. Then he headed west toward Petersburg, which controlled the only rail line into Richmond. When Grant reached Petersburg, he ordered his troops to put the city under siege.

Notes | Read to Learn

The Union Advances *(page 346)*

Identifying the Main Idea

Write the main idea of this passage.

While Grant fought Lee, the Union navy, led by David Farragut, closed the port of Mobile, Alabama. It was the last Confederate port on the Gulf of Mexico. As a result, blockade runners moving goods in or out of the South could no longer use any port on the Gulf east of the Mississippi.

General Sherman's forces pushed toward Atlanta. In August 1864, the troops cut the roads and railroads into the city. Confederate troops evacuated Atlanta on September 1 and Union troops occupied it. Sherman ordered all civilians to leave Atlanta. Then his troops burned everything of military value: mills, warehouses, factories, and railroads. Eventually, one-third of the city burned. In November, Sherman began his March to the Sea. His troops destroyed everything in their path, looting houses, burning crops, and killing cattle. They seized Savannah. Then they headed north into South Carolina. The troops burned and **pillaged,** or looted, nearly everything. They were determined to punish South Carolina for being the first to secede, which they saw as treason.

The South Surrenders *(page 347)*

Formulating Questions

What question could you ask that would help you learn more about the Thirteenth Amendment?

Lincoln's reelection in 1865 depended on the success of the military campaigns in the South. The Democrats nominated George McClellan, who promised to open negotiations with the South. The capture of Atlanta restored Northern support for the war. Lincoln won reelection with 55 percent of the popular vote. He believed his reelection was a **mandate,** or clear sign from the voters, to end slavery. The Thirteenth Amendment, banning slavery, passed in the House in 1865 and went to the states for ratification.

General Lee withdrew from Petersburg and tried to escape Grant's forces. Sheridan's cavalry got ahead of Lee's troops. They blocked the road at Appomattox Courthouse. With his troops surrounded and outnumbered, Lee surrendered to Grant on April 9, 1865. Grant promised the United States would not prosecute Confederate soldiers.

Though warned not to appear in public, Lincoln went to Ford's Theatre with his wife on April 14. During the play, John Wilkes Booth shot and killed the president. Lincoln's death shocked the nation.

The North's victory strengthened the power of the federal government over the states. It changed American society by ending slavery. The war also devastated the society and economy of the South.

Section Wrap-up

Answer these questions to check your understanding of the entire section.

1. Why were the Union victories in Virginia and the Deep South important to the outcome of the war?

2. When and where did Lee surrender, and what events followed the war?

Expository Writing

In the space provided write an essay briefly describing how the final days of the Civil War unfolded and the results of the war for the nation.

The Debate Over Reconstruction

Big Idea

As you read pages 356–363 in your textbook, complete the graphic organizer to show how each piece of legislation listed affected African Americans.

Legislation	Effect
black codes	1.
Civil Rights Act of 1866	2.
Fourteenth Amendment	3.
Fifteenth Amendment	4.

Notes

Read to Learn

The Reconstruction Battle Begins *(page 356)*

Problems and Solutions

List one solution offered by Lincoln and one offered by the Radical Republicans for how to bring the South back into the Union.

Lincoln's solution:

____

____

Radical Republicans' solution:

____

____

After the Civil War, the South's economy was in shambles. The president and Congress focused on Reconstruction, or rebuilding. President Lincoln wanted to bring the South into the Union without punishing it. His plan offered a general **amnesty,** or pardon, to all Southerners who took an oath of loyalty to the United States and accepted it's stand on slavery.

A group known as the Radical Republicans opposed Lincoln's plan. They wanted to prevent Confederate leaders from returning to power. They also wanted the Republican Party to become powerful in the South and the federal government to guarantee African Americans the right to vote in the South. Moderate Republicans thought the Radical Republicans were going too far, but they agreed to pass the Wade-Davis Bill. It called for most adult white men in a former Confederate state to take an oath of loyalty to the Union. Each state would have to abolish slavery, reject all Confederate debts, and deny former government and military officials the right to vote or to hold office. Congress passed the bill, but Lincoln blocked it with a **pocket veto.** He let the session of Congress end without signing the bill into law.

Notes | Read to Learn

Freedmen's Bureau *(page 358)*

Identifying the Main Idea

Congress established the Freedmen's Bureau ______________________.

After the war, newly freed African Americans, or freedmen, struggled to survive. Some Northerners believed that freedmen should be given Confederate land. Congress did not support the taking of land from plantation owners. Congress established the Freedmen's Bureau to help feed, clothe, and find jobs for African Americans. The Freedmen's Bureau also provided education for African Americans. It helped start colleges for training African American teachers.

Johnson Takes Office *(page 359)*

Making Generalizations

Circle sentences in the passage that support the following generalization.

The Civil War did not erase racial prejudice in the South.

Andrew Johnson became president after Lincoln was assassinated. His Reconstruction plan was similar to Lincoln's. He offered to pardon former Confederates who took an oath of loyalty to the Union and returned their property. Confederate officers, officials, and those who owned property worth more than $20,000 were excluded from receiving pardons.

To return to the Union, each state had to ratify the Thirteenth Amendment and reject all Civil War debts. Most states did so. However, Southern voters elected former Confederate leaders to the Senate, angering Congress members. Republicans were also angry about the **black codes** that had been passed in the South. These laws limited African Americans' rights.

Radical Republicans Take Control *(page 361)*

Determining Cause and Effect

What was the effect of the Fifteenth Amendment?

____

____

____

____

____

____

Republicans in Congress set their own Reconstruction plans, passing the Civil Rights Act of 1866. This allowed African Americans to own property and guaranteed equal treatment in court. Republicans also passed the Fourteenth Amendment, granting citizenship to all persons born in the United States. It also guaranteed them equal protection under the law.

The Republicans won control of Congress. They passed the Military Reconstruction Act. It required each former Confederate state to set up a new constitution that granted all male citizens the right to vote. Then each state had to ratify the Fourteenth Amendment before it could elect people to Congress. Worried that President Johnson would refuse to enforce their plans, Republicans **impeached** him, charging him with "high crimes and misdemeanors." Johnson was not convicted, but he did not run for reelection. Republicans kept control of Congress. They passed the Fifteenth Amendment, which gave African Americans the right to vote.

Section Wrap-up

Answer these questions to check your understanding of the entire section.

1. Describe President Lincoln's approach to Reconstruction.

2. How did the Republicans' control of Congress help them attain their Reconstruction goals?

Expository Writing

In the space provided write a short paragraph that compares and contrasts the different viewpoints and approaches toward Reconstruction by President Lincoln, President Johnson, and the Radical Republicans.

Chapter 10, Section 2 (Pages 366–371)

Republican Rule

Big Idea

As you read pages 366–371 in your textbook, complete by filling in each bubble.

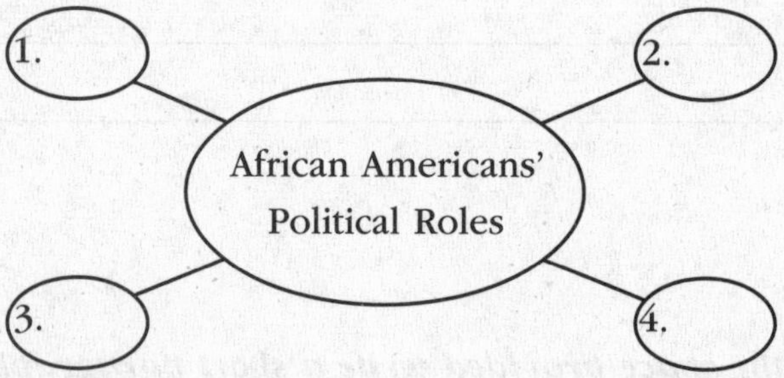

Notes

Read to Learn

Republican Rule in the South *(page 366)*

Distinguishing Fact from Opinion

Write* F *for fact or* O *for opinion next to the following statements.

___ *Southerners called Northerners who moved to the South after Reconstruction carpetbaggers.*

___ *All white Southerners who sided with Republicans betrayed the South.*

By late 1870 all the former Confederate states had rejoined the Union. Many Northerners moved to the South as Reconstruction began. Some Southerners called them **carpetbaggers**—for their suitcases made of carpet—and saw them as intruders trying to take advantage of the South's condition. Some carpetbaggers did attempt this, but others wanted to help.

Thousands of African Americans began to take part in governing the South, although they did not control the government. Many white Southerners joined with African Americans in supporting the Republican Party. This was mostly true of poor white farmers, who resented the planters and the Democratic Party. Southerners who supported Republicans were called **scalawags**—an old Scotch-Irish term for underfed, weak animals.

Republicans in the South ended the black codes. They set up state hospitals and institutions for orphans and the mentally ill. They rebuilt roads, railroads, and bridges. They paid for these improvements by borrowing money and setting high property taxes. Unfortunately, **graft,** or gaining money illegally through politics, was common in both the South and the North.

Notes | Read to Learn

African American Communities (page 369)

Making Inferences

What effect do you think education, churches, and other institutions had on the African American community?

Besides entering politics, African Americans aimed to improve their lives in other ways. Religion had always played a central role in their lives. Many African Americans started their own churches. These churches housed schools and hosted social and political events. The Freedmen's Bureau opened schools across the South. Public schools were also built. Academies offering advanced education were also started. Many of these academies grew into important African American colleges and universities that are still active today. Thousands of other groups were also started in the interest of creating support networks. These groups ranged from burial societies and debating clubs to drama societies and trade organizations.

The Ku Klux Klan Forms (page 371)

Determining Cause and Effect

Name the cause of the passage of the Enforcement Acts.

Cause:

Effect: Enforcement Acts are passed by Congress.

Many Southern whites resented African Americans. Some organized secret societies such as the Ku Klux Klan. The goal of the Ku Klux Klan was to drive out the Union troops and carpetbaggers and to have the Democratic Party control the South. Ku Klux Klan members terrorized Republican supporters. They burned African American homes and churches and tried to keep Republicans from voting.

President Grant and Republicans in Congress were outraged by these actions. As a result, Congress passed three Enforcement Acts in 1870 and 1871. One act made it a federal crime to interfere with a citizen's right to vote. The second act placed federal elections under the supervision of federal marshals. The third act, which was known as the Ku Klux Klan Act, outlawed the activities of the Ku Klux Klan. Under this law, thousands of Ku Klux Klan members were arrested. However, only a few hundred were actually convicted or served any time in prison.

Section Wrap-up

Answer these questions to check your understanding of the entire section.

1. How did Republicans change the South during Reconstruction?

2. How did African Americans work to improve their lives during Reconstruction?

Persuasive Writing

In the space provided write a short letter to President Grant using facts and other information to persuade him to respond to the activities of the Ku Klux Klan.

Chapter 10, Section 3 (Pages 372–377)

Reconstruction Collapses

Big Idea

As you read pages 372–377 in your textbook, complete the outline using the major headings.

Reconstruction Collapses

I. The Grant Administration
  A. ______________________
  B. ______________________
II. ______________________
  A. ______________________
  B. ______________________
III. ______________________

Notes

Read to Learn

The Grant Administration *(page 372)*

Detecting Bias

Why do you think wealthy people may not have opposed the sin tax?

____

____

____

____

____

____

During Grant's first term, the Republican-controlled Congress kept tariffs high, tightened banking regulations, and increased spending. Congress also kept taxes on alcohol and tobacco, called **"sin taxes."** These helped Congress pay off war bonds. Democrats argued that Republicans' economic policies, benefited only the wealthy. Wealthy people were often bondholders, but poor people paid most of the sin taxes. Some Republicans, known as Liberal Republicans, agreed with the Democrats and did not want Grant to be reelected. In the 1872 election, they ran Horace Greeley as their candidate. Grant won easily.

Scandals and economic troubles hurt Grant's second term. An economic crisis started in 1873 when a powerful bank went bankrupt. Smaller banks closed, businesses closed, and many people lost their jobs. These problems hurt the Republicans in the congressional elections of 1874. Then, in 1875, the "Whiskey Ring" scandal broke. It involved government officials and distillers in St. Louis who cheated the government. These scandals helped Democrats win control of the House and gain seats in the Senate.

Notes

Read to Learn

Reconstruction Ends *(page 374)*

Predicting

Reread the passage. What effects do you think the end of Reconstruction might have had on the South?

With more Democrats in Congress, it became more difficult for Republicans to carry out Reconstruction. Southern Democrats had worked to regain control of their state and local governments. They often intimidated African American and white Republican voters and used election fraud. Democrats defined the elections as a struggle between African Americans and whites. They gained the support of white owners of small farms' mostly former Republicans. By 1876 the Democrats had control of most of the South's state legislatures.

President Grant did not run for a third term in 1876. The Republicans nominated Rutherford B. Hayes, who wanted to end Reconstruction. The Democrats nominated Samuel Tilden. On election day, neither candidate won the majority of the electoral votes. Congress appointed a commission to solve the issue. It gave the electoral votes to Hayes. The commission's recommendations had to be approved by Congress.

After much debate, the Democrats in Congress voted with the Republicans to give the election to Hayes. Many people believed that some kind of deal had to have been made with the Democrats. The result of the election became known as the Compromise of 1877. Although no one is sure, the Compromise most likely included a promise by the Republicans to pull federal troops out of the South if Hayes was elected. In April 1877, Hayes did pull troops out, and Reconstruction ended.

A "New South" Arises *(page 377)*

Analyzing Information

Why were many African Americans trapped on the land they farmed after Reconstruction?

Many Southern leaders knew the South could not return to the agricultural economy it had before the war. Southern whites worked with Northern financiers to build railroads and industries across the South. However, the South remained mostly agricultural.

With the end of Reconstruction, many African Americans returned to plantations and became **tenant farmers,** paying rent for the land they farmed. Most of these farmers became **sharecroppers,** who paid a share of their crops rather than cash to cover rent and the cost of supplies. Many sharecroppers bought supplies on credit at high interest rates. Merchants could put liens on their crops. These **crop liens** meant merchants could take some of the sharecroppers' crops to cover debts. This led many tenant farmers into **debt peonage.** Sharecroppers could not make enough money to pay off their debts and leave. They could be imprisoned if they could not pay their debts.

Section Wrap-up

Answer these questions to check your understanding of the entire section.

1. What problems hurt Grant's administration?

2. How would you compare the New South and the Old South?

Informative Writing

In the space provided write a short essay explaining what events contributed to the end of Reconstruction in the South.

Chapter 11, Section 1 (Pages 386–393)

Miners and Ranchers

Big Idea

As you read pages 386–393 in your textbook, complete this graphic organizer by listing the locations of mining booms and the discoveries made there.

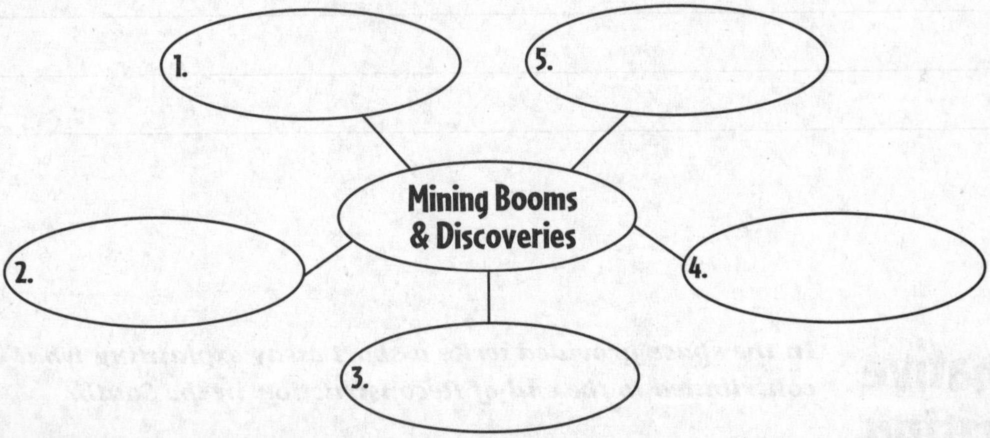

Notes

Read to Learn

Growth of the Mining Industry *(page 386)*

Comparing and Contrasting

Describe each mining method.

Placer mining

____

____

Hydraulic mining

____

____

Quartz mining

____

____

Throughout the 1800s, people flooded the West hoping to strike it rich by mining minerals such as gold and silver. Almost overnight, tiny frontier towns were transformed into small cities. These "boomtowns" were often rowdy places with rampant crime and lawlessness. Self-appointed volunteers, called **vigilance committees,** were the only law enforcers. Many boomtowns went "bust" when the exhausted mines closed. Mining spurred development in western states such as Nevada, Colorado, Arizona, the Dakotas, and Montana. Railroads came to these areas, and farmers and ranchers followed. By 1889, North Dakota, South Dakota, and Montana were admitted as states. Arizona's population grew more slowly, but it applied for statehood by 1912.

Early miners had extracted ore by hand in a process called placer mining. Later, miners sprayed hills or mountains with high-pressure water in a process called **hydraulic mining.** Although effective, this process devastated the environment. After 1884, most mining companies shifted to quartz mining, a process in which miners are sent down deep shafts to extract minerals.

Notes | Read to Learn

Ranching and Cattle Drives *(page 390)*

Determining Cause and Effect

What two causes prompted ranchers to undertake long drives?

1. ______________________

____

____

____

2. ______________________

____

____

____

Cattle ranching prospered in the Great Plains during the 1800s partly thanks to the **open range,** a vast, federally owned grassland where ranchers could graze their herds for free. Americans had long believed it was impossible to raise cattle in the Plains. Water was scarce, and the prairie grasses were too tough for cattle from the East to eat. But the longhorn, a breed of cattle from Texas, had adapted to life on the Plains.

During the Civil War, eastern cattle were slaughtered as food for armies. After the war, beef prices shot up. By this time, railroad lines also had reached the Great Plains. These factors made it worthwhile for ranchers to drive the longhorns north to the railroad, where they could be shipped east. In 1866, on the first **long drive** to Sedalia, Missouri, many of the cattle perished. The survivors, however, sold for 10 times their Texas price. Many trails, such as the Chisholm Trail, soon opened up between Texas and towns in states such as Kansas and Montana.

"Range wars" eventually broke out among ranchers, newly settled farmers, and sheep herders in Wyoming, Montana, and other territories. The open range was soon fenced off. This, along with an oversupply of cattle and blizzards in 1886 and 1887, meant the end of the open range.

Settling the Hispanic Southwest *(page 392)*

Identifying the Main Idea

Write the main idea of the passage.

____

____

____

____

____

____

____

____

Spain, and then Mexico, ruled the region now called the American Southwest before it came under U.S. control in 1848. The region's Spanish-speaking residents became American citizens. They were assured they would retain their property rights. However, the new Southwest attracted settlers from the East. They often clashed with the Mexican Americans, whose claims of land ownership dated back to centuries-old, vague Spanish land grants. American courts usually refused to accept these grants as proof of ownership.

In California, Hispanic landowners who owned **haciendas**—or huge ranches—clashed with "Forty-Niners." Elsewhere, English-speaking ranchers claimed large tracts of land of Mexican origin so they could expand their ranches. In some cases, the Hispanic population fought back, sometimes with violent force. In New Mexico, Hispanics retained their majority in the population and in the state legislature. Throughout the late 1800s, the Southwest also attracted immigrants from Mexico. They often settled in urban neighborhoods called **barrios.**

Section Wrap-up

Answer these questions to check your understanding of the entire section.

1. How did the mining industry help some territories become U.S. states?

2. Why did the open range disappear?

Persuasive Writing

Write a paragraph explaining your beliefs from either the point of view of a judge that does not see Spanish land grants as proof of ownership of land, or the point of view of a Mexican American who believes his land grant entitles him to the land.

Chapter 11, Section 2 (Pages 394–397)

Farming the Plains

Big Idea

As you read pages 394–397 in your textbook, complete this graphic organizer by listing the ways the government encouraged settlement.

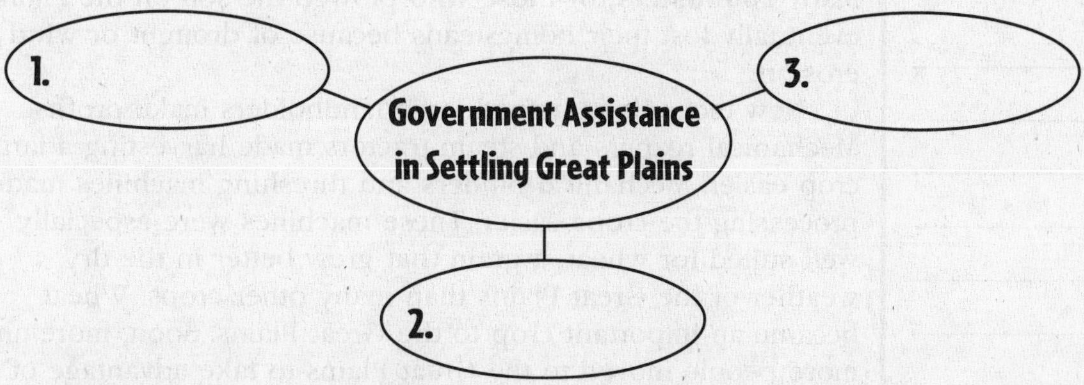

Notes

Read to Learn

The Beginnings of Settlement (page 394)

Problems and Solutions

List some of the problems faced by early Great Plains settlers.

____

____

____

____

____

____

____

The Great Plains region receives little rain, and has few trees. In 1819 Major Stephen Long traveled through the region and declared it to be a desert not fit for settlement. In the late 1800s, several factors helped change the Plains' desert image. Railroad companies sold land along the rail lines that they built through the Plains. They sold the land at low prices, attracting settlers there. Pamphlets and posters spread the news across the United States and Europe that the Plains were a ticket to prosperity. A Nebraskan claimed that farming the Plains would increase rainfall there, a claim seemingly supported by above average rainfall in the 1870s.

The government passed the Homestead Act in 1862. One could file for a **homestead,** or a tract of open public land, for a \$10 fee. A person could claim up to 160 acres of land and would own it after five years. The environment was harsh for Plains settlers. Summer temperatures soared above 100°F, and winters brought blizzards. Prairie fires were a danger, and sometimes grasshoppers destroyed crops.

Notes

Read to Learn

The Wheat Belt *(page 396)*

Determining Cause and Effect

What two factors caused many Plains farmers to take out loans on their property?

1. ______________________

____

____

2. ______________________

____

____

Formulating Questions

Write two questions you still have after reading the section.

1. ______________________

____

____

2. ______________________

____

____

____

New farming methods and inventions helped to make farming on the Great Plains profitable. One method was called **dry farming.** It involved planting seeds deep in the ground where there was enough moisture for them to grow. By the 1860s, farmers were using steel plows, reapers, and threshing machines. The new machines made dry farming possible. However, dry prairie soil could blow away in a dry season. Many **sodbusters,** or those who plowed the soil on the Plains, eventually lost their homesteads because of drought or wind erosion.

New technology helped large landholders make profits. Mechanical reapers and steam tractors made harvesting a large crop easier. Mechanical binders and threshing machines made processing the crops easier. These machines were especially well suited for wheat, a grain that grew better in the dry weather of the Great Plains than many other crops. Wheat became an important crop to the Great Plains. Soon, more and more people moved to the Great Plains to take advantage of the inexpensive land and the new technology. The Wheat Belt eventually included much of the Dakotas and the western parts of Nebraska and Kansas.

The new technology allowed some farms to become very large. These **bonanza farms** brought huge profits to their owners. By the 1880s, the Wheat Belt helped to make the United States the world's leading exporter of wheat.

However, Plains farmers also faced difficulties. A long drought that began in the late 1880s destroyed many crops and turned the soil to dust. The nation began to face competition from other wheat-producing countries. By the 1890s, an oversupply of wheat caused prices to drop. To make it through bad times, some farmers took out loans based on the value of their property. If they did not meet their payments, they had to give the land to the bank. Many then worked as tenant farmers for the new owner.

On April 22, 1889, the government opened for settlement one of the last large territories. Within hours, over 10,000 people raced to stake claims. This was called the "Oklahoma Land Rush." In 1890 the Census Bureau reported that there was no true frontier left in America, although there was still much unoccupied land. Many people believed that this was the end of an era.

Section Wrap-up

Answer these questions to check your understanding of the entire section.

1. Why and how did people begin to settle the Plains?

2. What was the Wheat Belt and how did it get its name?

Expository Writing

In the space provided write a paragraph about the advantages and disadvantages of participating in the Oklahoma Land Rush.

Chapter 11, Section 3 (Pages 398–403)

Native Americans

Big Idea

As you read pages 398–403 in your textbook, complete this time line by recording the battles between Native Americans and the United States government and the results of each.

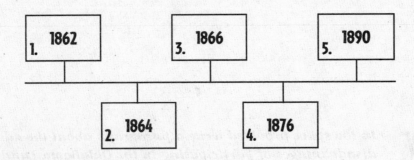

1. 1862
2. 1864
3. 1866
4. 1876
5. 1890

Notes

Read to Learn

Struggles of the Plains Indians *(page 398)*

Making Inferences

Why did the Indian Peace Commission's plan fail?

For centuries, many Native American groups lived on the Great Plains, most as **nomads** who roamed the land. As settlers moved onto the Great Plains, they clashed with the Native Americans. In 1862 in Minnesota, the Dakota Sioux faced starvation and lived in poverty after failing to receive **annuities,** or money promised to them by the U.S. government. They staged an uprising, waging war against both soldiers and settlers. The rebellion was suppressed.

From 1866 to 1868, the Lakota Sioux clashed with U.S. soldiers. This was called "Red Cloud's War." In one major battle known as Fetterman's Massacre, the Lakota wiped out an entire unit of the U.S. Army—about 80 soldiers. In 1864, in response to Native American raids and attacks, Colorado's territorial governor ordered their surrender at Fort Lyon. When several hundred Cheyenne came to negotiate a peace deal they were attacked by U.S. troops.

In 1867 Congress formed an Indian Peace Commission. It proposed creating two large reservations. However, this plan failed. Many Native Americans refused to move. Those who did move faced miserable conditions.

Notes

Read to Learn

The Last Native American Wars *(page 401)*

Predicting

Before you read, make a prediction about the passage based on the heading.

____

____

____

____

____

____

____

____

Detecting Bias

Complete the following sentence.

Based on the title of her book, I expect Helen Hunt Jackson to believe

____

____

____

____

____

______________________.

By the 1870s, many Native Americans left the reservations in disgust. They joined others who shunned reservations to hunt buffalo on the open plains. However, the buffalo were disappearing. Migrants crossing the plains, professional hunters, and sport hunters killed many buffalo. Railroad companies killed buffalo that were blocking rail lines.

In 1876 miners overran the Lakota Sioux reservation. Seeing that American settlers were violating the treaty, many Lakota left the reservation to hunt in Montana. In response, the government sent troops, including Lieutenant Colonel George A. Custer. On June 25, Custer and 210 soldiers attacked a very large group of Lakota and Cheyenne warriors camped along the Little Bighorn River. The warriors killed all but one of them. The army then stepped up its campaign against the Plains Indians. Some fled to Canada, while others were forced back on the reservation.

In 1877 the Nez Perce, led by Chief Joseph, refused to move to a smaller reservation in Idaho. When the army came to force them to move, they fled for more than 1,300 miles. However, Chief Joseph surrendered in October 1877. He and his followers were moved to Oklahoma.

Against government orders, some Lakota on a reservation continued to perform the Ghost Dance. This ritual celebrated, among other things, a hoped-for day when settlers would leave. Federal authorities blamed Chief Sitting Bull for this defiance and sent police to arrest him. He died in the ensuing gunfire. Some Ghost Dancers fled, but troops pursued them. On December 29, 1890, fighting broke out at Wounded Knee Creek. About 25 soldiers and 200 Lakota died.

Some Americans opposed the government's treatment of Native Americans. Helen Hunt Jackson, in her book *A Century of Dishonor,* described the government's injustices against Native Americans. Some people believed that Native Americans should **assimilate,** or be absorbed, into American culture as citizens and landowners. Congress in 1887 passed the Dawes Act. It gave each head of a household 160 acres of reservation land. Although some Native Americans succeeded as farmers or ranchers, many did not. Many found their **allotment** of land was too small to be profitable. Assimilation failed, and no good solution replaced it. The Plains Indians depended on the buffalo for food, clothing, fuel, and shelter. When the herds were wiped out, they could not continue their way of life, but few were willing to adopt the settlers' way of life.

Section Wrap-up

Answer these questions to check your understanding of the entire section.

1. What conflicts arose between the Plains Indians and American settlers?

2. What problems were caused by attempts to assimilate Native Americans?

Informative Writing

In the space provided write a newspaper account of one of the conflicts between Native Americans and U.S. soldiers.

Chapter 12, Section 1 (Pages 410–415)

The Rise of Industry

Big Idea

As you read pages 410–415 in your textbook, complete this graphic organizer by listing some of the causes of industrialization.

Causes

1.
2.
3.
4.

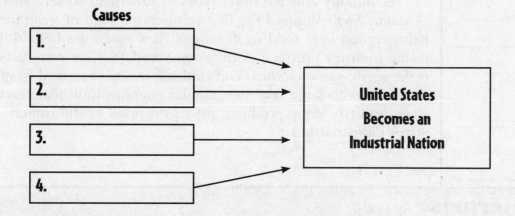

→ **United States Becomes an Industrial Nation**

Notes

Read to Learn

The United States Industrializes *(page 410)*

Determining Cause and Effect

List two causes of American population growth.

1. ______________

____

____

2. ______________

____

____

After the Civil War, many people left their farms to find work in factories. By the late 1800s, the United States had become the world's leading industrial nation. By 1914 the **gross national product (GNP)**—or the total value of all goods and services produced by a country—was eight times greater than in 1865.

One reason that industries expanded was an abundunce of natural resources such as coal and timber. Many resources were located in the West. The transcontinental railroad brought settlers to the West and resources to the East. A new resource, petroleum, was also being developed. It was turned into kerosene used in lanterns and stoves. In 1859 Edwin Drake drilled the first oil well near Titusville, Pennsylvania. Oil fields were soon developed across the country. Oil production helped to expand the nation's economy.

America's growing population provided industries with both a larger workforce and more demand for the goods they produced. The population increase resulted from large families and increased immigration. Between 1870 and 1910, over 20 million immigrants came to the United States.

Notes

Read to Learn

New Inventions (page 412)

Problems and Solutions

What problem did Gustavus Swift solve?

Inventions also contributed to the growth of industries. In 1876 Alexander Graham Bell developed the telephone. It changed both business and personal communication. Thomas Alva Edison invented the phonograph and the lightbulb, among others. In 1882 an Edison company began to supply electric power to New York City. Electric power changed American society.

Technology affected other parts of American society. In 1877 Gustavus Swift shipped the first refrigerated load of fresh meat. Refrigeration kept food fresh longer. New machines helped the textile industry produce cloth faster. Standard sizes were used to make ready-made clothes. The clothing business moved from small shops to large factories. Similar changes took place in the shoe industry. Many products' prices dropped as the United States industrialized.

Free Enterprise (page 414)

Identifying the Main Idea

Write the main idea of the passage.

The free enterprise system also helped industry in the United States expand. In the late 1800s, many Americans embraced a **laissez-faire** policy. This means government should not interfere in the economy, except to protect property rights and maintain peace. They believed a free market, in which companies compete, leads to more wealth for everyone. This policy promotes keeping taxes low and limiting government debt. The chance to gain wealth attracted **entrepreneurs.** These are people who risk their capital in organizing and running businesses. Many New Englanders invested capital in building factories and railroads. Foreign investors also invested in American industries.

In many ways, the U.S. government was laissez-faire in the late 1800s. In other ways, it actively aided industry. Congress passed the Morrill Tariff. It nearly tripled tariffs. This made imported goods cost more than American goods. The government gave land grants to western railroads and sold land with mineral resources for less than its true value.

High tariffs ran counter to laissez-faire policies. Tariffs also caused foreign countries to raise tariffs against American goods. This hurt Americans trying to sell goods abroad, particularly farmers. Despite this effect, many business and government leaders thought tariffs helped new American industries compete with large European industries. By the early 1900s, many American industries were large and competitive. Business leaders then began to push for free trade.

Section Wrap-up

Answer these questions to check your understanding of the entire section.

1. What effects did the expanding population have on industry?

2. How did Alexander Graham Bell and Thomas Alva Edison influence American society?

Persuasive Writing

In the space provided write a brief letter to a U.S. representative during the late 1800s arguing for or against passing the Morrill Tariff.

Chapter 12, Section 2 (Pages 416–421)

The Railroads

Big Idea

As you read pages 416–421 in your textbook, complete this graphic organizer by listing some of the effects of this rail network on the nation.

Nationwide Rail Network

Effects

1. ______________________
2. ______________________
3. ______________________
4. ______________________

Notes

Read to Learn

Linking the Nation *(page 416)*

Comparing and Contrasting

Compare and contrast workers hired to build the two railroads.

Union Pacific:

____

____

Central Pacific:

____

____

Both:

____

In 1862 President Lincoln signed the Pacific Railway Act. It called for a transcontinental railroad to be built by the Union Pacific and Central Pacific railroad companies. Each company got land along the route of the tracks. The Union Pacific started in Omaha, Nebraska, in 1865. It employed as many as 10,000 workers at one time, including Civil War veterans, immigrants, and ex-convicts. Because of a labor shortage in California, the Central Pacific hired about 10,000 workers from China.

Before 1860 the United States had hundreds of small railroad lines. Then, large rail lines began to take over and combine them. To fix scheduling and safety problems, in 1883 the American Railway Association divided the country into four **time zones.** The large railroads benefited the nation in other ways. They could shift railcars from one section of the country to speed long-distance transportation. New technology let railroads put longer and heavier trains on their lines. More powerful locomotives made operations more efficient. Railroads also united people from many regions.

Notes

Read to Learn

Robber Barons *(page 420)*

Evaluating Information

Complete the statements to evaluate the passage.

This passage included good information about

____

____

______________________.

This passage should include more information about

____

____

______________________.

Making Generalizations

Write a generalization about the Crédit Mobilier scandal.

____

____

____

____

____

____

____

____

The federal government encouraged railroad building by giving railroad companies **land grants.** Railroads then sold the land to settlers and businesses to raise the money they needed to build the railroad. By the 1860s, the railroads received land larger in area than New England, New York, and Pennsylvania combined. Some railroad companies earned enough money from the land grants to cover much of the cost of building their lines.

Some railroad entrepreneurs in the late 1800s got their wealth by cheating investors, bribing government officials, and cheating on their contracts. Corrupt railroad owner Jay Gould was infamous for manipulating stock.

Bribery also occurred often. This was partly because government helped fund railroads. Railroad investors knew that they could make more money by getting government land grants than by operating a railroad. As a result, investors bribed politicians to vote for more grants.

Crédit Mobilier was a construction company started by several stockholders in the Union Pacific. The investors set up contracts with themselves. Crédit Mobilier greatly overcharged the Union Pacific for the work it did. Because investors owned both companies, the railroad agreed to pay. The investors had made several million dollars by the time the Union Pacific was completed. However, the railroad had used up its land grants and was almost bankrupt. To convince Congress to give the railroad more grants, one of the investors gave members of Congress shares in the Union Pacific at a price well below what these shares were worth. In the 1872 election campaign, a letter to a New York newspaper listed the members of Congress who had accepted the shares. A further investigation into the scandal showed that the vice president at the time had also accepted shares from the railroad.

Not all railroad entrepreneurs were robber barons, or people who loot an industry and give nothing back. James J. Hill built the Great Northern Railroad without federal land grants. It ran between Minnesota and Washington state. He planned the route to pass near towns in the region. To increase business, he promised low fares to settlers who homesteaded along the route. He transported American products that were in demand in China to Washington, where they were shipped to Asia. In this way the railroad made money by transporting goods both east and west. The Great Northern became the most successful transcontinental railroad and the only one that did not eventually go bankrupt.

Section Wrap-up

Answer these questions to check your understanding of the entire section.

1. How were some railroad owners corrupt?

2. How were railroads financed, and how did they grow?

Expository Writing

In the space provided write a brief essay explaining how James J. Hill was different from the robber barons of the time.

Chapter 12, Section 3 (Pages 422–427)

Big Business

Big Idea

As you read pages 422–427 in your textbook, complete this graphic organizer to describe some steps larger business owners took to weaken or eliminate competition.

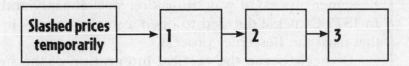

Slashed prices temporarily → 1 → 2 → 3

Notes | Read to Learn

The Rise of Big Business *(page 422)*

Predicting

Skim the passage. Predict what you will learn.

By 1900 big businesses dominated the economy. Big businesses became possible because of the **corporation,** an organization owned by many people but treated as one person by the law. Corporations sell shares of ownership called **stock.** By issuing stock, a corporation can raise money while spreading out the financial risk. Corporations use the money they receive from selling stock to invest in new technologies, hire workers, and buy machines. Corporations achieve **economies of scale,** in which they make goods cheaply by quickly making large quantities of them.

Businesses have two kinds of costs. A company pays fixed costs, such as taxes, whether or not it is operating. A company pays operating costs, such as wages and supplies, only when it is running. Before the Civil War, small companies usually had low fixed costs but high operating costs. If sales decreased, they usually shut down. Corporations had high fixed costs and low operating costs, so they could keep operating even during a recession. Corporations could cut prices to increase sales, rather than shutting down. Small businesses could not compete with big businesses, so many failed.

Notes

Read to Learn

Consolidating Industry *(page 424)*

Identifying the Main Idea

Write the main idea of the passage.

Comparing and Contrasting

Compare and contrast vertical integration with horizontal integration.

Vertical integration:

Horizontal integration:

Both:

Many corporate leaders disliked competition. Lower prices helped consumers but hurt corporations' profits. Many corporations organized **pools,** or deals to keep prices at a certain level. The courts disapproved of pools and would not enforce them. Pools usually fell apart when one company lowered prices to take business away from another.

Andrew Carnegie was a poor immigrant who became a business leader. While working for a railroad, he realized he could make money by investing in companies that served the railroad industry. Carnegie met Henry Bessemer, inventor of the Bessemer process, a way of making steel cheaply and efficiently. In 1875 Carnegie decided to open a steel company in Pittsburgh that used the Bessemer process.

Carnegie began the **vertical integration** of the steel industry. A vertically integrated company owns all the businesses that it depends on to run. Carnegie's company bought mines, quarries, and ore fields. Business leaders also pushed for **horizontal integration,** or combining similar companies into a large corporation. When one company controls a market, it is a **monopoly.** People who opposed monopolies believed they could charge whatever price they wanted for their products. Other people thought monopolies had to keep prices low to keep competition down.

Many states made it illegal for one company to own stock in another. In 1882 the Standard Oil Company formed the first **trust** to get around these laws. A trust lets one person, the trustee, manage another's property. Instead of buying a company, Standard Oil had the stockholders give their stock to Standard Oil trustees. In exchange, the stockholders received shares in the trust. In this way, the trustees ran many companies as if they were one.

In 1889 New Jersey passed a law allowing corporations to own stock in other businesses. Many companies soon formed new businesses called holding companies. A **holding company** does not produce goods itself, but owns the stock of companies that do and runs them like one large corporation.

American industries were producing many different products, and retailers needed to attract consumers to buy them. Advertising changed as large illustrated ads replaced small print ads in newspapers. Department stores changed how people shopped. Each sold a variety of products in one large, elegant building. Chain stores, or groups of similar stores owned by one company, offered low prices rather than variety. To reach people who lived in rural areas, retailers issued mail-order catalogs.

Section Wrap-up

Answer these questions to check your understanding of the entire section.

1. How did large corporations come to dominate American business?

2. How did the way retailers advertise goods to consumers change in the late 1800s?

Descriptive Writing

In the space provided write a description of how Andrew Carnegie's innovations transformed the steel industry.

Chapter 12, Section 4 (Pages 428–435)

Unions

Big Idea

As you read pages 428–435 in your textbook, complete this time line by filling in the incidents of labor unrest and the results of each incident.

1.	2.	3.

Notes

Read to Learn

Working in the United States *(page 428)*

Problems and Solutions

Explain how employers might respond to the problem.

Problem: Workers formed a union.

Solution:

____

____

____

____

____

The difference in their standard of living caused workers to resent the wealthy. In the late 1800s **deflation,** a rise in the value of money, also hurt relations between workers and owners. Deflation caused companies to cut wages, so workers earned less money for the same work. Many workers then decided to organize unions. Industries had two kinds of workers. Craft workers had special skills and training. Common laborers had few skills and earned lower wages. In the 1830s, craft workers began to form **trade unions.** Employers opposed unions, especially **industrial unions,** which represented all craft workers and common laborers in the same industry.

Employers sometimes put those who tried to start a union or strike on a **blacklist,** a list of "troublemakers" no company would hire. Employers could use a **lockout**—when employers locked workers out of the property and refused to pay them—to break up unions that did form. If the union called a strike, employers hired replacement workers. Courts often fined labor leaders who led strikes.

Notes | Read to Learn

Struggling to Organize *(page 431)*

Making Inferences

Why did the Knights of Labor union lose members after the Haymarket Riot?

In 1873, a recession forced many companies to cut wages. In 1877, one railroad cut wages again, and its workers went on strike. More than 80,000 railroad workers nationwide joined the protest. Some turned to violence, and President Hayes eventually ordered the army to open the railroads.

Founded in 1869, the Knights of Labor was the first nationwide industrial union. The Knights supported the eight-hour workday, equal pay for women, and the end of child labor. At first, the Knights preferred **arbitration,** in which a third party helps workers and employers reach agreements.

In 1886, about 3,000 protesters rallied at Chicago's Haymarket Square. When police arrived, someone threw a bomb that killed a police officer. Violence erupted, and about 100 people, including nearly 70 police officers, were injured in the Haymarket Riot. No one knew who threw the bomb, but eight men were convicted for it. One was a member of the Knights of Labor. The union lost members as a result.

Railroad workers formed the industrial American Railway Union (ARU) in 1893. The ARU unionized workers at the Pullman Palace Car Company in Illinois. The Pullman Company required workers to live in the town it built and to buy goods from its stores. When Pullman cut wages in 1893, workers could not afford their rent or the store's high prices. They began a strike. Other ARU members refused to pull Pullman cars. President Cleveland sent in troops, and a federal court issued an **injunction** ordering the strike to end. Both the strike and the union were ended.

New Unions Emerge *(page 434)*

Predicting

Make a prediction about women's working conditions in the 1800s.

Trade unions were more successful in the late 1800s. In 1886, several of them organized the American Federation of Labor (AFL). The AFL had three goals: to get companies to recognize unions and agree to negotiations; to create **closed shops,** which hired only union members; and to promote an eight-hour workday. By 1900, the AFL was the largest union in the country, but most workers were not union members.

After the Civil War, more women began earning wages. About one-third of them worked as domestic servants. One-third were teachers, nurses, and sales clerks. The final third were industrial workers, mostly in clothing and food processing factories. Women were paid less than men and could not join most unions. In 1903, two women founded the Women's Trade Union League to address women's labor issues.

Section Wrap-up

Answer these questions to check your understanding of the entire section.

1. What were some barriers to labor union growth?

2. What were some goals of labor unions?

Informative Writing

In the space provided write an encyclopedia entry about the growth of trade unions, including why they first formed and how the AFL originated.

Chapter 13, Section 1 (Pages 442–447)

Immigration

Big Idea

As you read pages 442–447 in your textbook, complete this graphic organizer by filling in the reasons people left their homelands to immigrate to the United States.

Reasons for Immigrating	
Push Factors	**Pull Factors**
1.	3.
2.	4.

Notes

Read to Learn

Europeans Flood Into America *(page 442)*

Identifying the Main Idea

Write the main idea of this section.

______

______

______

______

______

______

______

______

In the late 1800s, a major wave of immigration began. More than half of all immigrants were from eastern and southern Europe. They immigrated for a variety of reasons. Some came for jobs. Some came to avoid military service. Others, particularly Jews, fled religious persecution.

Most immigrants who came to the United States booked passage in **steerage.** This was the cheapest accommodations on a steamship. After about two weeks, they arrived at Ellis Island. This is a tiny island in New York harbor. Immigrants had to pass a medical exam. Most immigrants passed through Ellis Island in about a day.

Many immigrants settled in cities. There, they often lived in neighborhoods separated into ethnic groups, where they spoke their native languages, worshipped in familiar surroundings, and published ethnic newspapers. Immigrants who could learn English quickly and adapt to American culture generally adjusted well to life in the United States. So did those who had marketable skills or who settled among members of their own ethnic groups.

Notes

Read to Learn

Asian Immigration *(page 445)*

Making Generalizations

Complete the sentence to make a generalization.

Many Asian immigrants came to the United States because ______________

Chinese immigrants came to the United States for many reasons. They often came to escape poverty and famine or to find jobs. An 1850 rebellion in China also caused many Chinese to move to the United States. In the 1860s, demand for workers on the transcontinental railroad further increased Chinese immigration. Chinese immigrants mainly settled in cities on the West Coast. They often worked as laborers or servants or in skilled trades. Others became merchants or opened businesses.

Japanese immigration to the United States increased greatly between 1900 and 1910. As Japan industrialized, economic problems caused many Japanese people to leave.

At first, Asian immigrants arrived at a two-story shed at the wharf in San Francisco. In 1910, California opened a barracks on Angel Island for Asian immigrants. Most immigrants were young men. They were often kept at Angel Island for months awaiting the results of immigration hearings. Some immigrants wrote poems on the barracks walls.

Nativism Resurges *(page 446)*

Comparing and Contrasting

Complete the sentences.

1. The two laws from 1882 were similar because ______________

2. The two laws from 1882 were different because ______________

This new wave of immigration to the United States increased feelings of **nativism.** This is an extreme dislike for immigrants by native-born people. In the late 1800s, these feelings were mainly directed at Asians, Jews, and eastern Europeans.

Religious and ethnic prejudices and economic fears led to the desire to limit immigration. Some people feared the large number of Catholic immigrants from Europe. Labor unions argued that immigrants would work for low wages or accept jobs as strikebreakers. Some nativists formed anti-immigrant organizations. Members of the American Protective Association would not hire or vote for Catholic immigrants. The Workingman's Party of California worked to stop Chinese immigration.

Anti-immigrant feelings led Congress to pass new laws in 1882. One banned convicts, paupers, and the mentally disabled from immigrating. It also taxed new immigrants 50 cents. The other was the Chinese Exclusion Act. It barred Chinese immigration for ten years. It also prevented Chinese already in the country from becoming citizens. The Chinese in the country protested the law. They pointed out that laws did not ban European immigration. Yet Congress renewed the law and made it permanent in 1902. It was not repealed until 1943.

Section Wrap-up

Answer these questions to check your understanding of the entire section.

1. Describe the new wave of immigrants who came to the United States during the late 1800s.

____

____

____

2. How did nativism affect immigration policies in the United States?

____

____

____

Persuasive Writing

In the space provided write an editorial taking a position either for or against the immigration laws of 1882.

____

____

____

____

____

____

____

____

____

____

____

____

____

Chapter 13, Section 2 (Pages 450–455)

Urbanization

Big Idea

As you read pages 450–455 in your textbook, complete this graphic organizer by filling in some of the problems the nation's cities faced.

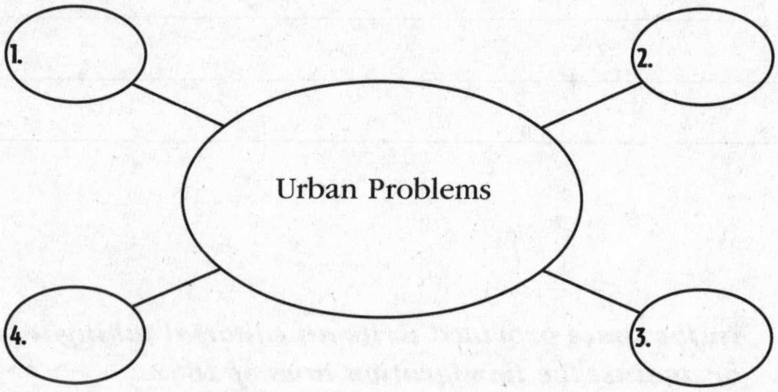

Notes | Read to Learn

Americans Migrate to the Cities *(page 450)*

Determining Cause and Effect

Explain the cause.

Cause: Cities offered

____

____

____

____

____

______________________.

Effect: Many people migrated to cities.

The urban population of the United States had increased greatly by 1900. Most immigrants had neither the money to buy farms nor the education to get high paying jobs. They settled in the nation's growing cities and worked in factories. American farmers also moved to cities, looking for better paying jobs. Cities offered other benefits, such as running water and modern plumbing. They also had libraries, museums, and theaters.

As city populations grew, the land prices increased. Land was limited, so builders began to build up instead of out. Tall, steel frame buildings called **skyscrapers** began to appear. Chicago's Home Insurance Building, built in 1885, was the first of many such buildings.

To move people around cities, different kinds of transportation developed. At first, railroad cars pulled by horses were common. San Francisco and other cities began using cars pulled by underground cables. Other cities began using electric trolley cars. When congestion on streets became a problem, cities built elevated railroads or subway systems.

Notes | Read to Learn

Separation by Class *(page 452)*

Comparing and Contrasting

As you read, complete the sentences.

1. Many middle class families lived in

____

2. Many working class families lived in

____

Wealthy, middle class, and working class people lived in different parts of the cities. The wealthy lived in fashionable districts in cities' hearts. They built large, beautiful houses modeled after stylish European homes. For example, merchant Potter Palmer chose to model his Chicago home after a castle. In New York, Cornelius Vanderbilt's grandson's home included a two-story dining room, a gymnasium, and a solid marble bathroom.

The growing middle class included doctors, lawyers, engineers, teachers, and social workers. Many moved away from the central city to its suburbs. New commuter rail lines helped them travel back and forth to their jobs.

The working class generally lived in **tenements.** These were dark and crowded multifamily apartments. Many working families sent their children to work in factories or took in boarders to supplement their incomes.

Urban Problems *(page 454)*

Analyzing Information

Why did some city dwellers support political machines?

____

____

____

____

____

____

____

____

____

People living in overcrowded city neighborhoods faced several problems, including crime, violence, fire, disease, and pollution. Both major and minor crimes increased as city populations grew.

Disease and pollution were even bigger threats. Improper disposal of sewage contaminated drinking water. This caused epidemics of diseases such as typhoid and cholera. Sources of pollution included horse manure on streets, chimney smoke, and soot and ash from coal or wood fires.

A new kind of political system took hold in cities. The **political machine** was an informal political group designed to gain and keep power. **Party bosses** provided people living in cities with jobs, food, housing, heat, and police protection. In exchange, they asked for votes. George Plunkett was one powerful New York City party boss.

Party bosses controlled the city's money. Machine politicians grew rich through fraud or **graft**—getting money by dishonest or questionable means. For example, a politician might find out where a park was being built. The politician would then buy the land and sell it to the city for a profit. Corrupt politicians often accepted bribes from contractors in exchange for city contracts.

One of the most famous political machines was Tammany Hall in New York City. William "Boss" Tweed was its corrupt leader. In some cities, the machines controlled all city services. Although corrupt, political machines provided necessary city services to the urban masses.

Section Wrap-up

Answer these questions to check your understanding of the entire section.

1. What technological developments made the growth of cities possible?

2. How did party bosses of the political machines grow wealthy?

Descriptive Writing

Suppose you are the child in a working class family, living in a large city around 1895. Describe some of the problems you face. Suggest possible solutions.

Chapter 13, Section 3 (Pages 458–467)

The Gilded Age

Big Idea

As you read pages 458–467 in your textbook, complete this graphic organizer by filling in the main idea of each of the theories and movements listed.

Theory or Movement	Main Idea
Social Darwinism	1.
Laissez-Faire	2.
Gospel of Wealth	3.
Realism	4.

Notes

Read to Learn

Social Darwinism *(page 458)*

Synthesizing Information

Explain what Social Darwinists would think about regulating business.

____

____

____

____

____

____

____

The Gilded Age lasted from around 1870 to around 1900 and was named for a term from a novel by Mark Twain and Charles Warner. It was a time of new inventions, industrial growth, and growing cities. Something "gilded" is covered with gold only on the outside but made of cheap material on the inside. The writers meant that there was corruption, poverty, and crime beneath the Gilded Age's shiny surface.

New ideas took hold at this time. One of the strongest beliefs of the time was **individualism,** the idea that any person could succeed if he or she worked hard enough. Another powerful idea of the time was Herbert Spencer's **Social Darwinism.** Spencer applied Charles Darwin's ideas about evolution to human society. He claimed that human society evolved through competition and natural selection. The laissez-faire doctrine opposed government interference in business. Andrew Carnegie's Gospel of Wealth held that the wealthy should engage in **philanthropy** to help the society that made them rich.

Notes

Read to Learn

A Changing Culture *(page 460)*

Evaluating Information

Would* The Adventures of Huckleberry Finn *be a good book to read in history class? Circle your answer. List two reasons.

Yes *No*

1. ____________

2. ____________

The nineteenth century was a time of great cultural change. Realism in art and literature became popular. This means artists and writers tried to portray the world more realistically. Thomas Eakins painted people doing everyday activities such as swimming. Realistic writers like Mark Twain tried to show the world as it was. His novel *The Adventures of Huckleberry Finn* presented realistic characters, dialect, and setting.

At this time, industrialization provided people with more money for recreation and entertainment. Saloons played a major role in the lives of workers and served as political centers. Families in the late 1800s enjoyed amusement parks. Many people enjoyed watching professional sports such as baseball and football. Some played tennis, golf, and basketball. Vaudeville and Scott Joplin's ragtime music also provided entertainment.

Politics in Washington *(page 462)*

Problems and Solutions

As you read, write the problem each act was intended to solve.

Pendleton Act:

____

____

Interstate Commerce Act:

____

____

Sherman Antitrust Act:

____

____

Under the spoils system, elected politicians had the power of patronage. This meant the winning party gave government jobs to those who had supported them. When Rutherford B. Hayes was elected President in 1877, he appointed reformers to his cabinet. His actions divided the Republican Party into two camps. The "Stalwarts" supported patronage. The "Halfbreeds," including Hayes, opposed patronage.

In 1880, Garfield, a Halfbreed, won the presidency. His vice president was a Stalwart. Garfield was assassinated by an unhappy job seeker. The assassin thought he could get a job at the White House if a Stalwart were President. Congress soon passed the Pendleton Act, which set up the civil service system. People applying for jobs had to pass an exam.

The Republicans and Democrats were very competitive in the late 1800s. In 1884, Democrat Grover Cleveland won the presidency. He faced many problems in office. Americans were upset about railroad rates and the power of big businesses such as Standard Oil. In 1887, Cleveland signed the Interstate Commerce Act, which limited railroad rates. Debate over tariff reduction was the major issue in the 1888 presidential election. Republican Benjamin Harrison won. In 1890, Congress passed the Sherman Antitrust Act to curb the power of trusts like Standard Oil. The law was ineffective.

Notes | Read to Learn

The Rebirth of Reform *(page 464)*

Identifying the Main Idea

Complete the sentence.

The purpose of the new reform movements was ______________________

____

____

____

The changes brought by industrialization led to debate over how to address society's problems. Henry George thought laissez-faire economics was making society worse, not better. Lester Frank Ward challenged Social Darwinism, too. He believed government regulation should replace wasteful competition. His ideas were called Reform Darwinism. A new style of writing called naturalism criticized industrial society. Its writers included Jack London and Stephen Crane. Jane Addams led the **settlement house** movement. It provided medial care, classes, and recreation programs for the poor. Increased public education furthered **Americanization,** in which immigrant children learned about American culture.

Section Wrap-up

Answer these questions to check your understanding of the entire section.

1. How did industrialism promote leisure time and new forms of entertainment?

____

____

2. Why was the Gilded Age a good description of this period in history?

____

____

Informative Writing

Suppose you just read a history book about the Gilded Age. Write a book review. Describe the main points of the book and how accurately the "author" described the period.

____

____

____

____

____

____

____

____

Chapter 13, Section 4 (Pages 470–475)

Populism

Big Idea

As you read pages 470–475 in your textbook, complete this outline by using the major headings of the section.

Populism

I. Unrest in Rural America
   A. ______
   B. ______
   C. ______
II. ______
   A. ______
   B. ______
III. ______
   A. ______
   B. ______

Notes

Read to Learn

Unrest in Rural America *(page 470)*

Determining Cause and Effect

As you read, complete the sentences.

Deflation hit farmers hard because

______

______

______.

______ ***because they were too small to affect prices.***

Populism was a movement to increase farmers' political power and to pass laws in their interest. During the Civil War, the government issued **greenbacks,** paper money not backed gold or silver. This caused **inflation,** a decline in the value of money. Prices of goods rose. After the war, the government stopped printing greenbacks, paid off bonds, and stopped minting silver coins. As the economy grew, **deflation** occurred. The value of money increased and prices fell.

Deflation hurt farmers. Many had to borrow money for seeds and supplies. Falling prices meant farmers sold their crops for less. Many farmers joined the Grange. It organized **cooperatives** that worked for the benefit of their members. The Grange pressured state legislatures to regulate railroad rates. Cooperatives pooled crops and kept them off the market to force prices up. Many Grange cooperatives failed, because they were too small to affect prices. Railroads and businessmen also refused to deal with them. In the 1880s, the Farmers' Alliance formed and organized larger cooperatives, which also failed.

Notes | **Read to Learn**

The Rise of Populism *(page 473)*

Comparing and Contrasting

List characteristics of Farmers' Alliance members in the South and the West.

South: ______________

____

West: ______________

____

Both:

____

____

Farmers' Alliance members in the West formed the People's Party, or the Populists. They nominated candidates for Congress and state offices. Alliance leaders in the South did not want a third party. They wanted to produce a list of demands and vote for candidates that supported them. Part of their strategy was the subtreasury plan. It asked the government to set up warehouses to store crops and provide farmers with low interest loans. Southern Alliance leaders also called for free coinage of silver, an end to protective tariffs and national banks, more regulation of railroads, and direct election of senators. That year, the Populists in the West elected representatives. Alliance members in the South elected Democrats. Many Southern Democrats did not support the Alliance program once they took office.

In 1892, the People's Party held a national convention in Omaha, Nebraska. Its platform called for coinage of silver and a **graduated income tax.** This taxes higher earnings more heavily. The Democrats and Grover Cleveland won the election.

The Election of 1896 *(page 474)*

Making Inferences

Complete the inference.

Populists supported Bryan instead of nominating their own candidate because

____

____

____

____

____

As the election of 1896 approached, leaders of the People's Party decided to make free coinage of silver an important issue. They held their convention after the Republican and Democratic conventions. The Republicans supported the gold standard, nominating William McKinley as their candidate. The Democratic Party nominated William Jennings Bryan, a strong supporter of free silver. The Populist Party decided to support Bryan instead of nominating a separate candidate. Bryan was a powerful speaker. In an electrifying address in defense of silver, Bryan said "you shall not crucify mankind on a cross of gold." He carried his campaign across the country. But this crusade only irritated many immigrants and city people.

McKinley launched a "Front Porch Campaign." He greeted delegations at his home. Many employers warned workers that if Bryan won, businesses would fail and unemployment would rise. Most workers and business leaders supported the Republican Party. McKinley won the election. Bryan and the Democrats lost in the northeastern industrial region. The Populist Party declined after 1896. Some of the reforms they favored were adopted later.

Section Wrap-up

Answer these questions to check your understanding of the entire section.

1. Why did the farmers form cooperatives after the Civil War? How successful were these organizations?

2. Who joined the Populist Party and what were its goals?

Expository Writing

In the space provided write an encyclopedia entry explaining the events that led to the rise of the Populist Party.

Chapter 13, Section 5 (Pages 476–481)

The Rise of Segregation

Big Idea

As you read pages 476–481 in your textbook, complete this web diagram by listing the ways states disenfranchised African Americans and legalized segregation.

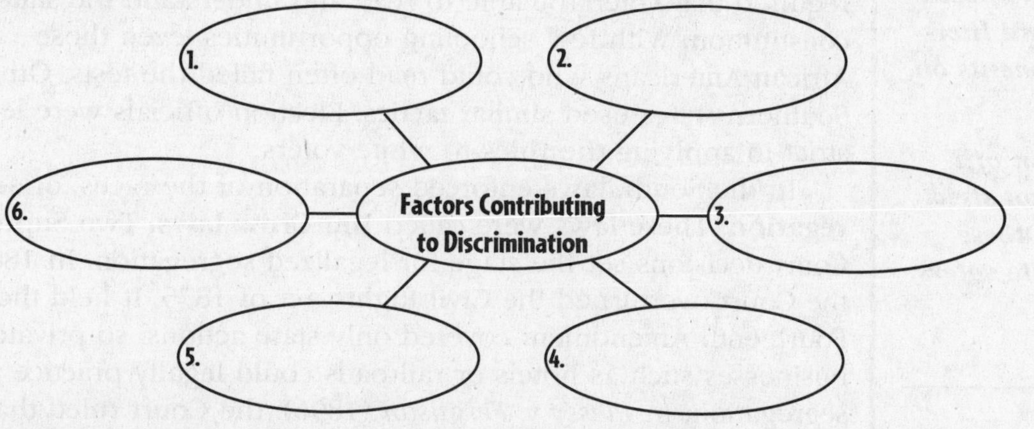

Notes

Read to Learn

Resistance and Repression *(page 476)*

Analyzing Information

Why did Democratic Party leaders fear the coalition of poor whites and African American Populists?

After Reconstruction, many African Americans were very poor and lived under great hardship. Most were sharecroppers, or landless farmers. They worked the land and turned over a large part of their crop to the landlord to pay for rent and supplies.

In 1879, Benjamin "Pap" Singleton, who had formerly been enslaved, organized a large migration of African Americans from the rural South to Kansas. They became known as the Exodusters. Some African Americans joined with the poor white farmers in the Farmers' Alliance. In 1886, a group formed the Colored Farmers' National Alliance. Many African Americans joined the Populist Party in 1891.

Democrats feared the coalition of poor whites and African American Populists. To break it up, Democratic leaders began to appeal to racism. They warned southern whites that the Populist Party would bring back "Black Republican" rule. They made it sound like the return of the Reconstruction period. In addition, election officials found ways to make it difficult for African Americans to vote.

Notes

Read to Learn

Imposing Segregation *(page 478)*

Drawing Conclusions

Draw a conclusion based on these facts:

Fact: States imposed poll taxes and literacy requirements on voters.

Fact: Election officials were not strict in applying these rules to white voters.

Conclusion:

____

____

____

The Fifteenth Amendment prohibited states from denying people the right to vote based on race, color, or former servitude, but not based on other grounds. Soon, states began imposing other voting restrictions that intended to keep African Americans from voting. Mississippi charged a $2 **poll tax,** a sum beyond the means of most poor African Americans. It also required that voters be able to read and understand the state constitution. With few schooling opportunities, even those African Americans who could read often failed the tests. Other Southern states used similar tactics. Election officials were less strict in applying the rules to white voters.

In the South, laws enforced separation of the races, or **segregation.** These laws were called **Jim Crow laws.** Two Supreme Court decisions set the stage for legalized segregation. In 1883, the Court overturned the Civil Rights Act of 1875. It held the Fourteenth Amendment covered only state actions, so private businesses such as hotels or railroads could legally practice segregation. In *Plessy* v. *Ferguson* (1896), the Court ruled that "separate but equal" facilities were legal. Separate facilities were often far from equal.

The African American Response *(page 480)*

Comparing and Contrasting

As you read, complete the sentences.

Booker T. Washington thought African Americans should

____

____

W.E.B. Du Bois believed African Americans should

____

____

African Americans increasingly faced mob violence or **lynchings.** These executions by mobs occurred without proper court action. In 1892, Ida B. Wells, an African American woman from Tennessee, started a campaign against lynching. She published a book condemning the mob violence. Wells called for a fair trial for those accused of crimes. The number of lynchings decreased in the 1900s due in part to her work.

Booker T. Washington was a well-known African American educator. He believed African Americans should try to achieve economic rather than political goals. In 1895, Washington summed up his views in a speech called the Atlanta Compromise. He urged African Americans to delay the fight for civil rights. He said they should focus instead on vocational education to prepare themselves for equal treatment.

Other African American leaders such as W.E.B. DuBois rejected Washington's ideas. DuBois believed African Americans could achieve equality only by demanding their rights especially voting rights. Many African Americans continued to work to restore the right to vote and to end discrimination.

Section Wrap-up

Answer these questions to check your understanding of the entire section.

1. How were African Americans in the South prevented from exercising their voting rights?

2. What was the Supreme Court's role in legalizing segregation?

Descriptive Writing

Write a journal entry giving your reaction to a speech by a major African American leader from the late 1800s about racial discrimination in the United States.

Chapter 14, Section 1 (Pages 490–495)

The Imperialist Vision

Big Idea

As you read pages 490–495 in your textbook, complete the outline below using the major headings of the section.

The Imperialism Vision

I. Building Support for Imperialism
   A. ______
   B. ______
   C. ______

II. ______
   A. ______
   B. ______

III. ______

Notes | Read to Learn

Building Support for Imperialism *(page 490)*

Determining Cause and Effect

List three causes of European expansion.

1. ______

2. ______

3. ______

In the 1800s, nations in Europe expanded overseas. This growth became known as the New Imperialism. **Imperialism** is a strong nation's economic and political domination over weaker ones. It had several causes. Europe needed more raw materials than it could produce. Tariffs hurt trade between industrial countries. These countries looked overseas for new markets. Europe was also running out of investment opportunities, so Europeans invested in other countries. To protect these investments, Europe made the countries into colonies and **protectorates.** In a protectorate, the imperial power let local rulers stay in control.

The United States also wanted to find new markets in other countries. Some Americans used the ideas of Social Darwinism to justify expansion. Others believed that English-speaking countries were naturally superior and should control other countries.

American leaders thought the United States needed a powerful navy. A navy could protect the country's merchant ships and defend its right to trade with other countries. By the late 1890s, the United States was becoming a great naval power.

Notes

Read to Learn

American Expansion in the Pacific *(page 493)*

Predicting

Complete the statement.

If Queen Liliuokalani had held on to power in Hawaii, ___________________

In the 1800s, Japan traded only with the Chinese and the Dutch. In 1853, President Fillmore decided to force Japan to trade with the United States. He sent a naval expedition to negotiate a treaty. When they saw the four warships, the Japanese knew they could not compete against such technology. Japan opened two ports to American trade.

Americans were also interested in Hawaii. Sugarcane grew well in Hawaii's climate. By the mid-1800s, there were many sugarcane plantations. In 1875, the United States removed tariffs on Hawaiian sugar. The islands' sugar industry boomed. Planters grew wealthy. In 1887, the planters made the Hawaiian king sign a constitution limiting his power. An 1890 tariff gave subsidies to U.S. sugar growers. Hawaiian sugar became more expensive than American sugar. Sales of Hawaiian sugar decreased, and the Hawaiian economy weakened.

In 1891, Queen Liliuokalani became the ruler of Hawaii. She disliked American influence in Hawaii and tried to create a new constitution that reestablished her authority. The planters responded by overthrowing the government and forcing the queen to give up power. Then they set up their own government. The United States annexed Hawaii five years later.

Diplomacy in Latin America *(page 495)*

Problems and Solutions

Write the solution James G. Blaine proposed.

Problem: Latin America was not buying enough products from the United States.

Solution: ___________________

The United States wanted more influence in Latin America. While the United States bought many raw materials from Latin American countries, those countries got most of their manufactured goods from Europe. The United States wanted to sell more products in Latin America. It also wanted Europeans to see the United States as the main power in the region. The idea that the United States and Latin American countries should work together became known as Pan-Americanism.

In 1889, the United States invited Latin American countries to a conference in Washington, D.C. James G. Blaine was secretary of state at that time. He had two goals for the conference. He wanted a customs union that would allow the countries to trade freely. He also wanted a system to solve disagreements among American nations. Latin American countries rejected these ideas. They did agree to create an organization to help countries in the Western Hemisphere work together. It was called the Commercial Bureau of the American Republics. Today it is known as the Organization of American States.

Section Wrap-up

Answer these questions to check your understanding of the entire section.

1. How did a desire for more trade and markets change the way the United States acted toward other countries?

2. What were the motivations for American expansion in the Pacific?

Informative Writing

In the space provided write a journal entry about the planters' overthrow of Queen Liliuokalani. Write from the point of view of either a planter or a native Hawaiian loyal to the queen.

Chapter 14, Section 2 (Pages 496–503)

The Spanish-American War

Big Idea

As you read pages 496–503 in your textbook, complete this graphic organizer by listing some of the circumstances that contributed to war with Spain.

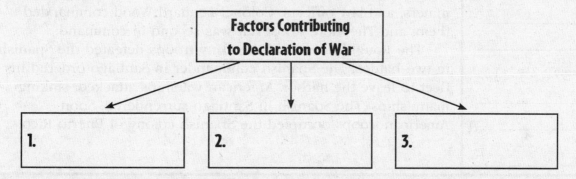

Factors Contributing to Declaration of War

1.

2.

3.

Notes

Read to Learn

The Coming of War *(page 496)*

Drawing Conclusions

Complete the sentence.

Spain offered Cuba autonomy because

Cuba began fighting for independence from Spain in 1868. In 1878, the rebellion collapsed. Many rebels fled to the United States. Americans had invested millions of dollars in Cuba's railroads and sugar plantations. They bought Cuban sugar. Then a new tariff on sugar caused the sale of Cuban sugar to fall. This hurt Cuba's economy. Rebels rose up against Spain again in February 1895 and declared Cuba independent.

Americans read stories of Spanish brutality in newspapers. This sensational reporting became known as **yellow journalism.** Although many stories were exaggerated, Cubans suffered greatly. President McKinley warned Spain that the United States might intervene. Spain removed the Spanish governor of Cuba and offered Cuba **autonomy,** or self-rule, if it agreed to remain part of the Spanish empire. The Cubans refused.

In 1898, riots started in Havana. McKinley sent the battleship *Maine* to evacuate Americans in Cuba. When it exploded in Havana's harbor, Americans blamed Spain. **Jingoism,** or aggressive nationalism contributed to the push for war. Congress declared war on Spain on April 19.

Notes

Read to Learn

A War on Two Fronts *(page 499)*

Comparing and Contrasting

Compare how the U.S. Army and Navy performed during war.

U.S. Army:__________

____

____

U.S. Navy:__________

____

____

Spain was not prepared for war, but the U.S. Navy was. A U.S. Navy fleet blockaded Cuba. Another fleet attacked and destroyed the Spanish fleet in the Philippines. With the help of local rebels, the navy fleet took control of the Filipino capital, Manila.

The U.S. Army was not as ready for war as the navy was. However, on June 14, 1898, about 17,000 soldiers landed in Santiago, Cuba. A volunteer cavalry regiment called the "Rough Riders" accompanied them. They were a group of cowboys, miners, and law officers. Colonel Leonard Wood commanded them, and Theodore Roosevelt was second in command.

The Rough Riders and the army troops defeated the Spanish in two battles. The Spanish commander in Santiago ordered his fleet to leave the harbor. American warships attacked, sinking many ships. The Spanish in Santiago surrendered. Soon American troops occupied the Spanish colony of Puerto Rico.

An American Empire *(page 501)*

Making Generalizations

Make a generalization about nations living under imperialist rule.

____

____

____

____

____

____

____

____

____

____

After the war, Cuba obtained its freedom, and the United States annexed Guam and Puerto Rico. The question of what to do with the Philippines remained open. Some Americans pushed for annexing the Philippines. Others opposed it. When the United States signed the Treaty of Paris with Spain in 1898, it agreed to pay $20 million to annex the Philippines.

Although Cuba became independent, President McKinley made sure it remained tied to the United States. He allowed Cuba to set up a new constitution under conditions that effectively made Cuba a protectorate of the United States. These conditions became known as the Platt Amendment. Cuba reluctantly added the amendment to its constitution.

The United States had to decide how to govern Puerto Rico. At first it was governed by a U.S.-appointed official. Congress gradually gave Puerto Rico more self-government. The debate over whether Puerto Rico should become a state, an independent country, or remain a commonwealth continues today.

In the Philippines, rebels fought the United States for control of the islands. The United States responded by treating the Filipinos much like Spain had treated the Cubans. Thousands died in reconcentration camps. The United States instituted reforms in the Philippines, which eased Filipino hostility toward it. Over the years, the United States gave the Filipinos more control. It finally granted independence to the Philippines in 1946.

Section Wrap-up

Answer these questions to check your understanding of the entire section.

1. What were two reasons that the United States went to war with Spain in 1898?

2. How did the war make the United States a world power?

Persuasive Writing

In the space provided write a newspaper editorial from the point of view of a person living in the United States in 1898. Express an opinion for or against annexing the Philippines. Give reasons to support your position.

Chapter 14, Section 3 (Pages 504–511)

New American Diplomacy

Big Idea

As you read pages 504–511 in your textbook, complete this graphic organizer by listing the reasons the U.S. wanted a canal through Central America.

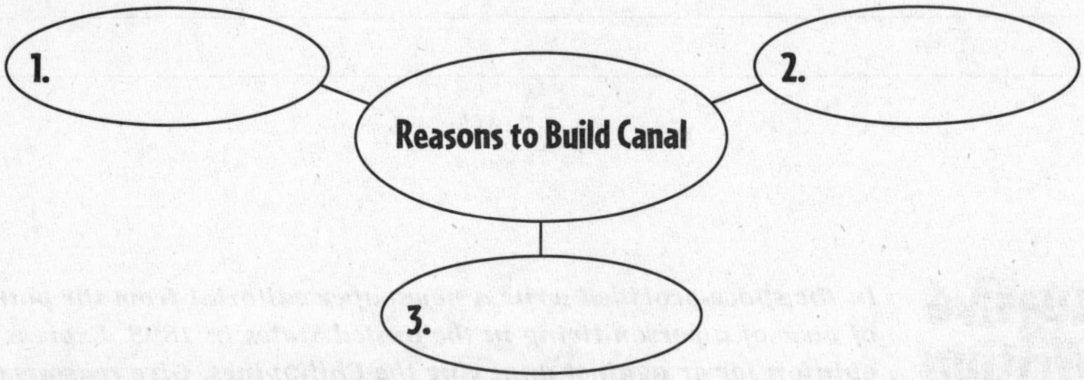

Notes

Read to Learn

American Diplomacy in Asia *(page 504)*

Identifying the Main Idea

Write the main idea of the first paragraph.

____

____

____

____

____

____

____

____

In 1894 China and Japan went to war over Korea, part of the Chinese empire. Japan easily defeated China. The peace treaty gave Japan a region of China called Manchuria. Russia opposed this because Manchuria bordered Russia. The Russians forced Japan to return Manchuria, then demanded that China lease it to Russia. The territory would still belong to China but be under Russian control. Then Germany, France, and Britain also wanted China to lease territory to them. Each leased area became the center of a **sphere of influence** where a foreign nation controlled economic development.

The United States supported an **Open Door policy** in which all countries could trade with China. The U.S. Secretary of State asked nations with leaseholds in China to allow other nations to trade freely within China. In the meantime, secret Chinese societies such as the Boxers were working to rid China of foreign control. In the 1900 Boxer Rebellion, the Boxers seized foreign embassies in Beijing and killed more than 200 foreigners. An international force crushed the rebellion.

Notes

Read to Learn

Roosevelt's Diplomacy *(page 506)*

Formulating Questions

Write a question you have about dollar diplomacy.

____

____

____

____

____

____

____

____

____

In the election of 1900, Theodore Roosevelt was President McKinley's running mate. They won. On September 6, 1901, McKinley was shot by an anarchist. He died a few days later. At 42, Roosevelt became the youngest president ever. Roosevelt supported the Open Door policy in China. He also helped to end a war between Japan and Russia in 1905.

In 1903, Roosevelt decided to build a canal through Panama, which was then part of Colombia. The United States offered Colombia $10 million and a yearly rent for the right to build the canal. Colombia refused the offer. The people of Panama, however, wanted the benefits of having a canal. They also wanted independence from Colombia. Officials in Panama planned an uprising. Roosevelt sent ships to prevent Colombia from interfering. The United States recognized Panama's independence, and the two nations signed a treaty allowing the canal to be built.

Roosevelt's approach to diplomacy came to be called the Roosevelt Corollary. It stated that the United States would intervene in Latin America when necessary to help the Western Hemisphere stay stable. President Taft continued Roosevelt's policies but focused more on industry development than military force. This became known as **dollar diplomacy.**

Woodrow Wilson's Diplomacy in Mexico *(page 510)*

Analyzing Information

List three reasons why Wilson's diplomacy in Mexico was unsuccessful.

1. ______________

____

2. ______________

____

3. ______________

____

Porfirio Díaz ruled Mexico until 1911. Under his rule, most Mexicans were poor and landless. They revolted. Francisco Madero replaced Díaz, but he proved to be a poor leader. General Victoriano Huerta had Madero murdered and seized power. President Wilson opposed imperialism, but he believed that the United States should promote democracy. He therefore refused to recognize Huerta's government. In April 1914, American sailors visiting Mexico were arrested for entering a restricted area. Mexico quickly released them, but refused to apologize. Wilson used this as an opportunity to overthrow Huerta. Anti-American riots followed this action. Venustiano Carranza became the Mexican president.

Mexican forces opposed to Carranza carried out raids into the United States. **Guerrillas** led by Pancho Villa burned the town of Columbus, New Mexico. Sixteen Americans died. Guerrilla fighters use surprise attacks and sabotage instead of open warfare. Wilson sent troops into Mexico to capture Villa, but they failed. Wilson's actions in Mexico damaged U.S. foreign relations. However, Wilson continued to intervene in Latin American countries in an attempt to promote democracy.

Section Wrap-up ***Answer these questions to check your understanding of the entire section.***

1. How did Theodore Roosevelt's foreign policy affect the role of the United States in the world?

2. What was the Open Door policy?

Expository Writing ***In the space provided compare Roosevelt's approach to diplomacy with Wilson's dealings with Mexico.***

Chapter 15, Section 1 (Pages 520–527)

The Roots of Progressivism

Big Idea

As you read pages 520–527 in your textbook, complete this graphic organizer by filling in the beliefs of the Progressives.

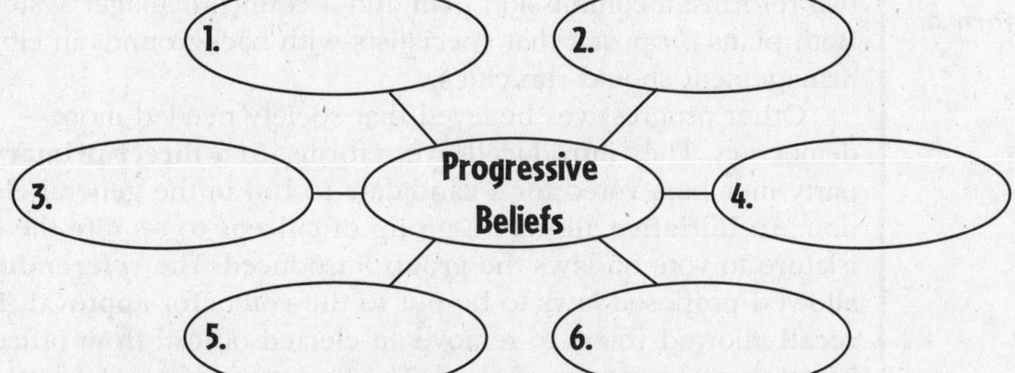

Notes | Read to Learn

The Rise of Progressivism *(page 520)*

Evaluating Information

Were muckrakers good for society? Circle your answer. Underline parts of the text to support your answer.

Yes   ***No***

Progressivism was a mix of ideas and views about how to fix the nation's problems. Most progressives believed that industrialism and urbanization had caused many social problems. Although they focused on different issues, they all believed that the government should play an active role in solving most of society's problems. They also believed people should fix society's problems by applying scientific principles to them.

Journalists were the first to express Progressive ideas. These journalists, known as **muckrakers,** examined social conditions and political corruption. They uncovered corruption in many areas. Some looked into the unfair practices of large corporations. Ida Tarbell published articles about the practices of the Standard Oil Company. Some investigated the government. Lincoln Steffens reported on vote stealing and other corrupt political practices. Others focused on social problems. Jacob Riis wrote about the poverty and disease that were part of many immigrant neighborhoods in New York City. The work of muckrakers pressured politicians to start reforms.

Notes

Read to Learn

Reforming Government (page 522)

Distinguishing Fact from Opinion

Underline one opinion held by progressives.

Circle one fact about progressive reforms.

In most cities, the mayor or city council chose the heads of city departments. They often hired political supporters and friends. These people often knew nothing about managing city services. Bosses of political parties controlled who ran for office. Political machines influenced the election of senators.

One group of progressives believed government should be more efficient and run by knowledgable experts. They proposed two reforms: a commission plan and a council-manager system. Both plans proposed that specialists with backgrounds in city management should run cities.

Other progressives believed that society needed more democracy. They introduced five reforms. In a **direct primary,** party members voted for a candidate to run in the general election. An **initiative** allowed a group of citizens to require the legislature to vote on laws the group introduced. The **referendum** allowed proposed laws to be put to the voters for approval. The **recall** allowed voters to remove an elected official from office before his or her term expired. The Seventeenth Amendment gave voters the right to elect their senators directly.

Suffrage (page 524)

Comparing and Contrasting

Tell how each group wanted to achieve women's suffrage.

National Woman Suffrage Association:

____

____

____

American Woman Suffrage Association:

____

____

____

The first women's rights convention met in Seneca Falls, New York, in 1848. It launched the **suffrage** (right to vote) movement. The convention's top goal, and that of many women progressives, was getting women the right to vote.

The movement got off to a slow start. It split into two groups when Congress passed the Fourteenth and Fifteenth Amendments to the Constitution. These amendments aimed to protect voting rights of African Americans. The National Woman Suffrage Association wanted Congress to pass an amendment guaranteeing women the right to vote. The American Woman Suffrage Association wanted state governments to grant women suffrage.

In 1890 the two groups joined to form the National American Woman Suffrage Association (NAWSA). NAWSA started slowly, but many women realized that they needed suffrage to push for social reform and for labor laws to protect them.

NAWSA threw its support behind President Wilson in the election of 1916. However, support for an amendment began to grow in Congress. In 1919, the Senate passed the Nineteenth Amendment guaranteeing women the right to vote. The states ratified it in 1920.

Notes | Read to Learn

Reforming Society *(page 526)*

Problems and Solutions

List three social problems that concerned progressives.

1. ______________

____

2. ______________

____

3. ______________

____

Many progressives focused on specific social problems. One was child labor. Many children worked in dangerous and unhealthy conditions. States began passing laws setting age and hour limits for working children. Progressives also pushed for health and safety codes for workers of all ages, such as laws to protect workers injured on the job. Some progressives believed alcohol caused many problems in American life. The temperance movement supported the moderation or elimination of alcohol consumption. The temperance movement later pushed for **prohibition,** or laws making it illegal to make, sell, or consume alcohol.

Many progressives wanted to reform the economy. They believed big businesses needed regulation and pushed the government to break up large companies. Some went further and supported socialism. This was the idea that the government should own and operate industry.

Section Wrap-up

Answer these questions to check your understanding of the entire section.

1. Why did the Progressive movement arise?

____

____

2. How were the Progressive and suffrage movements alike?

____

____

Persuasive Writing

In the space provided write a brief paragraph to include in a Progressive Era pamphlet either in favor of or against woman suffrage.

____

____

____

____

____

____

____

Chapter 15, Section 2 (Pages 528–535)

Roosevelt and Taft

Big Idea

As you read pages 528–535 in your textbook, use the major headings of the section to complete the outline below.

Roosevelt in Office

I. **Roosevelt Revives the Presidency**
   A. ______________________
   B. ______________________
   C. ______________________
   D. ______________________

II. ______________________
   A. ______________________
   B. ______________________
   C. ______________________

III. ______________________
   A. ______________________
   B. ______________________
   C. ______________________

Notes

Read to Learn

Roosevelt Revives the Presidency (page 528)

Identifying the Main Idea

Write the main idea in this passage.

____
____
____
____
____
____
____
____
____

President Roosevelt believed in both progressivism and **Social Darwinism.** He thought large corporations, helped the United States prosper. He also thought the government should balance the needs of groups in American society. His reforms programs were known as the Square Deal.

Roosevelt did not hesitate to enforce the law. When the railroad company Northern Securities tried to form a monopoly, Roosevelt sued them under the Sherman Antitrust Act. Other times he negotiated. He struck a deal with U.S. Steel that allowed the government to go over its books privately. This prevented a lawsuit and the disruption of the economy.

Roosevelt also felt it was his duty as the nation's "head manager" to prevent conflict. A union of coal mine workers—the United Mine Workers—launched a strike in eastern Pennsylvania. It led to a potential crisis in the supply of the nation's coal. As the strike wore on, Roosevelt asked the union and the owners to agree to **arbitration**—a settlement imposed by an outside party. The owners eventually agreed to a settlement.

Notes

Read to Learn

Conservation (page 532)

Detecting Bias

Put an X by the statement Roosevelt would most likely agree with.

___ ***The need for timber now outweighs the health of timber supplies.***

___ ***Protecting the environment is an investment in the future.***

Roosevelt also cared about environmental conservation. He was alarmed at the rate at which natural resources were being used. He introduced reform to save the nation's forests through timber management. He also added over 100 million acres to the protected national forests, established five new national parks, and established 51 federal wildlife reserves.

Taft's Reforms (page 533)

Making Generalizations

Make a generalization about Taft's presidency.

____

____

____

____

____

____

____

____

____

____

____

President Roosevelt and President Taft agreed on many Progressive issues and were close friends. However, they disagreed on some subjects. One was tariffs. Taft believed high tariffs limited competition and protected trusts. His attempt to lower tariffs divided progressives and conservative Republicans. Taft signed the Payne-Aldrich Tariff into law, but it reduced some tariffs only a little and actually raised others.

Taft replaced Roosevelt's conservationist secretary of the interior with a more conservative corporate lawyer, Richard A. Ballinger. This made some progressives unhappy. One official, Gifford Pinchot, accused Ballinger of wrongdoing. Although the attorney general found his charges groundless, Pinchot leaked the story to the press. Taft fired Pinchot for **insubordination,** or disobedience.

Taft did have some successes. He pursued progressive policies on child labor and established the Children's Bureau. Like Roosevelt, Taft was a dedicated conservationist. He expanded national forests and protected waterpower sites.

Yet his friendship with Roosevelt was damaged. Roosevelt was so annoyed by some of Taft's policies, he ran for president again in the 1912 election. Both he and Taft lost to Woodrow Wilson.

Section Wrap-up

Answer these questions to check your understanding of the entire section.

1. What efforts did Roosevelt make to regulate concentrated corporate power?

2. How did both Roosevelt and Taft promote environmental conservation?

Descriptive Writing

Suppose you are a journalist interviewing President Roosevelt about his political beliefs. Write a brief summary of your interview.

Chapter 15, Section 3 (Pages 536–541)

The Wilson Years

Big Idea

As you read pages 536–541 in your textbook, complete this chart by listing Wilson's progressive economic and social reforms.

Economic Reforms	Social Reforms
1.	5.
2.	6.
3.	7.
4.	

Notes

Read to Learn

The Election of 1912 *(page 536)*

Formulating Questions

Write one question you have based on the passage. Then write a short answer to it.

Question:

____

____

Answer:

____

____

____

The election of 1912 featured a current president, a former president, and an academic with limited political experience. Former President Roosevelt was disappointed with President Taft's performance. He decided to run as the leader of the newly formed Progressive Party. Because Taft had alienated so many groups, the race was truly between Roosevelt and Woodrow Wilson.

Both Roosevelt and Wilson supported progressivism. Yet they each had their own approach to reform. Roosevelt accepted the trusts as a fact of life. Roosevelt called his reform the New Nationalism. Wilson countered with his plan, the New Freedom. He argued that Roosevelt's approach gave the government too much power in the economy and did nothing to facilitate competition. He promised to restore this competition by breaking up the monopolies.

Roosevelt and Taft wound up splitting the Republican vote. This enabled Wilson to win the Electoral College and the election, even though he only won 42% of the popular vote.

Notes

Read to Learn

Wilson's Reforms *(page 538)*

Determining Cause and Effect

Write the effects of these three acts.

Underwood Tariff Act

____

____

____

Federal Reserve Act

____

____

____

Adamson Act

____

____

____

As president, Wilson continued to push for progressive reform. He reduced tariffs and levied an **income tax**—a direct tax on the earnings of individuals—with the Underwood Tariff Act, reformed the banks with the Federal Reserve Act, and created the Federal Trade Commission to help regulate the trusts. He also signed the Adamson Act, which established the eight-hour workday for railroad workers.

He lobbied members of Congress personally to pass the tariff act. The act reduced most tariffs by 30%, which Wilson believed would benefit the American economy. The Federal Reserve Act established regional federal banks, where other banks could put a portion of their deposits to protect them against losses.

Once Wilson was in office, he came to agree with Roosevelt's view regarding trusts. He felt that regulating the trusts was more efficient and safer than trying to break them up. To help do this, Wilson established the Federal Trade Commission (FTC). The FTC was a board that had the power to investigate companies and issue "cease and desist" orders to companies engaging in **unfair trade practices,** or those which hurt competition. Companies that disagreed with the FTC could take the commission to court.

Some progressives, unsatisfied by Wilson's approach, passed the Clayton Antitrust Act in 1914, which outlawed certain practices that restricted competition.

Progressivism's Legacy and Limits *(page 540)*

Analyzing Information

Explain one way Progressivism was limited.

____

____

____

____

____

____

Like Roosevelt, Wilson expanded the role of the president. He also broadened the role of the federal government. Before the Progressive Era, most Americans did not expect the government to pass laws to protect workers. They also did not expect it to regulate big business. In fact, many courts reversed such laws. However, by the end of the era both public opinion and legal opinion had shifted. Americans came to expect the federal government to play an active role in regulating the economy. They also expected the government to solve social problems.

Despite its successes, the Progressive movement failed to address racial issues. Even so, African Americans began to demand changes. In 1905 W.E.B. Du Bois and other African Americans met at Niagra Falls. They wanted to develop a plan that would help African Americans gain full rights. This meeting led to the foundation of the National Association for the Advancement of Colored People (NAACP) in 1909. Du Bois, as well as other NAACP founders, worked to ensure African Americans voting rights and to end lynching.

Section Wrap-up

Answer these questions to check your understanding of the entire section.

1. What were President Wilson's social and economic reforms?

2. How would you evaluate the legacy of the Progressive movement?

Informative Writing

In the space provided write a short address President Wilson might have given toward the end of his time in office. Explain how the president's views on trusts changed during his presidency.

Chapter 16, Section 1 (Pages 548–555)

The United States Enters World War I

Big Idea

As you read pages 548–555 in your textbook, complete this graphic organizer by identifying some factors that contributed to the conflict.

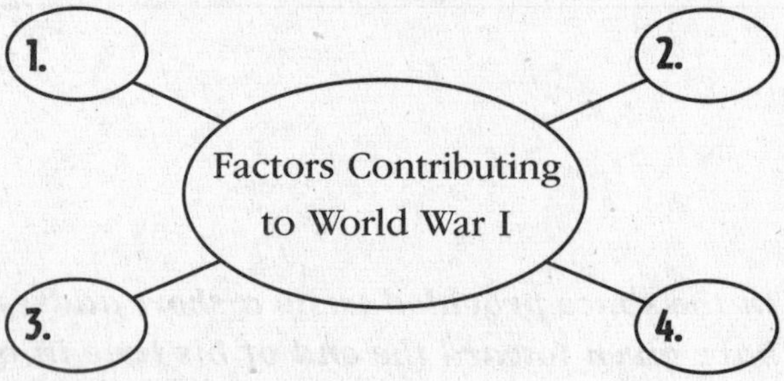

Notes | Read to Learn

World War I Begins *(page 548)*

Making Inferences

Explain why the heir to the Austro-Hungarian throne was killed.

____

____

____

____

____

____

____

____

In the late 1800s, Germany and France were enemies. Germany joined Italy and Austria-Hungary in the Triple Alliance. France, Russia, and Great Britain formed the Triple Entente. This system of alliances encouraged **militarism**—the buildup of armed forces.

Nationalism is intense pride in one's homeland. Imperialism led European powers to form empires. These factors led to conflict in southeastern Europe between the ruling Ottoman and Austro-Hungarian empires and the newly independent nation of Serbia. Austria-Hungary took control of the nation of Bosnia to stop the Serbs from uniting with it. The Serbs were angry. In June 1914, a Bosnian member of a Serbian nationalist group killed the heir to the Austro-Hungarian throne.

Several nations became involved. They formed alliances and declared war. France, Russia, Great Britain, and Italy became the Allies. Germany, Austria-Hungary, the Ottoman Empire, and Bulgaria became the Central Powers. Eventually, both sides became locked in a stalemate in France. In Russia, the Germans and Austrians swept across hundreds of miles of land and took thousands of prisoners.

Notes

Read to Learn

America Declares War *(page 552)*

Drawing Conclusions

List two reasons Americans supported the Allies as World War I began.

1. ____________________

____

____

2. ____________________

____

____

Write a conclusion about how this influenced U.S. policy.

3. ____________________

____

____

____

Determining Cause and Effect

Underline the sentence that describes why Americans became so angry about the Zimmerman Telegram.

As World War I began, President Wilson declared the United States neutral. However, many Americans supported one side or the other. Most Americans favored the Allies. Most of President Wilson's cabinet supported the Allies, too. The British worked to win U.S. support. They used **propaganda,** information designed to influence opinion. Britain also cut the transatlantic telegraph cable from Europe to the United States. This limited the news about the war mainly to British communications. Although many reports were exaggerated, many Americans believed them.

Businesses also supported the Allies because they had ties with businesses in the Allied countries. Many American banks loaned the Allies money. If the Allies won, the money would be paid back. If they lost, the money would be, too.

Although most Americans did not want to enter the war, many events drew the United States into it. The British navy had blockaded Germany. They stopped neutral ships to inspect them for **contraband,** or prohibited materials, headed for Germany or its allies. In response, Germany announced that it would sink without warning any ships in the waters around Britain. Attacking civilian ships without warning was against international law. In May, the British passenger ship *Lusitania* entered the war zone. A German U-boat—or submarine—sank the ship, killing nearly 1,200 people. About 128 were Americans.

President Wilson still tried to stay out of the war. However, he did send notes to Germany telling it to stop endangering the lives of civilians in war zones. After a U-boat shot at the French passenger ship *Sussex*, Wilson warned Germany to stop its submarine warfare or risk war with the United States. Germany did not want the United States to join the Allies. In the Sussex Pledge, Germany promised not to sink any merchant ships without warning.

In January 1917, a German official named Arthur Zimmermann told the German ambassador to Mexico to ask Mexico to ally itself with Germany in case of war between Germany and the United States. In return, Mexico would get back the territory it once held in Texas, New Mexico, and Arizona. The British intercepted the Zimmermann telegram. It was leaked to American newspapers. Many Americans now believed that war with Germany was necessary. In February 1917, Germany again began unrestricted submarine warfare. Finally, after Germany sank six American merchant ships, Wilson asked Congress to declare war on Germany. It did so on April 6, 1917.

Section Wrap-up ***Answer these questions to check your understanding of the entire section.***

1. How did intricate alliances contribute to the start of World War I?

2. Why did the United States eventually enter World War I?

Descriptive Writing ***In the space provided write a journal entry describing how you would react to reading the Zimmermann telegram for the first time in the newspaper.***

Chapter 16, Section 2 (Pages 556–561)

The Home Front

Big Idea

As you read pages 556–561 in your textbook, use the major headings of the section to complete the outline below.

The Home Front

I. Organizing the Economy
   A. ______________________
   B. ______________________
   C. ______________________
II. ______________________
   A. ______________________
   B. ______________________

Notes

Read to Learn

Organizing the Economy *(page 556)*

Identifying the Main Idea

Write the main idea of the passage.

____

____

____

____

____

____

____

____

Congress created special agencies to prepare the economy for war. The War Industries Board (WIB) coordinated the production of war materials. The Food Administration encouraged Americans to grow their own vegetables in **victory gardens.** The Fuel Administration introduced daylight savings time and shortened workweeks to conserve energy. The government raised money for the war through taxes and bonds.

The National War Labor Board (NWLB) tried to avoid labor strikes. For workers, it pushed for wage increases, an eight-hour workday, and the right to organize unions. In return, labor leaders agreed not to strike. Women took over many now-open industry. In the "Great Migration," many African Americans left the South to take jobs in northern factories. Many Mexicans came to the American Southwest to work for farmers and ranchers.

The Committee on Public Information (CPI) hired advertisers, artists, and others to sway public opinion in favor of the war. The government limited opposition to the war and **espionage,** or spying. Some civil liberties were suppressed.

Notes

Read to Learn

Building the Military *(page 560)*

Distinguishing Fact from Opinion

1. Underline one fact about draft boards.

2. Circle one opinion about draft boards.

Formulating Questions

Write two questions you have after reading the passage.

When the United States entered the war in 1917, it did not have enough soldiers. Although many people volunteered, more were needed. Many progressives believed that conscription, or forced military service, was against democratic principles. Congress, however, believed conscription was necessary. It set up a new system of conscription called selective service. It required all men between 21 and 30 to register for the draft. A lottery then randomly decided the order in which individuals were called before local draft boards. These boards selected or exempted men from military service. The members of the draft boards were local civilians. Progressives believed these community members could better decide which men to draft.

Eventually about 2.8 million Americans were drafted. About 2 million more volunteered. Some wanted to fight after hearing about German atrocities. Others wanted to fight for democracy. Many saw World War I as an opportunity for adventure and wanted to fight for their country. Troop morale was high for American soldiers during World War I, despite losses. During the war 50,000 Americans died in combat and more than 200,000 were wounded.

About 42,000 of the 400,000 African Americans who were drafted served in the war overseas. African American soldiers faced discrimination and prejudice in the army. They served in racially segregated units. They were almost always under the control of white officers. Despite this, many African Americans fought with distinction in the war. Two African American divisions fought in battles along the Western Front.

Women officially served in the armed forces for the first time in World War I. They served in noncombat positions. With men serving in combat, the armed forces faced a shortage of clerical workers. The navy enlisted women to serve as clerical workers, radio operators, electricians, chemists, and other occupations. The army, however, refused to enlist women. It hired women as temporary employees to fill clerical jobs. The only women to actually serve in the army were the army nurses. Women served as nurses in the navy, too.

Section Wrap-up

Answer these questions to check your understanding of the entire section.

1. How did the United States raise an army for World War I?

2. How did the government control the U.S. economy to support the war?

Informative Writing

Suppose you are serving in the military during World War I. In the space provided write a letter telling how you came to serve in the military.

Chapter 16, Section 3 (Pages 564–573)
A Bloody Conflict

Big Idea

As you read pages 564–573 in your textbook, complete this graphic organizer by listing some kinds of warfare and technology used in the fighting.

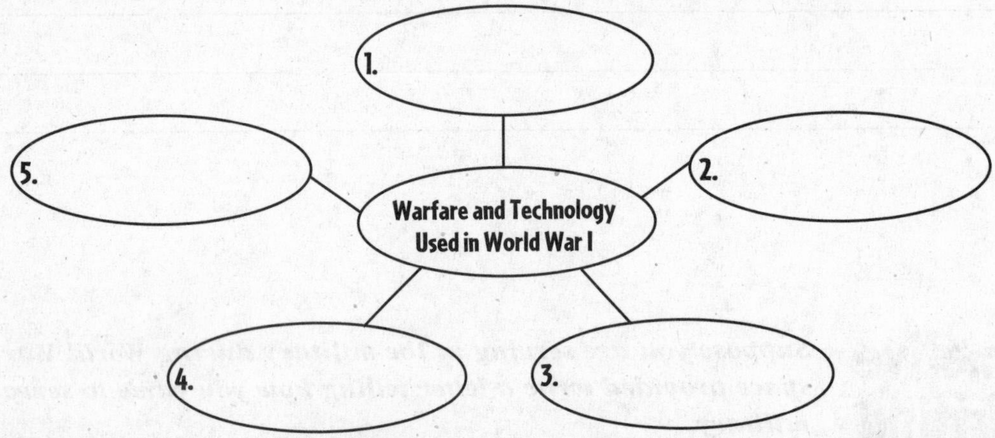

Notes

Read to Learn

Combat in World War I *(page 564)*

Making Inferences

Explain why the land between the trenches was called "no man's land."

During World War I, troops began using powerful artillery guns that hurled huge explosive shells long distances. They also used machine guns. Troops dug trenches to protect themselves from artillery. On the Western Front, troops dug a network of trenches that stretched from the English Channel to the Swiss border. The space between the opposing trenches became known as "no-man's-land." Soldiers from either side would race across no-man's-land while trying to dodge gunfire. Once across, they battled the enemy with grenades, bayonets, and sometimes even their fists. Combat was often brutal.

Both sides developed new technologies. The Germans began using poison gas. The fumes caused vomiting, blindness, and suffocation. The Allies also began using poison gas, and gas masks became necessary equipment. The British introduced the tank, which could roll over barbed wire and trenches. Airplanes were first used in World War I, first to observe enemy activities and then to shoot down German zeppelins and bomb enemy lines. Eventually, aircraft were used to shoot down other aircraft in air battles known as dogfights.

Notes

Read to Learn

The Americans Arrive *(page 566)*

Determining Cause and Effect

Write one effect of each cause.

1. Cause: U.S. ships traveled in convoys.

Effect:

____

____

2. Cause: Russia left World War I.

Effect:

____

____

About 2 million American soldiers fought in World War I. Although mostly inexperienced, they boosted the morale of the Allied forces. The admiral of the U.S. Navy suggested that merchant ships and troop transports headed for Europe be gathered in groups called **convoys.** Warships escorted the convoys. This system reduced shipping and troop losses.

In March 1917, riots broke out in Russia and its leader stepped down. A temporary government was unable to deal with the country's major problems. The Bolshevik Party led by Vladimir Lenin overthrew the Russian government. Lenin immediately pulled Russia out of the war, allowing Germany to concentrate its troops on the Western Front.

Germany launched a massive attack and pushed deeply into Allied lines. American and French troops twice blocked German drives on Paris. In September of 1918, American troops began a huge offensive against the Germans. By November, the Americans had destroyed the German defenses and pushed a hole in the German lines. Finally, on November 11, 1918, Germany signed an **armistice,** or cease-fire, that ended the war.

A Flawed Peace *(page 570)*

Analyzing Information

List reasons why this lesson is called "A Flawed Peace."

____

____

____

____

____

____

____

____

____

The peace conference started in January 1919 at the Palace of Versailles in France. The resulting treaty was called the Treaty of Versailles. The main people involved, known as the Big Four, were leaders of the Allied nations. President Wilson made a plan for peace known as the Fourteen Points. Five points sought to eliminate the causes of war. Eight addressed the right to **national self-determination.** The final point called for the formation of a League of Nations to keep peace and prevent future wars. The other Allied governments believed Wilson's plan was too easy on the Germans.

The Treaty of Versailles included many terms to weaken and punish Germany. It reduced Germany's military and forced it to pay **reparations,** or war damages. The war led to the end of the Russian, Ottoman, German, and Austro-Hungarian empires and the establishment of several new nations. The Treaty of Versailles did include Wilson's plan for the League of Nations, but many U.S. Congress members opposed it for that reason. They believed it would force the United States into many conflicts. After voting twice, the U.S. Senate refused to ratify the treaty. The League of Nations started without the United States.

Section Wrap-up

Answer these questions to check your understanding of the entire section.

1. What fighting techniques were used in World War I?

2. What was the American response to the Treaty of Versailles?

Expository Writing

In the space provided write a paragraph explaining the potential advantages and disadvantages to the United States of ratifying the Treaty of Versailles.

Chapter 16, Section 4 (Pages 576–581)

The War's Impact

Big Idea

As you read pages 576–581 in your textbook, complete this graphic organizer by listing some effects of the end of World War I on the American economy.

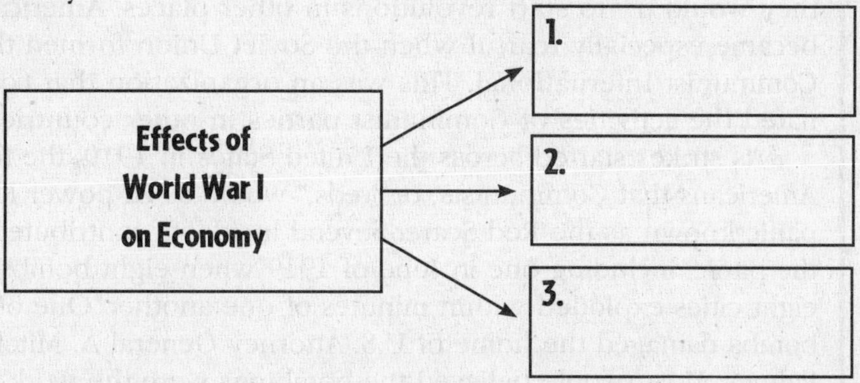

Notes

Read to Learn

An Economy in Turmoil *(page 576)*

Making Generalizations

The labor strikes of 1919 were

___ ***very***

___ ***somewhat***

___ ***not at all***

effective for the strikers.

After the war, the government removed economic controls. The result was inflation, which raised the **cost of living**—the cost of food, clothing, shelter, and other items people need to survive. Workers wanted higher wages, but business owners wanted to hold down operating costs. Unions were larger and more organized than before. As a result, there were many strikes in 1919.

Shipyard workers in Seattle organized the first big strike. Soon it became a **general strike,** or a strike that involves all workers in a location, not just workers in one industry. Although the strikers made no gains, the general strike worried many people because it was a technique used by radicals in Europe. When police officers in Boston went on strike, riots broke out in the city. The police commissioner fired the strikers and hired a new police force. A strike by workers at U.S. Steel was one of the largest strikes. The company hired replacement workers and the strike failed.

Many soldiers returned home looking for work. Many African Americans had moved to the North during the war to take factory jobs. Racism and frustration erupted into riots.

Notes | Read to Learn

The Red Scare *(page 579)*

Predicting

Before you read, complete this sentence.

I think the term "Red Scare" will mean

____

____

____

____

Synthesizing Information

Explain why the Palmer raids targeted immigrants.

1. ______________________

____

____

____

2. ______________________

____

____

____

The strikes in 1919 led many people to believe that Communists were trying to start a revolution in the United States. Many Americans felt betrayed when Russia withdrew from the war. Since the late 1800s, many Americans blamed immigrants for bringing Communist ideas into the United States. They also blamed immigrants for labor problems and violence. When Communists took control of Russia, Americans feared they would try to start revolutions in other places. Americans became especially fearful when the Soviet Union formed the Communist International. This was an organization that coordinated the activities of Communist parties in other countries.

As strikes started across the United States in 1919, the fear of Americans that Communists, or "reds," would seize power led to a panic known as the Red Scare. Several incidents contributed to the panic, including one in June of 1919 when eight bombs in eight cities exploded within minutes of one another. One of these bombs damaged the home of U.S. Attorney General A. Mitchell Palmer. Most people believed the bombings were the work of radicals trying to destroy the American way of life.

Palmer set up a special division within the Justice Department. The General Intelligence Division was headed by J. Edgar Hoover, and it later became the Federal Bureau of Investigation (FBI). Although evidence pointed to no one group as the bombers, Palmer organized raids on the foreign-born and on radicals. Palmer rounded up many immigrants and had them **deported,** or expelled from the country.

The Palmer raids were carried out without concern for people's civil rights. Homes were entered without search warrants. People were jailed indefinitely and not allowed to talk to their attorneys. Palmer was first praised for his work. However, when he failed to find any real evidence of a revolutionary conspiracy, his popularity faded. The Red Scare led to anti-immigrant feelings and a call for Congress to limit immigration.

By 1920, most Americans wanted an end to the unrest within the country. In the 1920 election, the Democrats ran James M. Cox and Franklin D. Roosevelt. They ran on the ideals of progressivism. The Republicans ran Warren G. Harding. He called for a return to "normalcy." He wanted the United States to return to the simpler days before the Progressive Era reforms. Many voters agreed with Harding, and he won by a landslide.

Section Wrap-up

Answer these questions to check your understanding of the entire section.

1. What were the main causes of the wave of strikes after World War I?

2. What were the causes of and reaction to the Red Scare?

Persuasive Writing

In the space provided write a short campaign speech Warren Harding might have given to persuade voters to vote for him in the 1920 election.

Chapter 17, Section 1 (Pages 590–595)

The Politics of the 1920s

Big Idea

As you read pages 590–595 in your textbook, complete the outline using the major headings of the section.

The Politics of the 1920s

I. The Harding Administration
   A. ______
   B. ______
II. ______
III. ______
   A. ______
   B. ______
   C. ______
   D. ______

Notes

Read to Learn

The Harding Administration *(page 590)*

Determining Cause and Effect

Write the cause.

Cause:

______

______

______

______

______

______.

Effect: Scandals plagued the Harding administration.

Warren G. Harding was elected president in 1920. He ran on the campaign promise to return the country to normalcy. This meant a return to "normal" life after the war. Harding appointed many friends from Ohio to cabinet positions and high-level jobs. They were known as the Ohio Gang. Some used their positions to sell jobs, pardons, and protection from prosecution. They caused several scandals.

The most famous was Teapot Dome. Secretary of the Interior Albert B. Fall secretly allowed private companies to lease lands containing Navy oil reserves. Fall became the first cabinet officer to go to prison. Another scandal involved Attorney General Daugherty. He was suspected of taking bribes from a German agent.

In a 1923 tour of the West, President Harding fell ill and died. Vice President Calvin Coolidge became president and distanced himself from corruption. He restored integrity to the presidency. Coolidge believed his job was to make sure government interfered as little as possible with business. In 1924 he easily won the election.

Notes | Read to Learn

Policies of Prosperity *(page 593)*

Problems and Solutions

Complete the sentences.

1. To balance the budget, Mellon

____

____

_______________.

2. To provide extra income to people and businesses, Mellon

____

____

_______________.

Presidents Harding and Coolidge both opposed government regulation of business. Harding appointed two cabinet members who contributed to the economic growth and prosperity of the 1920s: Andrew Mellon and Herbert Hoover.

Mellon had three major goals as secretary of the treasury: balance the budget, reduce government debt, and cut taxes. Mellon convinced Congress to create agencies to prepare the budget and track expenses. He then cut government spending. Mellon argued that if taxes were lower, businesses and consumers would spend and invest more. As the economy grew, the government would collect more taxes at a lower rate than if taxes were high. This idea is known today as **supply-side economics.** In 1928 Congress drastically cut tax rates.

Secretary of Commerce Hoover tried to encourage economic growth. His policy of **cooperative individualism** encouraged businesses to form trade associations. These groups would then share information with the government. Hoover believed this would reduce costs and increase efficiency. Hoover also tried to help companies find new markets and supported the growth of the airline and radio industries.

Trade and Arms Control *(page 594)*

Synthesizing Information

Complete the statement based on the last paragraph. After World War I, many countries

____

____

____

____

____

_______________.

Before World War I, the United States was a debtor nation. By the end of the war, allies owed the United States more than $10 billion. Many Americans at this time favored **isolationism.** This was a policy of staying out of world affairs. However, the nation was too involved economically and politically with other countries to be truly isolationist. America's former allies struggled to repay their war debts. High import taxes made it hard for foreign countries to sell products in the United States. The war reparations, Germany paid to European nations crippled its economy. In 1924 a U.S. diplomat negotiated the Dawes Plan. American banks loaned Germany money to pay reparations. Britain and France agreed to accept less in reparations and to pay more on their war debts.

Secretary of State Charles Evans Hughes spoke to the major world powers at a conference in Washington. The conference led to a treaty between Britain, France, Italy, Japan, and the United States to reduce the naval arms race. This supported the idea that written agreements could end war. The United States and fourteen other nations signed the Kellogg-Briand Pact. In it they agreed to settle all disputes peacefully.

Section Wrap-up

Answer these questions to check your understanding of the entire section.

1. How did two of President Harding's cabinet appointees contribute to the economic growth and prosperity of the 1920s?

2. Why was it impossible for the United States to maintain an isolationist stand after World War I?

Descriptive Writing

In the space provided write a newspaper obituary for Warren G. Harding. Use words that reflect feelings about him and his administration at the time of his death.

Chapter 17, Section 2 (Pages 596–603)

A Growing Economy

Big Idea

As you read pages 596–603 in your textbook, complete this graphic organizer to analyze the causes of economic growth and prosperity in the 1920s.

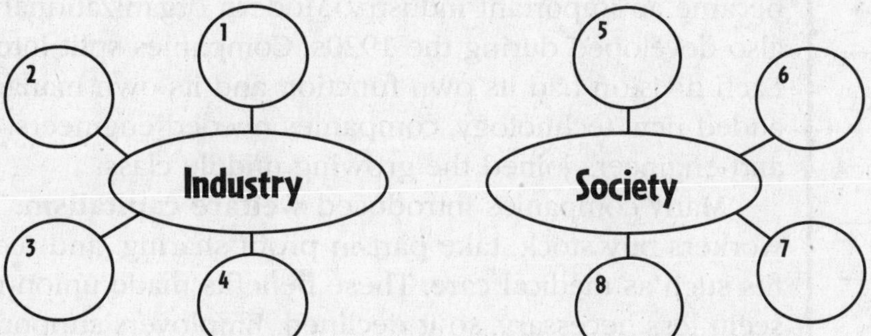

Notes

Read to Learn

The Rise of New Industries *(page 596)*

Making Generalizations

Complete the statement.

During the 1920s,

____

____

____

____

____

____

______________________.

During the 1920s, Americans earned more money than ever before while working fewer hours. **Mass production,** or large-scale product manufacturing done mainly by machinery, made more products available and lowered costs. This reshaped American economics and industry.

Henry Ford used the **assembly line** to build cars. This system divided operations into simple tasks unskilled workers could do. It reduced the time needed and the cost. By lowering the price of his mass-produced car, the **Model T,** Ford created a huge demand. The automobile reduced the isolation of rural areas and allowed people to live farther from work.

With their greater incomes, people bought new products such as frozen foods, household cleaners, washing machines, and cosmetics. During the 1920s, the airlines and radio industries expanded. The government used airlines to deliver mail and began building airports. Lindbergh's transatlantic solo flight gave the idea of commercial flights a boost. NBC and CBS began creating networks of radio stations.

Notes

Read to Learn

The Consumer Society *(page 600)*

Making Inferences

Make two inferences based on the passage.

1. ______________

____

____

2. ______________

____

____

Before the 1920s, most Americans thought that going into debt was shameful. This attitude changed, and more Americans went into debt to buy items such as furniture and bought cars on credit.

Inventors at this time had trouble getting people to buy products they did not know they needed. Advertising stepped in to convince consumers to buy new products and itself soon became an important industry. Modern organizational structures also developed during the 1920s. Companies split into divisions. Each division had its own function and its own manager. As they added new technology, companies needed engineers. Managers and engineers joined the growing middle class.

Many companies introduced **welfare capitalism.** They let workers buy stock, take part in profit sharing, and receive benefits such as medical care. These benefits made union membership seem less necessary, so it declined. Employers supported **open shops,** which did not require union membership. Not all Americans shared in the economic boom. African Americans, Native Americans, women, immigrants, and farmers struggled.

The Farm Crisis *(page 603)*

Drawing Conclusions

Draw a conclusion about how tariffs affected American farmers.

____

____

____

____

____

____

____

During the war, the government had encouraged farmers to grow more to meet the need for food in Europe. Many farmers went into debt to buy more land and machinery to raise more crops. Sales and prices were high, so farmers prospered. After the war, Europeans began producing more farm products, so profits fell for American farmers. New technologies such as fertilizers, machinery, and new seed varieties allowed farmers to produce more, but demand for the products did not increase, so farmers received lower prices for their goods.

In 1922 Congress passed the Fordney-McCumber Act. This law raised tariffs to protect American industries from competition. Europeans reacted by buying fewer American agricultural products. Prices dropped even more when farmers could not sell their products overseas.

Some congressmen tried to help the farmers sell their surpluses. They proposed a plan in which the government would buy the crop surpluses to sell abroad at a loss. However, President Coolidge vetoed the bill. He thought it would encourage farmers to produce greater surpluses. As a result, American farmers stayed in a recession throughout the 1920s.

Section Wrap-up

Answer these questions to check your understanding of the entire section.

1. How did the growth of the automobile industry and the rise of other new industries improve Americans' standard of living?

2. What factors contributed to the economic crisis in farming during the 1920s?

Expository Writing

In the space provided write an advertisement for a 1920s Ford Model T.

Chapter 17, Section 3 (Pages 604–609)

A Clash of Values

Big Idea

As you read pages 604–609 in your textbook, complete this graphic organizer by filling in some causes and effects of anti-immigrant prejudices.

Causes		Effects
1 ______	Anti-Immigrant Prejudices	4 ______
2 ______		5 ______
3 ______		6 ______

Notes

Read to Learn

Nativism Resurges (page 604)

Synthesizing Information

Write two reasons Mexican immigrants filled agriculture, mining, and railroad jobs.

1. ______

______

______

2. ______

______

______

During the 1920s, anti-immigrant feelings grew because of an influx of immigrants, cultural tensions, and recession. **Nativism,** the belief that one's native land needs to be protected against immigrants, also grew. In 1920 two Italian immigrants named Nicola Sacco and Bortolomeo Vanzetti were arrested for armed robbery and murder. It was widely reported that they were **anarchists,** people who oppose all forms of government. Despite thin evidence, Sacco and Vanzetti were found guilty and later executed. One of the biggest efforts to restrict immigration came from the Ku Klux Klan. It targeted groups it felt did not represent traditional American values.

In 1921 Congress passed the Emergency Quota Act to limit immigration. The National Origins Act of 1924 made the quotas stricter and permanent. These acts favored people from northwestern Europe and exempted those from Central and South America. The reduction in immigration caused a shortage of workers for agriculture, mining, and railroad work. Mexican immigrants filled these jobs. Large numbers arrived after the Newlands Reclamation Act of 1902 funded projects in the Southwest.

Notes | Read to Learn

A Clash of Cultures *(page 606)*

Identifying the Main Idea

Write the main idea.

Distinguishing Fact from Opinion

Write one opinion held by Fundamentalists in the 1920s. Then write one fact about them.

Opinion:

Fact:

During the 1920s, a "new morality" took over the nation. The new morality challenged traditional ways of thinking. It glorified youth and personal freedom and changed American society.

Women won the right to vote in 1920. This encouraged many women to break free of their traditional roles and behaviors. Attitudes toward marriage changed. The ideas of romance, pleasure, and friendship became linked to successful marriages. The automobile also played a part in the new morality. It gave young people more freedom. Single women began working for their own financial independence as employment opportunities increased during the 1920s. Women's colleges encouraged students to pursue careers. Many professional women made contributions in fields such as science, medicine, law, and literature.

Many groups wanted to preserve traditional values against the new morality. A religious movement called Fundamentalism stressed the teachings of the Bible as literally true history. Fundamentalists rejected the theory of **evolution,** which argued that human beings had developed from lower forms of life over the course of millions of years. Fundamentalists believed in **creationism,** which says that God created the world as described in the Bible. In 1925 Tennessee outlawed the teaching of evolution. A high school biology teacher named John T. Scopes was tried and convicted of breaking this law. The Scopes Trial helped illustrate the struggle between the new morality and traditional beliefs.

In January of 1920 the Eighteenth Amendment went into effect. This amendment prohibited, or banned, the sale of alcohol. Many people felt prohibition would reduce unemployment, violence, and poverty. Congress passed the Volstead Act to enforce the law, but many Americans violated it. Organized crime supplied illegal alcohol to secret bars called **speakeasies.** In 1933 the Twenty-first Amendment later repealed prohibition.

Section Wrap-up

Answer these questions to check your understanding of the entire section.

1. What factors contributed to the rise in nativism during the 1920s?

2. How did the status of women change during the 1920s?

Persuasive Writing

In the space provided write a magazine article in favor of or against the new morality. Give reasons to support your position.

Chapter 17, Section 4 (Pages 610–613)

Cultural Innovations

Big Idea

As you read pages 610–613 in your textbook, complete this chart by filling in the main characteristics of art, literature, and popular culture from the 1920s.

Cultural Movement	Main Characteristics
Art	1.
Literature	2.
Popular Culture	3.

Notes

Read to Learn

Art and Literature *(page 610)*

Making Generalizations

Make a generalization about art and literature of the 1920s.

Many artists and writers of the 1920s were attracted by the lifestyle of Manhattan's Greenwich Village and Chicago's South Side. This unconventional and artistic lifestyle was known as **bohemian.** Artists explored the meaning of the modern world.

European art movements influenced American art. American artists expressed modern experiences in a diverse range of styles. Painter John Marin was inspired by both nature and urban New York. Edward Hopper painted haunting, realistic scenes. Georgia O'Keeffe painted landscapes and flowers.

Poets and writers of the 1920s also varied greatly in their styles and subject matter. Poet Carl Sandburg used common speech to glorify the Midwest. Edna St. Vincent Millay wrote about women's equality. Playwright Eugene O'Neill wrote about realistic characters in tragic situations. Ernest Hemingway described the experience of war. Sinclair Lewis wrote about the follies of small town America. F. Scott Fitzgerald's novel *The Great Gatsby* exposed the emptiness of modern society.

Notes

Read to Learn

Popular Culture *(page 612)*

Determining Cause and Effect

List three effects of the prosperity of the 1920s.

1. ________________

____

2. ________________

____

3. ________________

____

Formulating Questions

Write one question you have based on the passage.

____

____

____

____

Many Americans in the 1920s had more leisure time and spending money than before. They used this time to watch sports and enjoy movies, radio, and other types of popular entertainment.

Motion pictures were very popular during the 1920s. People rushed to see films starring Mary Pickford, Charlie Chaplin, Rudolph Valentino, and Douglas Fairbanks. Theaters hired piano players to provide music during silent pictures. Subtitles told the storyline. In 1927 the first "talking" movie was produced.

Radio was also popular at this time. Radio stations broadcast popular music as well as radio shows such as *Amos 'n' Andy*. Radio, movies, newspapers, and magazines, or the **mass media,** did more than entertain people. They helped spread new ideas and unify the nation.

Radio and films also popularized sports such as baseball and boxing. Baseball star Babe Ruth became a national hero. Sports fans idolized boxer Jack Dempsey. They followed his heavyweight matches against Gene Tunney. Newspaper coverage helped create interest in college football stars such as Red Grange. He was called the "Galloping Ghost" because of his speed and agility. Other sports celebrities included golfers, tennis players, and even swimmers.

Section Wrap-up

Answer these questions to check your understanding of the entire section.

1. How did the art and literature of the 1920s reflect the disillusionment of the era?

2. How did many Americans spend their leisure time during the 1920s?

Expository Writing

In the space provided write a paragraph comparing the sports stars, movies, or radio of the 1920s with those of today.

Chapter 17, Section 5 (Pages 616–621)

African American Culture

Big Idea

As you read pages 616–621 in your textbook, complete this graphic organizer by filling in some causes and effects of the Harlem Renaissance.

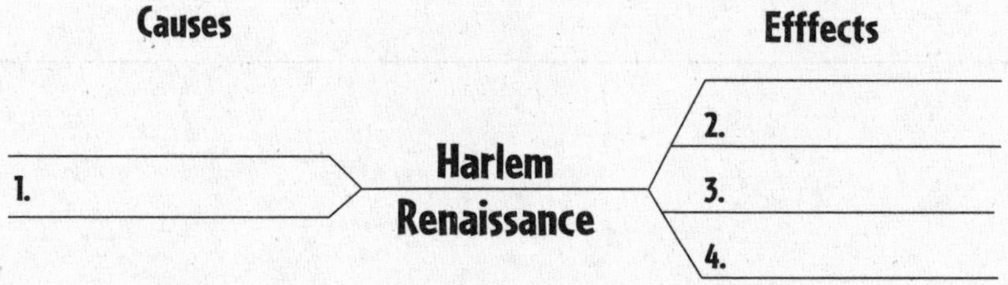

Notes | Read to Learn

The Harlem Renaissance *(page 616)*

Comparing and Contrasting

List major figures in these genres of the Harlem Renaissance.

Literature:

____

____

Music:

____

____

Theater:

____

____

Many African Americans joined the Great Migration from the rural South to northern cities. They hoped to escape segregation, find jobs, and improve their lives. As the North's African American population grew, it influenced culture and the arts. New York City's Harlem neighborhood became the center for the flowering of African American arts known as the Harlem Renaissance. Two of its writers were Claude McKay and Langston Hughes. McKay's verses reflect defiance and contempt for racism, which were major characteristics of the movement. Hughes became the leading voice of the African American experience.

Louis Armstrong introduced an early improvisational style of **jazz** music influenced by Dixieland and ragtime. Bandleader Duke Ellington got his start at the Harlem Cotton Club. He soon created his own sound. Bessie Smith performed the **blues,** soulful music evolved from spirituals.

The theater also thrived. Paul Robeson gained fame for his roles in *Emperor Jones* and *Show Boat*. Josephine Baker was a well-known singer and dancer. This artistic flowering inspired pride in African American culture and its roots.

Notes

Predicting

Skim the passage. Make a prediction about what you will learn.

____

____

____

____

Analyzing Information

Give two reasons why middle class African Americans may have distanced themselves from Garvey.

1. ______________________

____

____

____

2. ______________________

____

____

____

Read to Learn

African Americans and 1920s Politics *(page 619)*

The Great Migration influenced politics in the North. The African American population became an important voting bloc that often affected the outcomes of elections in the North.

Many African Americans voted for Republicans, the party of Abraham Lincoln. In 1928 African American voters in Chicago elected Oscar DePriest to Congress. He was the first African American congressman from a Northern state. DePriest introduced laws against racial discrimination and lynching.

The National Association for the Advancement of Colored People (NAACP) worked against segregation and injustice. Its main tactic was lobbying politicians, but also worked through the courts. In 1922 the NAACP helped get an anti-lynching law passed in the House of Representatives. The Senate did not pass the bill, but the NAACP's work kept the issue in the news. In 1930 the NAACP helped defeat a Supreme Court nominee known for his racist positions. His nomination was defeated. This proved the NAACP had the political strength to affect national politics.

Other groups stressed black pride and nationalism. Marcus Garvey was a dynamic leader from Jamaica. He founded a group called the Universal Negro Improvement Association (UNIA). Garvey believed African Americans could gain economic and political power through education. He also called for separation from white society. Garvey planned to lead his followers back to Africa.

The growing African American middle class distanced itself from this movement. The FBI thought the UNIA was dangerous. Garvey insulted some key figures in the Harlem Renaissance. Garvey was convicted of mail fraud in 1923, and in 1927 President Coolidge had him deported. In the end, Garvey's movement inspired many people with pride in their African heritage.

Section Wrap-up

Answer these questions to check your understanding of the entire section.

1. How did the Harlem Renaissance lead to a rediscovery of African American cultural roots?

2. Why was there an increase in African American political activism in the postwar period?

Descriptive Writing

In the space provided write letter as someone living in Harlem during the 1920s. Describe your reactions to Marcus Garvey's back to Africa proposal.

The Causes of the Great Depression

Big Idea

As you read pages 628–633 in your textbook, complete this graphic organizer by comparing the backgrounds and issues of the 1928 presidential candidates.

1928 Presidential Campaign		
Candidate	**Background**	**Issue**
1.	2.	3.
4.	5.	6.

Notes

Read to Learn

The Long Bull Market *(page 628)*

Making Inferences

Read the third paragraph again. Make an inference about 1920s stock prices compared with their actual values.

____

____

____

____

____

____

In the 1928 presidential election, Herbert Hoover ran as the Republican nominee. The Democrats nominated Alfred E. Smith, a Catholic. Many Protestants feared the Catholic Church would rule the White House if he was elected. Hoover and the Republicans also took credit for the prosperity of the 1920s. As a result, Hoover won.

After the election, stock prices continued to increase. The **stock market** was a system for buying and selling shares of companies. The late 1920s saw a **bull market,** or a long period of rising stock prices. Many investors began buying stocks on **margin.** They made a small down payment on the stock and took out a loan from a stockbroker to pay for the rest. If stock prices fell, the stockbroker issued a **margin call,** a demand for the investor to repay the loan.

Before the late 1920s, the prices that investors paid for stocks had to do with the company's profits. This was no longer true by the late 1920s. Many buyers hoped to make a quick profit and practiced **speculation.** They were betting that the stock market would continue to climb.

Notes	Read to Learn

The Great Crash *(page 630)*

Determining Cause and Effect

List two causes of bank closures. Then list two effects of the closures.

Causes: ____________

____

____

____

Effects: ____________

____

____

____

By mid-1929, the stock market was running out of new customers. Professional investors began selling off their holdings. Prices decreased. Other investors sold their shares to pay the interest on loans from brokers. Prices fell further. On October 29, 1929, which became known as Black Tuesday, stock prices took their steepest dive. The crash was not a major cause of the Great Depression, but it undermined the economy.

Many banks had lent money to stock speculators. They had also invested depositors' money in the stock market. When stock prices fell, many banks lost money on their investments, and speculators could not repay their loans. The banks had to cut back on the number of loans they made. As a result, people could not borrow as much money as they once did. This helped send the economy into a recession.

Many banks were forced to close. People who had deposits in these banks lost all their savings. Some Americans began **bank runs.** This takes place when many people withdraw money at the same time out of fear the banks will close. This caused many more banks to collapse.

The Roots of the Great Depression *(page 632)*

Identifying the Main Idea

What is the main idea of the passage?

____

____

____

____

____

____

____

____

____

____

The Great Depression had several causes. One was overproduction. Most Americans did not have enough money to buy all the goods that were made. During the 1920s, many Americans bought high-cost items on the **installment** plan. This allowed people to pay for items in monthly installments. Some people had to reduce their purchases in order to pay their debts. When sales slowed, manufacturers cut production and laid off employees. This effect rippled through the economy.

Americans were also not selling many goods to foreign countries. In 1930, Congress passed the Hawley-Smoot Tariff. It raised the tax on many imports. Foreign countries then raised their tariffs against American goods, which caused fewer American products to be sold overseas.

The Federal Reserve had kept interest rates low in the 1920s, encouraging banks to make risky loans. Low rates also misled many business leaders into thinking that the economy was still growing. They borrowed more money to expand production. This led to overproduction when sales were actually decreasing. When the Depression hit, companies had to lay off workers to cut costs.

Section Wrap-up *Answer these questions to check your understanding of the entire section.*

1. How did buying stocks on margin cause problems?

____

____

____

2. How did overproduction cause unemployment to rise?

____

____

____

Descriptive Writing *In the space provided write a letter describing what happened on Black Tuesday. Imagine that you are someone who witnessed the events of the day firsthand.*

____

____

____

____

____

____

____

____

____

____

____

____

Chapter 18, Section 2 (Pages 634–637)

Life During the Great Depression

Big Idea

As you read pages 634–637 in your textbook, use the major headings of the section to complete the outline.

Life During the Great Depression

I. The Depression Worsens
   A. ______
   B. ______
II. ______
   A. ______
   B. ______
   C. ______

Notes

Read to Learn

The Depression Worsens *(page 634)*

Evaluating Information

Which paragraph contains the best information about the Depression's impact on farmers?

______
______
______
______
______
______
______

The Depression grew worse during Hoover's administration. Thousands of banks failed, and thousands of companies went out of business. Millions of Americans were unemployed. Many relied on bread lines and soup kitchens for food.

Many people could not afford to pay their rent or mortgage and lost their homes. Court officers, called **bailiffs,** evicted non-paying tenants. Homeless people put up shacks on public lands, forming shantytowns throughout the country. Many called the shantytowns "Hoovervilles" because they blamed the president for their problems. Some homeless and unemployed people wandered around the country. Known as **hobos,** they traveled by sneaking onto open boxcars on freight trains.

Great Plains Farmers soon faced a new problem. When crop prices decreased in the 1920s, farmers left many fields unplanted. In 1932, the Great Plains experienced a severe drought. The unplanted soil turned to dust. Much of the Plains became a Dust Bowl. Many families packed their belongings and headed west to California. Still, many remained homeless and poor.

Notes | Read to Learn

Art and Entertainment *(page 636)*

Making Generalizations

Make a generalization about how movies and radio affected people's lives during the Depression.

____

____

____

____

____

____

____

____

Analyzing Information

Give two examples of how art and literature reflected the realities of the Great Depression.

1. _______________

____

____

____

2. _______________

____

____

____

Americans turned to entertainment to escape the hardships of the Depression. Many went to the movies. Comedies featuring child stars such as Shirley Temple provided people with a way to escape their daily worries. Americans also enjoyed cartoons. Walt Disney produced the first feature-length animated film in 1937. Even films that focused on the serious side of life were generally optimistic.

Two movies from this period were *The Wizard of Oz* and *Gone with the Wind,* both produced in 1939. *Gone with the Wind* is a Civil War epic that won nine Academy Awards. One went to Hattie McDaniel, who won Best Supporting Actress. She was the first African American to win an Academy Award.

Americans also listened to the radio. They listened to news, comedy shows, and adventure programs like *The Lone Ranger.* Short daytime dramas were also popular. Some of these dramas were sponsored by the makers of laundry soaps and were nicknamed **soap operas.** Talking about the lives of radio characters provided Americans with a common ground.

Art and literature in the 1930s reflected the realities of life during the Depression. Painters such as Grant Wood showed traditional American values, particularly those of the rural Midwest and the South. His painting *American Gothic* is one of the most famous American works of art.

Novelists such as John Steinbeck wrote about the lives of people in the Depression. In *The Grapes of Wrath,* Steinbeck told the story of an Oklahoma farm family who fled the Dust Bowl to find a better life in California. He based his writing on visits to and articles about migrant camps in California.

Some writers during the Depression influenced literary style. In a technique known as stream of consciousness, William Faulkner showed what his characters were thinking and feeling without using conventional dialogue. Faulkner explored the issue of race in the American South.

Photographers traveled around the nation taking pictures of life around them. In 1936, *Life* magazine was introduced. It was a weekly magazine that showcased the work of photojournalists, such as Dorothea Lange and Margaret Bourke-White, who documented the hardships of the Great Depression.

Section Wrap-up

Answer these questions to check your understanding of the entire section.

1. What was the Dust Bowl and what caused it?

2. How did the Great Depression affect American families?

Expository Writing

In the space provided write an essay comparing real life during the Depression to life as it was portrayed in movies and on radio programs.

Chapter 18, Section 3 (Pages 640–643)

Hoover Responds to the Depression

Big Idea

As you read pages 640–643 in your textbook, complete this graphic organizer by listing President Hoover's three major initiatives and their results.

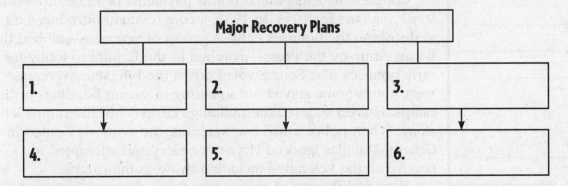

Major Recovery Plans

1.	2.	3.
4.	5.	6.

Notes

Read to Learn

Promoting Recovery *(page 640)*

Identifying the Main Idea

What is the main idea of this passage?

Publicly, President Hoover declared the economy to be on the right track soon after Black Tuesday. Privately, he was worried. He brought together business, as well as government and labor leaders. Industry leaders promised not to cut factories or cut wages. By 1931, they had broken these promises.

Hoover increased **public works,** or government-financed building projects, to create jobs. It wasn't enough. For public works to make a dent, Hoover needed to massively increase government spending. He would have to either raise taxes or run a deficit. Either way, Hoover was afraid it would only delay economic recovery.

Hoover set up the National Credit Corporation and the Reconstruction Finance Corporation to provide money to banks and businesses, but neither met the nation's needs. Hoover opposed **relief,** money given directly to destitute families. By the spring of 1932, local and state governments were running out of money. Congress passed an act to provide loans to states for direct relief. Hoover signed it, but the program could not reverse the economy's downward spiral.

Notes

Read to Learn

In an Angry Mood *(page 642)*

Determining Cause and Effect

What caused the Bonus March? What was an effect of the march?

Cause:

____

____

____

Effect:

____

____

____

After the stock market crash in 1929, people were prepared to accept bad times. By 1931, people wanted more government help. The suffering nation grew restless and people began to revolt.

Farms were heavily mortgaged to pay for supplies. Many lost their farms when creditors **foreclosed** and took ownership. Other farmers began destroying crops, hoping the lack of supply would raise prices. Some even blocked food deliveries or dumped milk into ditches.

Congress had scheduled bonus payments of $1,000 to World War I veterans for 1945. In 1931, a congressman introduced a bill to distribute the bonuses early. A group of veterans—dubbed the Bonus Army by the press—marched to the Capitol to lobby for early bonuses. The Senate voted down the bill. Many veterans went home. Some stayed on, squatting in vacant buildings or in camps. Hoover ordered the buildings cleared but the camps left alone. When police killed two veterans, the army was called in. General Douglas ignored Hoover's orders and attempted to remove all the veterans—including those in the camps.

Newsreel images of troops assaulting veterans further damaged Hoover's reputation and haunted him throughout the 1932 campaign. Although Hoover failed to end the Depression, he expanded the role of the government more than any president before him.

Drawing Conclusions

What could you conclude about the mood of the public?

____

____

____

____

____

____

____

____

Section Wrap-up

Answer these questions to check your understanding of the entire section.

1. How would you evaluate President Hoover's attempts to revive the economy?

2. What were the limitations of Hoover's recovery plans?

Persuasive Writing

In the space provided write a newspaper editorial arguing for or against the government's providing money for relief.

Chapter 19, Section 1 (Pages 650–659)

The First New Deal

Big Idea

As you read pages 650–659 in your textbook, complete this time line by recording the major problems Roosevelt addressed during his first 100 days in office.

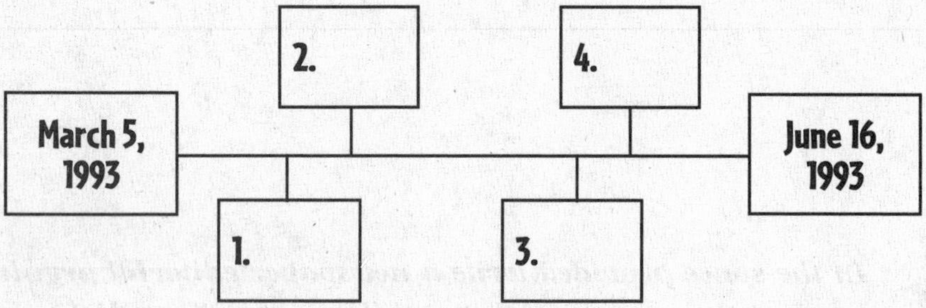

Notes

Read to Learn

Roosevelt's Rise to Power *(page 650)*

Determining Cause and Effect

Identify the cause.

Cause:

____

____

____

Effect: Roosevelt's popularity paved the way for his presidential nomination.

The Republicans nominated Herbert Hoover to run for a second term. The Democrats choose the popular New York Governor Franklin D. Roosevelt. He pledged himself "to a new deal for the American people." The New Deal became the name for his policies to end the Depression.

Roosevelt was a distant cousin of President Theodore Roosevelt. He was born into a wealthy New York family and attended Harvard and Columbia Law School. After school, Roosevelt went into politics. He served in the New York legislature. Under President Wilson, he was assistant secretary of the navy. Roosevelt ran as the vice-presidential candidate in the 1920 election. He lost. A year later, Roosevelt came down with **polio,** a paralyzing disease. Eleanor Roosevelt, his wife, kept his political career alive through public speeches while he recovered.

By 1928, Roosevelt was active again in politics. As governor of New York, Roosevelt oversaw the creation of a relief agency to help the unemployed. His popularity paved the way for his presidential nomination. In November 1932, he won the election by a landslide.

Notes | Read to Learn

The Hundred Days *(page 652)*

Distinguishing Fact from Opinion

Complete the sentences.

1. The opinion that Roosevelt would

____

____

led to bank runs.

2. It is a fact that under the gold standard

____

____

Between Roosevelt's election and his inauguration, unemployment continued to rise. Bank runs increased. Some people feared Roosevelt would lower the value of the dollar to fight the Depression. Under the **gold standard,** one ounce of gold equaled a set number of dollars. To lower the value of the dollar, the United States would have to stop exchanging dollars for gold. Depositors in American banks took out money. They wanted to convert deposits to gold before the dollar lost value. Thirty-eight state governors declared **bank holidays.** They closed banks before runs could put them out of business.

Roosevelt began his term by sending bill after bill to Congress. During the first three months of his administration, Congress passed 15 major acts to attack the economic crisis. Roosevelt chose advisors with different points of view. One group believed business and government should work together. A second group distrusted business and wanted government to run important parts of the economy. A third group wanted to break up companies to introduce competition.

Banks and Debt Relief *(page 653)*

Identifying the Main Idea

Write the main idea of the passage.

____

____

____

____

____

____

____

____

President Roosevelt realized that one of the first things he needed to do was restore people's confidence in the banks. He declared a national bank holiday and then called a special session of Congress. On the day Congress met, the House and Senate passed the Emergency Banking Relief Act. The president signed it into law. It said federal officials would check the nation's banks and license those that were financially sound.

On March 12, Roosevelt addressed the nation on radio in the first of many **fireside chats**—talks in which he told the American people what he was trying to accomplish. He told them it was safe to put their money back into banks. The next day there were more deposits than withdrawals.

Roosevelt's advisors pushed for regulation of the bank industry and the stock market. The Securities Act of 1933 required companies to provide investors with complete and truthful information. The Glass-Steagall Banking Act created the Federal Deposit Insurance Corporation. It insured bank deposits up to a set amount. Roosevelt asked Congress to establish the Homeowners Loan Corporation to help people pay their mortgages. Congress also created the Farm Credit Administration to help farmers refinance their mortgages.

Notes

Read to Learn

Farms and Industry *(page 656)*

Formulating Questions

Write two questions you have about the passage.

1. ____________________

____

____

2. ____________________

____

____

To help farmers hurt by the Depression, Roosevelt started a new farm program. Under the program, the government paid farmers not to raise certain livestock and crops. The Agricultural Adjustment Administration ran the program. Over the next two years, the farm surplus fell sharply. Prices and farm income rose. The program mostly benefited large commercial farmers who grew one crop. Many poor tenant farmers became homeless.

In June 1933, Roosevelt turned his attention to industry. Congress enacted the National Industrial Recovery Act (NIRA). It suspended antitrust laws. It let business, labor, and government set up voluntary rules for each industry. These rules were known as codes of fair competition. Some codes set prices, minimum wages, and limited factories to two shifts per day. The National Recovery Administration (NRA) ran the program. Participating businesses displayed signs with the NRA symbol. NRA codes were difficult to administer and tended to favor large corporations. By the time the Supreme Court declared the NRA unconstitutional in 1935, it had lost much of its support.

Relief Programs *(page 658)*

Comparing and Contrasting

As you read, complete the sentences.

1. The PWA and the CWA both

____

____

2. Only the PWA

____

____

3. Only the CWA

____

____

Some presidential advisors thought the major cause of the Depression was a lack buying power. They supported work programs for the unemployed, which would get money into the hands of individuals. One such relief program was the Civilian Conservation Corps (CCC). The CCC employed young men 18 to 25 years old under the direction of the forestry service. They planted trees, fought forest fires, and built reservoirs. The young men lived in camps near their work areas, earning $30 per month. The program put about 3 million people to work.

Congress set up the Federal Emergency Relief Administration (FERA). The FERA provided federal money to state and local agencies to fund their relief projects. The Public Works Administration (PWA) was a federal relief agency. The PWA built highways, dams, sewer systems, schools, and government buildings. It gave contracts to construction companies. The PWA broke down racial barriers in construction trades.

The Civil Works Administration (CWA) hired workers directly and placed them on the federal payroll. It built roads, airports, schools, playgrounds, and parks before Roosevelt ordered it shut down. The New Deal programs inspired hope and restored faith in the country.

Section Wrap-up ***Answer these questions to check your understanding of the entire section.***

1. What events and experiences were part of Franklin Roosevelt's early political career?

2. Why did New Deal advisors feel it is sometimes necessary to regulate industry and labor?

Persuasive Writing ***In the space provided write a letter to President Roosevelt explaining whether he should or should not have signed NIRA into law. Give reasons for your position.***

Chapter 19, Section 2 (Pages 662–667)

The Second New Deal

Big Idea

As you read pages 662–667 in your textbook, complete this graphic organizer by filling in Roosevelt's main legislative successes of the Second New Deal and their provisions.

Legislation	Provisions
1.	2.
3.	4.
5.	6.

Notes

Read to Learn

Launching the Second New Deal *(page 662)*

Analyzing Information

Why do you think Roosevelt asked Congress to fund the Second New Deal?

By 1935, the New Deal was facing criticism from the right and the left. The right opposed Roosevelt's **deficit spending.** He borrowed money to finance programs. Other challenges came from the left. Three opponents threatened to draw enough votes to stop Roosevelt's reelection in 1936.

Roosevelt soon began a series of programs called the Second New Deal. He asked Congress for funds to provide work relief and jobs. One such program created a new federal agency called the Works Progress Administration (WPA). Its workers built highways, roads, public buildings, and parks. A program called Federal Program Number One gave jobs to artists, musicians, and writers. They created murals and sculptures and gave concerts. Writers recorded oral history and stories.

In May 1935, the Supreme Court struck down the National Recovery Administration, finding the NRA codes unconstitutional. Roosevelt called upon Congress to pass his new programs to keep the voters' support.

Notes

Read to Learn

Reforms for Workers and Senior Citizens *(page 665)*

Identifying the Main Idea

Complete the sentences to identify the main idea.

1. The Wagner Act protected workers' rights to

____

____

____

2. One result of its passage was

____

____

____

Synthesizing Information

Complete the statement.

The Social Security Act was meant to help

____

____

____

____

____

____

____

The Supreme Court ruling against the NRA also struck down the part of the NIRA that protected the right to form unions. The President and Congress knew the labor vote would be important in the 1936 election. They also believed higher union wages gave workers more money to spend to help the economy. Opponents argued that high wages meant higher costs and less money to hire workers.

In July 1935, Congress passed the National Labor Relations Act, or the Wagner Act. It guaranteed workers' rights to form unions and bargain collectively. It set up the National Labor Relations Board (NLRB), which organized secret ballots to form unions. The Wagner Act provided for **binding arbitration.** This meant that both sides to an argument could be heard by a third party who would decide the issue.

The Wagner Act stimulated more union activity. The United Mine Workers worked with other unions to organize other industrial workers. They formed the Committee for Industrial Organizations (CIO) in 1935. The CIO organized the automotive and steel workers.

Union organizers started using new tactics such as the **sit-down strike.** In this strike, workers stopped work inside the factory and refused to leave. Companies could not send in replacement workers. The United Auto Workers (UAW) union organized many successful sit-down strikes.

Roosevelt and his advisors spent months preparing the Social Security Act. They viewed it as an insurance measure. This law provided some security for older Americans and unemployed workers.

In the Social Security system, workers pay premiums. These premiums are a tax paid to the federal government. The government then distributes this money. Retired workers over the age of 65 could collect a monthly retirement benefit. Unemployed workers looking for jobs could receive temporary income. Poor mothers with children and the disabled could receive welfare payments.

The Social Security Act helped many people, but not all. It did not cover farmers and domestic workers. About 65 percent of African Americans fell into those two groups. Security Security established the idea that government should take care of those who were unable to work.

Section Wrap-up

Answer these questions to check your understanding of the entire section.

1. What challenges did Roosevelt face in the mid-1930s?

2. Why is the Social Security Act considered one of the most important laws passed by the New Deal?

Descriptive Writing

Write a journal entry in the voice of someone who was recently employed through the WPA. Describe the work you do and how it has affected your life.

Chapter 19, Section 3 (Pages 668–673)

The New Deal Coalition

Big Idea

As you read pages 668–673 in your textbook, complete this outline by using the major headings of the section.

The New Deal Coalition

I. Roosevelt's Second Term
   A. ______________________
   B. ______________________
   C. ______________________
II. ______________________
   A. ______________________
   B. ______________________

Notes

Read to Learn

Roosevelt's Second Term (page 668)

Analyzing Information

Based on the passage, explain how government spending relates to recessions.

1. ______________________

2. ______________________

The New Deal caused shifts in party loyalties. People in the South had been the core of the Democratic Party. New supporters of the Democratic Party included farmers, industrial workers, immigrants, African Americans, women, and ethnic minorities. Roosevelt won the 1936 election against Alf Landon.

In 1936, the Supreme Court struck down the Agricultural Adjustment Act as unconstitutional. Other New Deal programs seemed threatened. Roosevelt proposed changing the balance of the Court by adding more justices. This **court-packing** plan was a political mistake. Roosevelt appeared to be threatening the Court's independence. Many people opposed the idea, and the court-packing bill never passed.

In 1937 the economy seemed on the verge of recovery. Roosevelt decided to balance the budget. Then unemployment surged again. This recession led to a debate in his cabinet. Treasury Secretary Morgenthau favored cutting spending. Others wanted to spend heavily to jump-start the economy. Roosevelt was reluctant to start deficit spending but decided to ask for more funds in 1938.

Notes

Read to Learn

The New Deal Ends *(page 672)*

Identifying the Main Idea

Write the main idea of the passage.

____

____

____

____

____

____

____

____

In Roosevelt's second term, Congress passed laws to build low-cost housing, give loans to tenant farmers, abolish child labor, and set a 44-hour workweek.

The New Deal had only limited success in ending the Depression. Unemployment remained high until after World War II. The New Deal did give Americans a stronger sense of security. The Roosevelt recession enabled more Republicans to win seats in the 1938 elections. With some conservative Democrats, they began blocking New Deal legislation. By 1939, the New Deal had ended.

The New Deal worked by balancing competing interests. As a result, business leaders, farmers, workers, and consumers expected the government to protect their interests. Two Supreme Court rulings encouraged the government to take on this role. One was the 1937 case of *NLRB* v. *Jones and Laughlin Steel*. In it, the Court held that the interstate commerce clause gave the federal government authority to regulate production in states. Another case was *Wickard* v. *Filburn* in 1942. This time the Court allowed the government to regulate consumption. These decisions increased federal power over the economy and gave the government a mediator role. The New Deal set up this role of **broker state.** This means the government brokers, or works out, conflicts between different interest groups.

Drawing Conclusions

Identify the three elements that contributed to the creation of the broker state.

1. ________________________

____

2. ________________________

____

3. ________________________

____

The biggest change brought about by the New Deal is Americans' view of government. New Deal programs created a **safety net** for average Americans. Safeguards and relief programs protected them against economic disaster. People wanted the government to keep this safety net in place. Some critics thought the New Deal gave the government too much power. People still debate today whether the government should intervene in the economy. Another issue still debated today is how much the government should support disadvantaged people.

Section Wrap-up

Answer these questions to check your understanding of the entire section.

1. What were the achievements and defeats of Roosevelt's second term?

2. What new role did the federal government take on during the New Deal era?

Informative Writing

In the space provided write a pamphlet to describe the coalition that helped reelect Roosevelt in 1936.

Chapter 20, Section 1 (Pages 682–687)

America and the World

Big Idea

As you read pages 682–687 in your textbook, complete the outline below by using the major headings of the section.

America and the World

I. The Rise of Dictators
   A. ______
   B. ______
   C. ______
   D. ______
II. ______
   A. ______
   B. ______
   C. ______

Notes

Read to Learn

The Rise of Dictators (page 682)

Analyzing Information

Read the first paragraph. How did Mussolini and Hitler rise to power?

______
______
______
______
______
______
______
______

Many countries struggled economically after World War I. This made room for dictators in Europe, Russia, and Japan. Benito Mussolini founded Italy's Fascist Party. **Fascism** was an aggressive nationalist movement. It was also strongly anticommunist. Adolph Hitler rose to power in Germany when he worked to elect the Nazis to the Reichstag. He claimed Jews were responsible for Germany's defeat in the war. Mussolini and Hitler exploited people's fears and racism. By 1932, the Nazi party dominated the Reichstag. They later voted to give Hitler dictatorial powers.

Vladimir Lenin led the Communist Party in Russia. The party established communist control throughout the Russian Empire and renamed these territories. Setting up a one-party system, they suppressed individual rights and punished opponents. When Joseph Stalin came into power, he combined family farms and turned them into **collectives.** Between 8 and 10 million people died from hunger or false trials during Stalin's rule. Japan fell under military rule. Its army invaded Manchuria, a resource-rich region in China. Officers assassinated Japan's prime minister. The military now controlled Japan.

Notes

Read to Learn

American Neutrality *(page 686)*

Identifying the Main Idea

Identify the main idea in this passage.

Detecting Bias

What words tell you Roosevelt opposed the dictators' policies?

American isolationism grew after World War I. European nations could not repay the money they had borrowed during World War I. Books and articles claimed arms manufacturers had tricked the United States into going to war. This impression was only furthered when the Nye Committee held hearings that documented the huge profits these businesses made during the war. This suggested they had influenced the United States to enter the war. After the Nye Report, even more Americans turned toward isolationism.

In response to these feelings, Congress passed three neutrality acts between 1935 and 1937. The Neutrality Act of 1935 made it illegal for the United States to sell arms to any country at war. In 1936, a rebellion erupted in Spain, which quickly became a civil war. Hitler and Mussolini helped the rebels. A second neutrality act was passed after the Spanish Civil War began. The act made it illegal for the United States to sell arms to either side in a civil war.

Soon after, Italy, Germany, and Japan formed the Axis Powers. Congress passed the Neutrality Act of 1937 in response. This required warring nations to buy all nonmilitary supplies from the United States on a "cash and carry" basis. Loans were not allowed. The countries had to send their ships to the United States to pick up the supplies. This was to prevent attacks on neutral American ships that would pull the country into a European or global conflict.

President Roosevelt knew that ending the Depression was the nation's first priority. He understood his countrymen's feelings, but he was not an isolationist. Roosevelt believed in **internationalism,** the idea that trade between nations helped to prevent war. When Japan attacked Manchuria, Roosevelt decided to help China. He authorized the sale of weapons to China. He argued that the Neutrality Act did not apply, since neither country had declared war. He warned the nation that it was dangerous to stand by and let "an epidemic of lawlessness" infect the world.

Section Wrap-up

Answer these questions to check your understanding of the entire section.

1. How did postwar conditions contribute to the rise of antidemocratic governments in Europe?

2. Why did many Americans support a policy of isolationism in the 1930s?

Expository Writing

In the space provided write an essay about the advantages and disadvantages of the United States following a policy of isolationism in the 1930s.

Chapter 20, Section 2 (Pages 688–693)

World War II Begins

Big Idea

As you read pages 688–693 in your textbook, complete the time line below by recording the events leading up to the beginning of World War II.

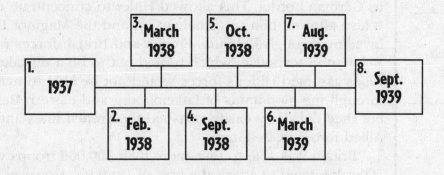

1. 1937
2. Feb. 1938
3. March 1938
4. Sept. 1938
5. Oct. 1938
6. March 1939
7. Aug. 1939
8. Sept. 1939

Notes

Read to Learn

Path to War *(page 688)*

Making Inferences

Make an inference about the success or failure of the policy of appeasement.

European leaders tried to avoid war by negotiating with Germany. In 1938, Hitler threatened to invade Austria unless Nazis were given important government posts. Austria's chancellor put the matter to a democratic vote. Fearing the outcome, Hitler sent troops into Austria and announced the unification of Austria and Germany. Then Hitler claimed the Sudetenland, a German-speaking area of Czechoslovakia. Though Czechoslovakia opposed his claim, Britain and France agreed to Hitler's demands at the Munich Conference. The resulting policy became known as **appeasement.**

Hitler next demanded German control of the Polish city of Danzig. This convinced Britain and France to prepare for a military intervention. They announced that they would aid Poland if it defended its territory. In May 1939, Hitler ordered his army to prepare to invade Poland. He also began negotiating with the USSR. Hitler proposed to Stalin a nonaggression treaty. Stalin agreed—shocking the world. However, Britain and France understood that Hitler was freeing himself to fight them. The pact also included a deal to divide Poland between Germany and the USSR.

Notes | # Read to Learn

The War Begins *(page 690)*

Determining Cause and Effect

1. What caused Hitler to invade through Belgium?

___

___

2. What were the effects of this invasion route?

___

___

Hitler invaded Poland on September 1, 1939. Two days later, Britain and France declared war on Germany. World War II had begun. Poland bravely resisted the invasion. Germany's new way of fighting **blitzkrieg,** or lightning war, proved too advanced for Poland's outdated army. By October 5, Germany had defeated Poland. Hitler prepared to invade France.

The British sent troops to France. Instead of attacking Germany, French forces waited behind the Maginot Line, along its German border. This allowed Hitler to concentrate on Poland. It also allowed him to maneuver around the Maginot Line by invading through Belgium. French and British forces raced into Belgium in response, which turned out to be a mistake. The Allies assumed Hitler's forces would not be able to make it through the mountains of Luxembourg and eastern Belgium—but they did. They easily smashed the French lines and trapped Allied forces in Belgium.

Britain was able to save more than 300,000 troops when Hitler hesitated to attack the port of Dunkirk. However, France surrendered to Germany in June of 1940. After installing a puppet government, Hitler then set his sights on Britain.

Britain Remains Defiant *(page 693)*

Predicting

Predict the fate of the British had they not had the advantage of radar.

___

___

___

___

___

___

___

Hitler expected Britain to negotiate peace after France surrendered. For British Prime Minister Winston Churchill, however, the war was now a fight to defend civilization. When Hitler realized Britain would not surrender, he prepared to invade. Getting across the English Channel would be a challenge, though, for Germany did not have many transport ships. To invade, Hitler had to defeat the British Royal Air Force. In June 1940, the *Luftwaffe* launched a fierce air battle—the Battle of Britain—to destroy the British air force.

On August 23, German bombers accidentally bombed London, enraging the British, who in turn bombed Berlin the following night. Furious, Hitler then ordered the *Luftwaffe* to continue bombing London. Hitler's goal was now to terrorize the British people into surrendering. He failed. Londoners took refuge in the city's subway tunnels whenever German planes attacked.

Germany had thousands of fighter planes. Britain had a few hundred, but it also had radar, which let British fighters detect and intercept incoming German planes. The German air force suffered greatly as a result. On October 12, 1940, Hitler cancelled the invasion of Britain.

Section Wrap-up

Answer these questions to check your understanding of the entire section.

1. Why was Hitler able to take over Austria and Czechoslovakia?

2. Describe the early events of the war. Why was Britain able to resist the Nazis?

Descriptive Writing

In the space provided write a journal entry about the German air raids on London from the point of view of a British citizen living in London during World War II.

Chapter 20, Section 3 (Pages 694–699)
The Holocaust

Big Idea

As you read pages 694–699 in your textbook, complete the graphic organizer below by listing some examples of Nazi persecution of European Jews.

Examples of Persecution	
	1.
	2.
	3.
	4.
	5.

Notes | Read to Learn

Nazi Persecution of the Jews *(page 694)*

Problems and Solutions

Identify two problems faced by Jewish immigrants who wanted to enter the United States.

European Jews had experienced anti-Semitism before World War II. They had sometimes been set apart in ghettos and prohibited from owning land. Persecution of Jews during World War II reached alarming heights. In September of 1935, the Nuremberg Laws took citizenship away from Jewish Germans. It also banned marriage between Jews and other Germans. Soon after, Jewish people were barred from voting. Their passports were marked with a red "J." By 1938, they could not practice law or medicine or operate businesses.

On *Kristallnacht,* "the night of broken glass," anti-Jewish violence erupted in Germany and Austria. The result was 90 Jewish deaths and hundreds of serious injuries. The Gestapo arrested thousands of wealthy Jews. German and Austrian Jews now lived in terror.

The United States had huge backlogs of visa applications from Jews in Germany. U.S. immigration laws barred officials from granting visas to anyone "likely to become a public charge," a description custom officials felt fit Jewish immigrants who had to leave any wealth behind. As a result, millions of Jews remained trapped in Europe.

Notes

Read to Learn

The Final Solution *(page 698)*

Making Inferences

What was meant by the term "final solution" to the Jewish question?

____

____

____

____

____

____

Determining Cause and Effect

List three causes that help explain why the Holocaust occurred.

1. ______________________

____

____

2. ______________________

____

____

3. ______________________

____

____

In 1942, Nazi leaders met at the Wannsee Conference to determine the "final solution of the Jewish question." Previous "solutions" included rounding up Jews and other "undesirables," such as the disabled, Gypsies, and Slavs from conquered territories, and shooting them. They were then piled into mass graves. Nazis also forced Jewish people into trucks and piped in exhaust fumes to kill them. But the Nazis considered these methods slow and inefficient.

The Nazis made plans to round up Jews from areas of Nazi-controlled Europe. They built **concentration camps,** or detention centers throughout Europe. Healthy individuals from these camps worked 12-hour shifts as slave laborers in nearby factories until they dropped dead from the living conditions. The elderly, disabled, and young children, who could not work, were sent directly to **extermination camps.** Here, they were executed in huge gas chambers, where the whole process could be done more efficiently. The bodies of these victims were burned.

The first concentration camps, which the Nazis built in 1933, were used to jail their political opponents. Buchenwald was built in 1937 near the town of Weimar, Germany. It was one of the largest concentration camps of the World War II era. Even without gas chambers, hundreds of prisoners died there every month from exhaustion and harsh conditions.

Extermination camps did even more damage. Most were located in Poland. At these camps, including the infamous Treblinka and Auschwitz, Jews were the main victims. More than 1,300,000 Jews died at Auschwitz. In only a few years, Jewish culture was virtually wiped out in Nazi-controlled regions of Europe.

People continue to debate why and how the Holocaust happened. Most historians believe several factors contributed to it. The German people felt they had been unjustly treated by the harsh treaty terms of World War I. Germany faced severe economic problems. Hitler had a strong hold over Germany and people feared his secret police. Resistance was difficult and dangerous. Germany did not have a strong tradition of representative government before the Nazi era. Europe had a long history of anti-Jewish prejudice and discrimination, which fed into the Nazi propaganda and racial program.

Section Wrap-up

Answer these questions to check your understanding of the entire section.

1. Describe the early persecutions of Germany's Jewish population.

2. What methods did the Nazis use to try to exterminate Europe's Jewish population?

Informative Writing

In the space provided write a brief encyclopedia article about the Holocaust. Include an explanation of what led to this shocking episode in history.

Chapter 20, Section 4 (Pages 702–707)

America Enters the War

Big Idea

As you read pages 702–707 in your textbook, complete the graphic organizer by listing two events that shifted American opinion toward helping the Allies.

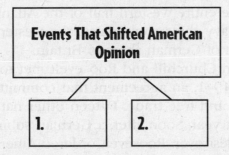

Events That Shifted American Opinion

1.

2.

Notes

Read to Learn

FDR Supports England *(page 702)*

Formulating Questions

What is a question you could ask to understand the Neutrality Act of 1939?

The United States was divided at the beginning of Germany's war with Britain and France. President Roosevelt declared the United States neutral two days after Britain and France declared war. Despite this, Roosevelt wanted to help the two nations in their struggle against Hitler. He asked Congress to revise the neutrality laws to eliminate the ban on arm sales to nations at war. The result was the Neutrality Act of 1939. The law was similar to the 1937 Neutrality Act governing the sale of nonmilitary items by allowing countries to buy weapons on a cash-and-carry basis. The public supported the president's decision to help the allies as long as the arms sales were not carried on American ships.

Soon U.S. neutrality would be tested. Britain had lost nearly half its naval destroyers. It needed to purchase destroyers from the United States, but lacked the cash. Roosevelt created a loophole. He exchanged 50 American destroyers for the right to build American bases in British-controlled parts of Bermuda and in the Caribbean. The act did not apply because the deal did not involve a sale or any purchases.

Notes | Read to Learn

Edging Toward War *(page 704)*

Analyzing Information

How did the hemispheric defense zone concept help Britain?

After President Roosevelt was reelected, he began to expand the nation's role in the war. He removed the cash requirement of the Neutrality Act with the Lend-Lease Act. This allowed the United States to lend or lease arms to any country "vital to the defense of the United States." Congress passed the act by a wide margin. The United States began leasing weapons to Britain.

Technically, the United States was still neutral and could not protect British cargo ships, hindering getting the arms to Britain. Roosevelt then introduced the **hemispheric defense zone.** He declared the entire western half of the Atlantic to be neutral. This way, U.S. Navy ships could patrol the western Atlantic and reveal the location of German ships to Britain.

Winston Churchill and Roosevelt met to discuss the Atlantic Charter in 1941, an agreement that committed their nations to democracy and free trade. Fifteen other nations signed the charter that year. Soon after, a German submarine fired on an American destroyer. Roosevelt ordered American ships to "shoot on sight" German ships. Germany retaliated, and the United States found itself drawn further into the war.

Japan Attacks *(page 705)*

Problems and Solutions

As you read, write Roosevelt's solution to the following problem.

Problem: Great Britain's ships in Asia were threatened by Japanese attacks.

Solution:

Britain needed much of its navy in Asia to protect itself against a Japanese attack. Japan depended on the United States for key materials, including steel and oil. Wanting to hinder Japanese aggression, Roosevelt restricted the sale of **strategic materials,** including fuel and iron. Furious, the Japanese signed an alliance to become a member of the Axis.

Japan sent troops into Indochina, now a direct threat to Great Britain. Roosevelt responded by freezing Japanese assets in the United States. He reduced the amount of oil sent to Japan and sent General Douglas MacArthur to the Philippines to build American defenses there. Roosevelt made it clear the oil embargo would end only if Japan withdrew its troops from Indochina. Japan continued to prepare for war while it negotiated with the United States. Neither side would back down. On December 7, 1941, Japan attacked Pearl Harbor.

Although Germany and Japan were allies, Hitler was under no obligation to aid Japan. He was frustrated, though, with the American naval attacks on German submarines. He believed the time had come to declare war. On December 11, Germany and Italy both declared war on the United States. Hitler had greatly underestimated U.S. strength.

Section Wrap-up

Answer these questions to check your understanding of the entire section.

1. How did Roosevelt help Britain while maintaining official neutrality?

2. What events led to increasing tension, and ultimately war, between the United States and Japan?

Persuasive Writing

In the space provided write a newspaper editorial arguing for or against the United States becoming involved in World War II.

Chapter 21, Section 1 (Pages 714–721)

Mobilizing the War

Big Idea

As you read pages 714–721 in your textbook, complete the graphic organizer below by filling in the agencies the U.S. government created to mobilize the nation's economy for war.

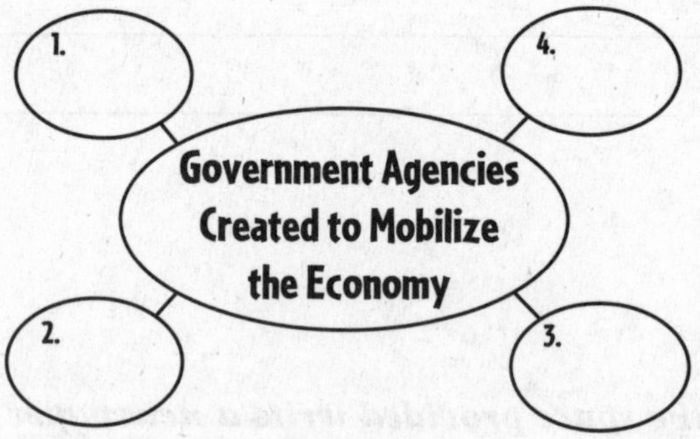

Notes

Read to Learn

Converting the Economy *(page 714)*

Identifying the Main Idea

What is the main idea of this passage?

Even before the attack on Pearl Harbor, the United States had begun to mobilize the economy. When the German blitzkrieg hit France in May 1940, President Roosevelt declared a national emergency. He announced a plan to build 50,000 warplanes a year.

Roosevelt and his advisors believed that giving industry an incentive to move quickly was the best way to convert the economy to war production. Normally, companies would bid for a contract to make military equipment. That system was now too slow. Instead, the government signed **cost-plus** contracts, agreeing to pay a company whatever it cost to make a product, plus a guaranteed percentage of the cost as profit. Under this system, the more a company produced and the faster it did the work, the more money it would make.

Congress gave the Reconstruction Finance Corporation (RFC) new authority. Congress did this to help convince companies to switch their factories to make military goods. The government gave the agency permission to make loans to companies to help them cover the cost of converting to war production.

Notes | Read to Learn

American Industry Gets the Job Done *(page 716)*

Determining Cause and Effect

Fill in the effect.

Cause: Clashes occurred between the WPB and the military.

Effect: ______________________

____

____

____

____

____

By the summer of 1942, most major industries had changed to war production. Automobile companies began to make trucks, jeeps, and tanks. They also made rifles, mines, helmets, and other military equipment. The Ford Company created an assembly line to build the B-24 bomber. By the end of the war, the company had built more than 8,600 aircraft.

Henry Kaiser's shipyards built ships. They were best known for making Liberty ships. These were the basic cargo ships used during the war. They were welded instead of riveted, making them cheap, easy to build, and difficult to sink.

To make mobilization more efficient, President Roosevelt set up the War Production Board (WPB). This agency had the authority to set priorities and production goals. It also controlled the distribution of raw materials and supplies. Almost immediately, the WPB clashed with the military. Military agents continued to sign contracts without consulting the WPB. In 1943, Roosevelt set up the Office of War Mobilization (OWM) to settle arguments among the different agencies.

Building an Army *(page 718)*

Drawing Conclusions

How did the participation of women and minorities affect the U.S. war effort?

____

____

____

____

____

____

____

____

Before the defeat of France, Congress had opposed a peacetime draft. Congress approved the Selective Service and Training Act in September 1940. This peacetime draft prepared people to fight the war.

The military was segregated. Minorities served in noncombat roles. Because they were **disenfranchised,** or could not vote, some African Americans did not want to support the war. African American leaders launched the "Double V Campaign." This campaign urged African Americans to support the war effort in order to fight racism abroad and at home. Roosevelt had to order the military to recruit women and minorities.

The 99th Pursuit Squadron was the army's first African American unit. The pilots trained in Tuskegee, Alabama. They became known as the Tuskegee Airmen and helped win the Battle of Anzio in Italy. Later, three new African American squadrons, the 332nd Fighter Group, protected American bombers without losing a single aircraft to enemy forces.

The Women's Army Corps (WAC) brought women into the army, although women were barred from combat. Oveta Culp Hobby was assigned the rank of colonel. The Women Airforce Service Pilots (WASPs) formed in 1943 and made more than 12,000 deliveries of planes over the next year.

Section Wrap-up

Answer these questions to check your understanding of the entire section.

1. How did the United States change to a wartime economy?

2. What were the issues involved in raising an army for the United States?

Persuasive Writing

In the space provided write a letter to the editor arguing for or against peacetime recruitment for the military.

Chapter 21, Section 2 (Pages 722–727)

The Early Battles

Big Idea

As you read pages 722–727 in your textbook, complete the time line below by listing some of the major battles discussed and the victor in each.

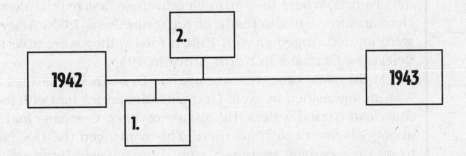

1942 — 1. — 2. — 1943

Notes | Read to Learn

Holding the Line Against Japan *(page 722)*

Making Inferences

Make an inference about how poor conditions affected the outcome at Bataan.

The Japanese continued to win victories in the Pacific until the Battle of Midway. Two days after their attack on Pearl Harbor, Japanese troops landed on the Philippine Islands, strongly outnumbering American and Filipino forces. General Douglas MacArthur decided to retreat to the Bataan Peninsula.

Conditions were horrible. Soldiers starved, and malaria, scurvy, and dysentery ran rampant. Eventually the defenders of Bataan surrendered. They were forced to march 65 miles to a Japanese prison camp. Almost 10,000 troops died on the way. The march was later called the Bataan Death March.

By early 1942, the United States was preparing to drop bombs on Tokyo. President Roosevelt ordered Lieutenant Colonel James Doolittle to command the mission. America bombed Japan for the first time in April of that year. Doolittle's raid sent Japanese strategy into a tailspin. Thanks to the work of code breakers, American forces were able to decode Japan's plan to attack both New Guinea and Midway. This allowed Admiral Chester Nimitz to ambush the Japanese fleet at Midway and win the battle. The Battle of Midway was a turning point.

Notes | Read to Learn

Stopping the Germans *(page 725)*

Analyzing Information

Complete the sentence.

The Battle of Stalingrad was a turning point in the war because

____

____

____

____

____

____

Predicting

Based on the passage, make two predictions about World War II.

1. ______________________

____

____

____

2. ______________________

____

____

____

In 1942, Joseph Stalin wanted President Roosevelt to directly attack Germany in Europe. Winston Churchill, however, wanted to attack the **periphery,** or edges, of the German empire. Roosevelt agreed and ordered troops to invade Morocco and Algeria in North Africa. These were French territories under German control.

General Patton led the American forces in Morocco. They quickly captured the city of Casablanca. Then they headed east into Tunisia, where they struggled in their first real battle with German forces. In the Battle of Kasserine Pass, 7,000 Americans were injured. Together with British forces, they were able to defeat the Germans in North Africa in 1943.

At the same time, the war against German submarines in the Atlantic intensified as well. German submarines had entered American coastal waters. By August of 1942, Germans had sunk about 360 American ships there. This convinced the U.S. Navy to set up a **convoy system.** Cargo ships traveled in groups escorted by navy warships. American and British shipyards also upped production of cargo ships. Soon they were producing more ships than the German submarines were sinking. The United States was also using new technology such as radar, sonar, and depth charges against the submarines. The war slowly turned in favor of the Allies.

In the spring of 1942, Hitler was confident he could beat the Soviets by wrecking the Soviet economy. He considered the city of Stalingrad central to his efforts. Hitler ordered his troops to capture and hold the city at all costs. In September of that year, German troops entered Stalingrad, but they were not equipped for the cold in ways the Soviet army was. The Germans lost thousands of soldiers. In November, Soviet reinforcements arrived and trapped almost 250,000 German troops within the city. The Germans surrendered the city in February of 1943. Germany was now on the defensive.

Section Wrap-up

Answer these questions to check your understanding of the entire section.

1. How were the Allies able to fight a war on two fronts and turn the war against the Axis Powers in the Pacific, Russia, and the North Atlantic?

2. How did generals MacArthur and Patton and Lieutenant Colonel James Doolittle contribute to the war effort?

Informative Writing

In the space provided write a news account of the Battle of Stalingrad.

Chapter 21, Section 3 (Pages 728–735)

Life on the Home Front

Big Idea

As you read pages 728–735 in your textbook, complete this graphic organizer by listing opportunities for women and African Americans before and during the war. Also evaluate what progress still needed to take place after the war.

Opportunities

	Before War	After War	Still Needed
Women	1.	2.	3.
African Americans	4.	5.	6.

Notes

Read to Learn

Women and Minorities Gain Ground *(page 728)*

Evaluating Information

Does the passage do a good job explaining how women and minorities gained ground? Circle your answer. Then explain it.

Yes *No*

____

____

____

____

____

Before the war, most Americans believed married women should not work outside the home. However, the labor shortage during the war forced factories to hire married women. "Rosie the Riveter" was the symbol of the campaign to hire women. Images of Rosie appeared on posters and in newspaper ads. Although most women left the factories after the war, their work permanently changed American attitudes about women in the workplace.

Many factories did not want to hire African Americans. A. Philip Randolph was the head of the Brotherhood of Sleeping Car Porters—a major union for African American railroad workers. He told President Roosevelt that he was going to organize a march on Washington. Roosevelt responded by issuing an order saying that discrimination in hiring workers in defense industries would not be tolerated. He created the Fair Employment Practices Commission to enforce the order.

To help farmers in the Southwest overcome the labor shortage, the government started the Bracero Program in 1942. It arranged for Mexican farm workers to help in the harvest.

Notes | Read to Learn

A Nation on the Move *(page 730)*

Making Generalizations

How were minorities treated during the war?

____

____

____

Underline three facts that support your generalization.

The wartime economy created millions of new jobs. However, people who wanted them did not always live near the factories. Many workers moved to the **Sunbelt,** a region including southern California and the Deep South. African Americans, however, were moving north in the Great Migration. They were often met with suspicion and intolerance.

In California, **zoot-suit** wearers—often Mexican American teenagers—faced prejudice. The baggy zoot suit used more material than the **victory suit.** Some thought that wearing it was unpatriotic. In June of 1943, 2,500 soldiers and sailors stormed Mexican American neighborhoods in Los Angeles. They attacked Mexican American teenagers. Police did not intervene.

After Japan attacked Pearl Harbor, all people of Japanese ancestry on the West Coast were ordered to move to internment camps. In *Korematsu* v. *the United States,* Fred Korematsu argued that his civil rights had been violated. He took his case to the Supreme Court, but he lost. After the war, the Japanese American Citizens League (JACL) tried to help Japanese Americans who had lost property during the relocation.

Daily Life in Wartime *(page 734)*

Problems and Solutions

Identify one problem in the passage. List one solution to it.

Problem:

____

____

____

____

Solution:

____

____

____

____

Wages and prices rose quickly during the war. To stabilize prices, President Roosevelt created the Office of Price Administration (OPA) and the Office of Economic Stabilization (OES). They regulated prices and controlled inflation. The demand for raw materials and supplies created shortages. To keep products available for military use, the OPA **rationed** them, or limited their availability. Meat, oil, sugar—even gasoline—were all rationed. Households received ration coupons each month that limited the amounts of rationed goods they could purchase. Americans also planted **victory gardens** to produce more food. The government ran scrap drives to collect the spare rubber, tin, aluminum, and steel the military needed.

The United States raised taxes to help pay for the war. Because most Americans opposed a high tax increase, the taxes raised during World War II paid for only 45 percent of the war's cost. People bought bonds issued by the government as a way to make up the difference. The government promised to pay back the money, plus interest, at a later date. Individuals bought nearly $50 billion worth of war bonds. Banks, insurance companies, and other financial institutions bought the rest—more than $100 billion worth of bonds.

Section Wrap-up

Answer these questions to check your understanding of the entire section.

1. How did the wartime economy create opportunities for women and minorities?

2. How did Americans cope with shortages and rapidly rising prices?

Descriptive Writing

Suppose you are a woman living during the war. Write a journal entry describing a typical day in your life.

Chapter 21, Section 4 (Pages 736–743)

Pushing Back the Axis

Big Idea

As you read pages 736–743 in your textbook, complete this graphic organizer by filling in the names of some of the battles. Where possible, indicate whether each was an Allied or Axis Powers victory.

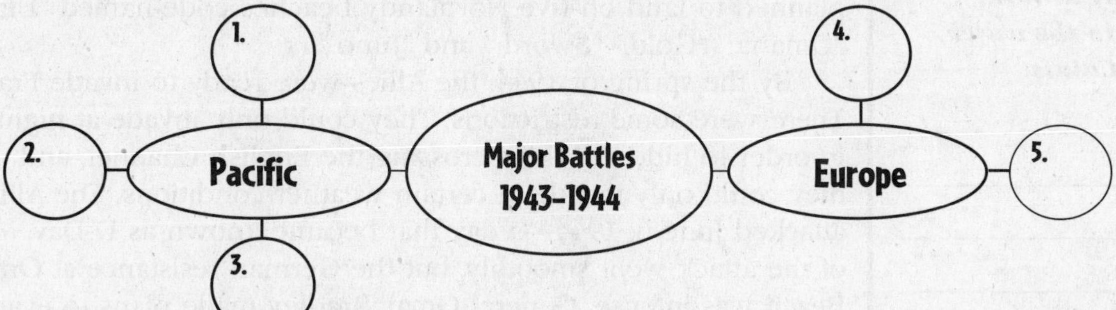

Notes

Read to Learn

Striking Germany and Italy *(page 736)*

Predicting

Skim the passage. Make two predictions about what the section will be about.

1. ____________________

____

____

____

2. ____________________

____

____

____

In January 1943, President Roosevelt met with Prime Minister Winston Churchill at the Casablanca Conference in Morocco. The two leaders agreed to step up the bombing of Germany. The Allies also agreed to attack the Axis forces in Sicily.

Between 1943 and 1945, the air forces of Britain and the United States dropped about 53,000 tons of explosives on Germany every month. The bombing created an oil shortage and destroyed the railroad system, as well as many German aircraft factories. Germany's air force could not replace the planes they lost. The Allies now had total control of the air.

General Eisenhower was in charge of the Sicily invasion. Allied troops captured the western half of the island. The Germans were defeated in Sicily. Italy's king arrested Mussolini and began to negotiate a surrender to the Allies. But German troops seized northern Italy and returned Mussolini to power.

Roosevelt and Churchill met with Stalin in late 1943. They reached several agreements—one being that Germany would be broken up after the war. Stalin also agreed to attack Germany once the Allies landed in France.

Notes

Read to Learn

Landing in France *(page 739)*

Determining Cause and Effect

Fill in the effect.

Cause: The Allies placed inflated rubber tanks and dummy landing craft in the water near Calais.

Effect: ______________

____

____

____

____

____

Roosevelt and Churchill met in Egypt to continue planning the invasion of France—otherwise known as Operation Overlord. Roosevelt selected General Eisenhower to command the invasion. The Germans knew the Allies were planning to invade France, so Hitler fortified the coast. The Germans guessed that the Allies would land in Pas-de-Calais. To fuel this misconception, the Allies placed inflated rubber tanks and dummy landing craft along the coast across from Calais. They actually planned to land on five Normandy beaches code-named "Utah," "Omaha," "Gold," "Sword," and "Juno."

By the spring of 1944, the Allies were ready to invade France. There were some restrictions. They could only invade at night in order to hide the ships crossing the English Channel, and they could only invade in certain weather conditions. The Allies attacked June 6, 1944—a day that became known as D-Day. Most of the attack went smoothly, but the German resistance at Omaha Beach was intense. General Omar Bradley made plans to evacuate, but American forces soon began knocking out the German defenses. By the end of the day, the invasion was successful.

Driving Japan Back *(page 741)*

Identifying the Main Idea

Write the main idea of this passage.

____

____

____

____

____

____

____

____

The United States also developed a strategy to defeat Japan. It had two parts. In the first, Admiral Nimitz commanded the Pacific Fleet as it hopped from one central Pacific island to the next. This campaign started in the fall of 1943, but the Pacific's geography posed a problem. Many of the islands were coral reef atolls, and the water over the reefs was often shallow. U.S. ships ran aground before reaching the shore, forcing troops to wade to shore. Many died from Japanese gunfire before reaching the shore. One vehicle, called an **amphtrac,** successfully crossed the reefs to deliver troops.

In the second part of the plan, General MacArthur's troops invaded Guadalcanal, in the southwest Pacific, in 1942. By early 1944, MacArthur's troops had captured enough islands to surround Japan's main military base in the region. U.S. troops turned their focus to recapturing the Philippines. In response, Japan attacked from the north and west. Some Japanese fighters were **kamikaze** pilots—those who deliberately flew their planes into American ships. The pilots died, but also inflicted severe damage. The Japanese eventually retreated, but the battle to recapture the Philippines was long. It was still going on when word came in August 1945 that Japan had surrendered.

Section Wrap-up

Answer these questions to check your understanding of the entire section.

1. What were the goals of the two major offensives the Allies launched in Europe in 1943?

2. What was the American strategy for pushing back the Japanese in the Pacific?

Expository Writing

Suppose you will debate the effectiveness of the Allies' strategies for defeating the Axis Powers. Summarize the arguments you would make in a brief paragraph.

Chapter 21, Section 5 (Pages 746–753)

The War Ends

Big Idea

As you read pages 746–753 in your textbook, complete the outline below using the major headings of the section.

The War Ends

I. The Third Reich Collapses
 A. ______
 B. ______
II. ______
 A. ______
 B. ______
 C. ______
 D. ______
 E. ______
 F. ______
III. ______
 A. ______
 B. ______

Notes

Read to Learn

The Third Reich Collapses *(page 746)*

Formulating Questions

Write two questions you have based on the passage.

1. ______

______

______

______

2. ______

______

______

______

Hedgerows, or dirt walls covered in shrubbery, surrounded many fields in Normandy, enabling the Germans to defend their positions. On July 25, 1944, American bombers blew a hole in German lines and America tanks raced through the gap. Then, on August 25, the Allies liberated Paris.

Hitler staged one last desperate offensive by cutting off Allied supplies coming through the port of Antwerp, Belgium. His attack, known as the Battle of the Bulge, caught the Americans by surprise. Three days later, however, General Patton and his troops slammed into German lines. Allied aircraft bombed German fuel depots. Patton's troops soon broke through the German lines. The United States won the battle.

By the time the Battle of the Bulge ended, the Soviets had pushed Hitler's troops out of Russia and across Poland. As Soviets drove toward Berlin from the east, American forces pushed toward it from the west. Soviet troops arrived in Berlin on April 21, 1945, and by April 30, Hitler had killed himself. His successor, Karl Doenitz, surrendered unconditionally to the Allies on May 7.

Notes | Read to Learn

Japan Is Defeated *(page 748)*

Distinguishing Fact from Opinion

List one fact and one opinion from the passage about the atomic bomb.

Fact:

____

____

____

____

Opinion:

____

____

____

____

President Roosevelt died on April 12, 1945, after suffering a stroke. Harry S. Truman became president and had to end the war in Japan. The United States tried sending B-29s to bomb Japan, but they ran out of fuel by the time they reached Japan and could not hit their targets. U.S. troops invaded Iwo Jima so they could establish a place for the bombers to refuel. Iwo Jima's geography was difficult. American troops succeeded in capturing the island, but more than 6,800 marines died in the process.

While American engineers prepared airfields on Iwo Jima, General Curtis LeMay decided to change plans. He ordered B-29s to drop bombs filled with **napalm,** which exploded and ignited fires. The firebombs killed many civilians. Japan still refused to surrender. American troops invaded Okinawa in April of 1945 and captured it in late June.

President Truman knew the United States had a new weapon that could force Japan's unconditional surrender—the atomic bomb. The American program to build it, code-named the Manhattan Project, had started under Roosevelt. After much debate, President Truman ordered the bomb dropped. He believed doing so was justified because it would save American lives. On August 6, 1945, an atomic bomb was dropped on Hiroshima. Three days later, another was dropped on Nagasaki. The bombs killed tens of thousands of people. Japan surrendered on August 15, V-J Day. World War II was over.

Building a New World *(page 752)*

Analyzing Information

Circle the names of the five permanent members of the Security Council. How were these members probably chosen?

____

____

____

____

In 1944, delegates from 39 countries met in Washington, D.C. They discussed forming a new organization, the United Nations. It would have a General Assembly in which every member nation would have one vote. It would also have an eleven-member Security Council. Britain, France, China, the Soviet Union, and the United States would be the council's permanent members. They would have veto power. In 1945, representatives from 50 countries came to San Francisco to officially organized the United Nations. They designed its **charter,** or constitution. The General Assembly would vote on resolutions and choose the nonpermanent security group's members. The Security Council attended to international peace and security.

In August 1945, the United States, Britain, France, and the Soviet Union created the International Military Tribunal (IMT). At the Nuremberg trials, the IMT tried German leaders for war crimes. Many of these leaders were executed. Several Japanese leaders were also tried and executed.

Section Wrap-up

Answer these questions to check your understanding of the entire section.

1. What tactics did the Allies use to defeat Japan?

2. Why did the Allies create the United Nations and hold war crimes trials?

Informative Writing

In the space provided write a brief newspaper article about the formation of the United Nations. Include details about its members and its purpose.

Chapter 22, Section 1 (Pages 760–765)

The Origins of the Cold War

Big Idea

As you read pages 760–765 in your textbook, complete the graphic organizer by filling in the names of the conferences held among the "Big Three" Allies and the outcomes of each.

Conferences	Outcomes
1.	2.
3.	4.

Notes

Read to Learn

The Yalta Conference (page 760)

Making Generalizations

Read the passage. Underline two statements that support this generalization:

The Soviet Union was against spreading democracy in Europe.

In February 1945, Roosevelt, Churchill, and Stalin met at Yalta. There, they discussed Poland. Churchill and Roosevelt wanted the Poles to choose their own government. Stalin supported the Communist government it had set up during the war. They compromised. The Communist government stayed, but Stalin agreed to hold free elections quickly. They also divided Germany into four zones. Great Britain, the United States, the Soviet Union, and France each controlled a zone. Just two weeks after Yalta, the Soviet Union forced Romania to form a Communist government. They also refused to allow elections in Poland.

Relations between the United States and the Soviet Union were strained from 1946 to 1990, an era known as the Cold War. The conflict arose because the countries had different goals. The Soviet Union was worried about its security and wanted to keep Germany weak. The Soviets also wanted to spread communism to other nations. The United States focused on economic problems. Americans believed economic growth and democracy were important in order to keep world peace.

Notes

Read to Learn

Truman Takes Control *(page 763)*

Analyzing Information

Read the statements. Write T by the one Truman might have said. Write S by the one Stalin might have said.

1. ___ Poland and Czechoslovakia can have their own governments, but they must remain friendly to the Soviet Union.

2. ___ The people of Poland and Eastern Europe must be allowed to elect their own governments.

Problems and Solutions

Write Truman's solution.

Problem: Stalin wanted reparations from Germany.

Solution:

____

____

____

____

____

____

____

Vice President Harry S. Truman became the president after Roosevelt died in 1945. Truman was anticommunist and did not trust Stalin. He also did not want to appease Stalin. He demanded that Stalin hold free elections as promised. Truman finally met Stalin in July 1945 at the Potsdam Conference, where they worked out a deal on Germany. Truman believed that Germany's industrial economy had to be revived. He thought this was necessary for all of Europe's recovery. Truman also thought that if its economy stayed weak, Germany might turn to communism. Stalin wanted reparations from Germany. He felt that the Germans should pay for the damage they caused to the Soviet Union.

Truman suggested that the Soviet Union take reparations from the zone under its own control. He also offered small amounts of industrial equipment from other zones, which the Soviets could pay for with agricultural goods from their zone. Stalin did not like Truman's proposal. However, Truman hinted that he had an atomic bomb. Stalin accepted.

The Soviets refused to uphold the Declaration of Liberated Europe. They set up pro-Soviet Communist governments in Eastern Europe. These countries were called **satellite nations.** They had their own governments, but remained Communist and friendly to the Soviet Union. Churchill later called the Communist takeover of Eastern Europe an **iron curtain** that separated Eastern Europe from the West.

Section Wrap-up

Answer these questions to check your understanding of the entire section.

1. How did Stalin support the spread of communism in Europe?

2. Why did President Truman disagree with Stalin about German reparations?

Persuasive Writing

Suppose you are living in the Soviet Union after World War II. Write a letter to American President Truman. Explain why the Germans should pay high reparations to your country. Include examples to support your position.

Chapter 22, Section 2 (Pages 766–773)

The Early Cold War Years

Big Idea

As you read pages 766–773 in your textbook, complete the time line by recording some major events involving the Korean War.

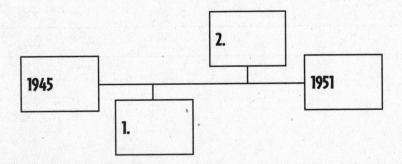

1945

1.

2.

1951

Notes

Read to Learn

Containing Communism (page 766)

Determining Cause and Effect

Write the cause.

Cause:

____

____

____

____

____

Effect: The Soviets blockaded Berlin in anger.

In 1945 Britain and the United States pushed the Soviets to hold free elections in Eastern Europe, but they refused. One diplomat suggested the use of diplomacy, economics, and military action to stop Soviet expansion. This policy became known as **containment.** Soon after, Soviet-related crises erupted Iran and in Turkey. The Soviets backed down only under threats of force from the United States. In 1947 Truman asked Congress for money to help Greece and Turkey fight communism. To weaken the appeal of communism, the United States also created the Marshall Plan. It gave Europe aid to rebuild its economies.

In 1948 the United States, France, and Britain combined their zones with West Berlin to create West Germany. The Soviets blockaded Berlin in anger. Truman ordered the Berlin airlift, in which cargo planes brought food and other supplies to the city. Stalin finally lifted the blockade, but Americans and Western Europe were moved to form NATO, the North Atlantic Treaty Organization. Twelve nations agreed to help each other if attacked. The Soviets set up the Warsaw Pact alliance.

Notes | Read to Learn

The Korean War *(page 770)*

Detecting Bias

Reread the passage. Place an X next to the statement or statements that show how MacArthur may have felt about Truman's leadership.

Identifying the Main Idea

Reread the passage. Which best states the main idea of the passage? Circle it.

1. The Korean War made the UN focus on the containment policy.

2. The spread of the Cold War to Asia forced a change in American foreign policy.

The Cold War spread to Asia. In China, Mao Zedong led Communist forces in a revolt against Chiang Kai-shek's Nationalist government. Their fight began in the 1920s. However, the two sides stopped fighting during World War II and joined forces to stop the Japanese invasion. After the war ended, the two groups began fighting again. The United States wanted to stop the spread of communism in Asia. It sent Chiang Kai-shek $2 billion in aid. However, the Communists captured the capital Beijing and moved south. The Nationalists left the mainland and fled to Taiwan. In 1949 the Communists set up the People's Republic of China.

In the same year, the Soviet Union tested its first atomic weapon. In 1950 it signed a treaty of alliance with China. Americans feared that these allies would support Communist revolutions around the world. The United States set up formal relations with the Nationalists on Taiwan. The United States also changed it policy toward Japan. General Douglas MacArthur was put in charge of occupied Japan, where he encouraged democracy and quick economic recovery. Americans saw Japan as a way to defend Asia against communism.

After World War II, the Allies divided Korea at the 38th parallel. The Soviet-controlled north became Communist. In the U.S.-controlled south, an American-backed government was set up. The Soviets gave military aid to North Korea, which built a huge army and invaded South Korea on June 25, 1950. President Truman saw this as a test of the containment policy. He sent MacArthur and the American military to Korea. Truman also asked the United Nations for troops to help. In September 1950, MacArthur ordered an invasion. The North Koreans were taken by surprise, and they retreated across the 38th parallel. MacArthur pushed the North Koreans toward the Chinese border. The Chinese were afraid of a UN invasion and warned the UN troops to retreat. Then the Chinese invaded Korea and pushed UN troops south.

General MacArthur wanted to expand the war into China. He criticized Truman for wanting a **limited war,** a war fought to achieve limited goals. In response, Truman fired MacArthur. By 1951 the UN forces drove the Chinese and North Koreans back over the 38th parallel. An armistice was signed in July 1953. By then more than 35,000 Americans had died in the war. During the Korean War, the United States began a military buildup. In the past, the United States focused on Europe to contain communism. Now it had to focus its military on Asia. Defense agreements were signed and aid was given to those fighting communism in Asia.

Section Wrap-up

Answer these questions to check your understanding of the entire section.

1. How did the Korean War change the American view of containment?

2. What steps did the United States take toward containing communism after World War II?

Persuasive Writing

In the space provided write a report to President Truman summarizing the crises that involved Communist forces from 1945 to 1953. Include American responses to each crisis into your report.

Chapter 22, Section 3 (Pages 774–781)

The Cold War and American Society

Big Idea

As you read pages 774–781 in your textbook, use the major headings of the section to complete the outline.

The Cold War and American Society

I. A New Red Scare
    A. The Loyalty Review Program
    B. ______________________
    C. ______________________
II. ______________________
    A. ______________________
    B. ______________________
    C. ______________________
III. ______________________
    A. ______________________
    B. ______________________

Notes

Read to Learn

A New Red Scare *(page 774)*

Formulating Questions

Read the questions below. Circle the question that is answered in the passage. Underline the question that requires further study.

1. How did the loyalty review program impact federal employees?

2. How did Chambers know that Hiss was a spy?

During the 1950s, Americans were caught up in the Red Scare. It began in September 1945 with a Soviet defector who reported that Soviet spies were inside the United States looking for information about the atomic bomb. This led to fear of a Communist **subversion,** or a plot to overthrow the government.

In 1947 Truman set up a **loyalty review program** to screen federal employees to test their loyalty. Over 2,000 people lost their jobs. The FBI infiltrated groups and wiretapped telephones. FBI Director J. Edgar Hoover also urged the House Un-American Activities Committee to hold public hearings on subversion. One of the hearings focused on the film industry. Many in Hollywood refused to testify and were blacklisted.

In 1948 Whittaker Chambers, a magazine editor, testified that several government officials were spies. One the spies was Alger Hiss of the State Department. Hiss denied this charge, but was later found guilty. Hiss was also convicted of **perjury,** or lying under oath. In another case, Ethel and Julius Rosenberg were found guilty of passing along atomic secrets to the Soviets and they were executed.

Notes

Read to Learn

McCarthyism *(page 777)*

Drawing Conclusions

Place an X next to the statements in the passage that support this conclusion:

McCarthy's investigative methods ruined the careers of many government employees.

In 1949 the Red Scare grew worse. The Soviet Union tested an atomic bomb, and China fell to the Communists. Many Americans believed that they were losing the Cold War and that Communists had infiltrated the government. In February of 1950, Senator Joseph McCarthy claimed that he had a list of 205 Communists working in the State Department. He accused many politicians and others of being Communists. He never produced the list as proof.

The McCarran Act was passed in 1950. This law required all Communist organizations to register with the government. The groups were also forced to share their records with the government. The law stopped Communists from getting passports or traveling abroad. It stated that they could be arrested during emergencies. Truman tried to veto the bill, but Congress overrode the veto. The bill became law.

In 1952 McCarthy became chairman of the Senate subcommittee on investigations. Then he forced government officials to testify about Communist influences. McCarthy turned the investigations into witch hunts based on weak evidence and fear. He destroyed reputations with unfounded charges. This became known as McCarthyism. McCarthy would badger witnesses and refuse to accept their answers. His methods left a sense of suspicion and guilt about the witnesses.

In 1954 McCarthy began to question members of the United States Army. McCarthy's investigation was aired on television, and millions of Americans watched. McCarthy's popularity decreased as people finally challenged him and his methods. In 1954 the Senate passed a vote of **censure,** or formal disapproval, against McCarthy. His influence was gone. He faded from public view.

Life During the Early Cold War *(page 778)*

Predicting

Read this section's title. What do you think this passage will cover?

____

____

____

____

The Red Scare and the spread of nuclear weapons shaped everyday life in the United States during the 1950s. Americans were upset when the Soviet Union tested the powerful hydrogen, or H-bomb. They began to prepare for a surprise Soviet attack. They set up special areas as bomb shelters. Students also practiced bomb drills called "duck-and-cover" drills. Experts warned that these measures would not protect people from the initial blast or the **fallout**—the radiation left after the blast. For each person killed by the blast, four more would die from fallout.

The fear of communism influenced American movies and fiction. Many movies focused on FBI activities in spy cases. Novels described the effects of nuclear war.

Section Wrap-up

Answer these questions to check your understanding of the entire section.

1. Why did President Truman set up the loyalty review program?

2. Why were American preparations for a Soviet attack unlikely to be successful?

Expository Writing

In the space provided write a newspaper editorial that includes the disadvantages of the government's loyalty review program and the McCarren Act.

Chapter 22, Section 4 (Pages 782–787)

Eisenhower's Cold War Policies

Big Idea

As you read pages 782–787 in your textbook, complete the graphic organizer by filling in aspects of Eisenhower's Cold War policies.

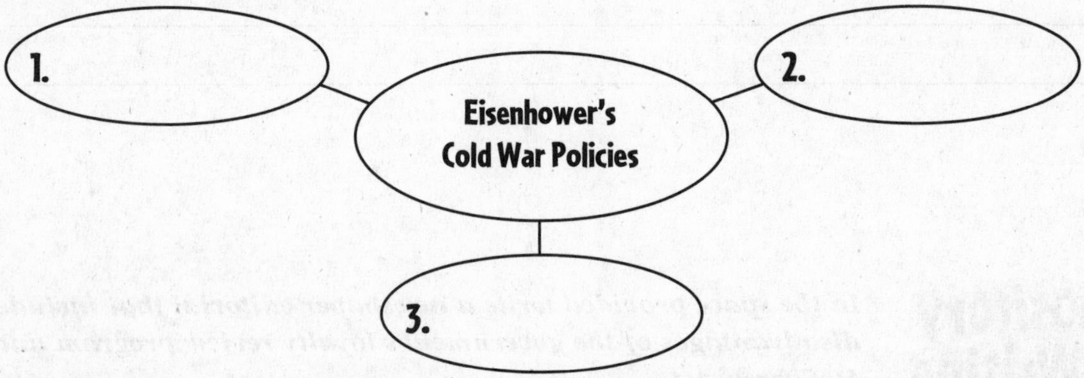

Notes

Read to Learn

Massive Retaliation *(page 782)*

Problems and Solutions

Write one problem addressed by the massive retaliation policy.

____

____

____

____

____

____

____

____

Republican Dwight D. Eisenhower won the 1952 presidential election in a landslide. He believed a strong military and economy were essential to win the Cold War. He also thought that conventional wars cost too much money. Eisenhower believed the United States had to prevent wars by threatening nuclear war. This policy became known as **massive retaliation.** It allowed him to cut military spending by billions of dollars. Eisenhower shrunk the army but invested in nuclear weapons and new technology to deliver them.

Eisenhower supported **brinkmanship**—the willingness to go to brink of war to force another nation to back down. Some thought this policy was dangerous, but Eisenhower used the threat to end the Korean War and protect Taiwan.

In 1955 Egypt seized the Suez Canal from an Anglo-French company that controlled it. Egypt wanted to use the profits from the canal to pay for a dam. In response, Britain and France invaded Egypt. The Soviet Union offered to help Egypt by attacking Britain and France. Eisenhower threatened a nuclear war with the Soviets. Britain and France retreated.

Notes

Read to Learn

Covert Operations *(page 785)*

Synthesizing Information

Number the events below in the order in which they occurred.

____ ***An uprising in Hungary was crushed by the Soviet Union.***

____ ***The Shah of Iran was put back in power by a CIA coup.***

____ ***Khrushchev cancelled the Paris Summit.***

Making Generalizations

Reread the paragraph about Guatemala. What do you think the CIA feared would happen if they did not launch a covert operation?

____

____

____

____

____

____

____

____

Eisenhower knew that brinkmanship would not work all the time. He knew it would not stop Communists from starting revolutions within countries. Eisenhower used **covert**—or hidden—operations to prevent revolutions. These were run by the Central Intelligence Agency, or CIA. Many of these operations took place in **developing nations,** or nations with mostly agricultural economies. Many of these nations blamed American capitalism for their problems. They looked to the Soviet Union as a model for industrialization. Americans feared that these nations would stage Communist revolutions, so Eisenhower offered financial aid to many of these nations. In places where the Communists were stronger, the CIA used covert operations. The CIA overthrew anti-American leaders. They replaced them with pro-American leaders.

Covert operations worked in Iran. There the prime minister overthrew the Shah of Iran and then wanted to make an oil deal with the Soviet Union. The CIA organized riots and a coup, and the prime minister was overthrown. The Shah returned to power.

In Guatemala, the president won his office with Soviet support. His programs took over large estates. Some of the estates were owned by Americans. Then Guatemala received weapons from Czechoslovakia. The CIA armed and trained rebels to overthrow the pro-Communist president.

Sometimes covert operations did not work. Nikita Khrushchev took over the Soviet Union after Stalin died. The CIA got a copy of a speech Khrushchev made in which he attacked Stalin's policies. The CIA broadcast the speech in Eastern Europe. In 1956 a revolt in Hungary began. The Soviets moved troops into Hungary and stopped the revolt.

In 1957 Eisenhower asked Congress to allow the use of the military to stop communism in the Middle East. This became known as the Eisenhower Doctrine. American troops went to Lebanon to protect its government. In 1958 Khrushchev demanded that the United States and its allies take their troops out of West Berlin. The United States threatened to use military force to protect Berlin. The Soviet Union backed down again.

Khrushchev visited Eisenhower in the United States in late 1959. They planned to hold a summit in Paris in 1960. Before the summit began, an American U-2 spy plane was shot down over the Soviet Union. Eisenhower refused to apologize. Khrushchev cancelled the summit. As Eisenhower prepared to leave office, he delivered a farewell address. In his speech, he pointed out a new relationship between the military and defense industries. He warned Americans to guard against the influence of this **military-industrial complex** in a democracy.

Section Wrap-up

Answer these questions to check your understanding of the entire section.

1. What did Eisenhower think was necessary to win the Cold War?

2. What was one example of how covert operations did not work?

Informative Writing

In the space provided write an essay that compares the advantages of covert operations with those of brinkmanship.

Chapter 23, Section 1 (Pages 794–799)

Truman and Eisenhower

Big Idea

As you read pages 794–799 in your textbook, complete the graphic organizer by listing the characteristics of the postwar economy of the United States.

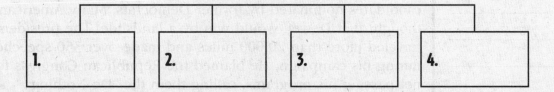

Characteristics of a Postwar Economy			
1.	2.	3.	4.

Notes

Read to Learn

Return to a Peacetime Economy *(page 794)*

Predicting

Read the first two paragraphs. Then predict what happened next.

Americans feared that the end of military production and the return of soldiers would bring unemployment and recession. Instead, Americans who had lived with shortages during the war helped to grow the economy after the war by buying consumer goods. Demand for goods led to inflation and labor unrest. Strikes occurred in the automobile, steel, and mining industries. President Truman tried to prevent energy shortages and railroad strikes by forcing miners and others back to work.

Labor unrest and inflation led to a change in leadership. In the 1946 elections, the Republicans took control of both houses of Congress. To decrease the power of unions, the new Congress proposed the Taft-Hartley Act. The act outlawed the **closed shop,** or the practice of forcing business owners to hire only union members. It allowed states to pass **right-to-work laws** to outlaw **union shops** in which workers were forced to join unions. The law also prohibited featherbedding, or limiting output in order to create more jobs. President Truman vetoed the bill, but Congress passed the act in 1947 over his veto. Labor leaders claimed the law ended many of the gains unions made since 1933.

Notes

Read to Learn

Truman's Program *(page 796)*

Determining Cause and Effect

List two reasons why the Democrats took control of the Congress in 1948.

1. ______________________

____

____

____

____

2. ______________________

____

____

____

____

The Republicans controlled Congress, but President Truman pushed for his programs anyway. He tried to increase Social Security benefits and the minimum wage, and to create more government jobs and a national health insurance system. The president planned public works projects such as new public housing. Truman pressed Congress to pass a civil rights bill to protect African Americans' rights. Then he ended segregation in the military and discrimination in hiring for federal jobs. Several of these plans were stopped by the Republicans and Southern Democrats in Congress.

Few people believed that Truman would win the 1948 election. He faced Republican Governor Thomas Dewey and two candidates nominated by former Democrats. Many Americans thought that Dewey would win by a landslide. The president traveled more than 20,000 miles and made over 350 speeches during his campaign. He blamed the Republican Congress for not passing his programs, calling them the "Do-Nothing Congress." Americans soon believed him, and he won by a small margin. The Democrats also won control of Congress.

The president pushed the new Congress to pass his Fair Deal programs, and they responded by passing parts of it. Congress increased the minimum wage and expanded Social Security benefits. It also approved the National Housing Act of 1949. However, Congress did not pass national health insurance and civil rights laws.

The Eisenhower Years *(page 798)*

Making Inferences

Reread the passage. Underline the examples that support this inference:

Eisenhower wanted to help people in need.

In 1952, the Republicans chose General Dwight Eisenhower as their candidate for president. Eisenhower was very popular and went by the name "Ike." He easily won the election against Democrat Adlai Stevenson.

President Eisenhower believed in **dynamic conservatism.** This was a balance of conservative economics and social activism. The president made many conservative decisions. He chose business leaders for his cabinet and stopped government price controls. Furthermore, he halted aid to businesses, schools, and public housing.

However, the president increased Social Security benefits and the minimum wage. Eisenhower's programs also helped farmers and people without jobs. He pushed for public works projects. The Federal Highway Act of 1956 spent $25 billion to build interstate highways. These programs helped him win a second term in 1956.

Section Wrap-up

Answer these questions to check your understanding of the entire section.

1. What were the results of the 1946 election?

2. What changes did President Eisenhower's dynamic conservatism bring to the economy?

Persuasive Writing

Write a letter to your neighbor asking him or her to vote for President Truman in the upcoming 1948 election. Include several reasons why you think that President Truman should be reelected.

Chapter 23, Section 2 (Pages 800–807)

The Affluent Society

Big Idea

As you read pages 800–807 in your textbook, complete the time line by recording some major events of scientific, technological, and popular culture during the 1950s.

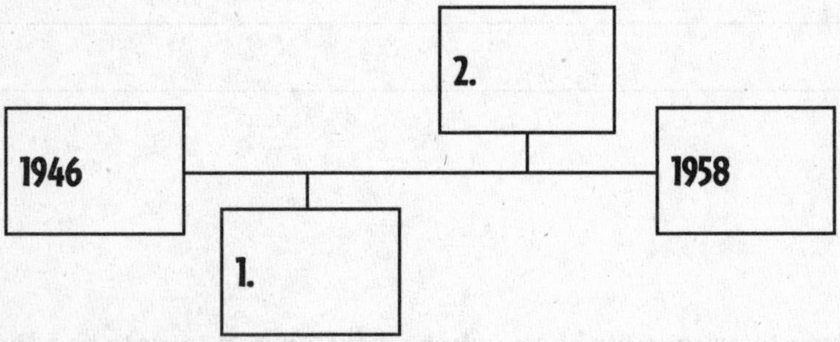

Notes | Read to Learn

American Abundance *(page 800)*

Identifying the Main Idea

Write the main idea of the passage.

____

____

____

____

____

____

____

____

The 1950s was a decade of wealth. New businesses and technology produced many new goods and services. Americans earned more money than ever before, and they spent it on new goods such as refrigerators. Advertising increased as businesses pressed Americans to buy their goods. Much of it was aimed at people living in new mass-produced suburbs that grew around large cities. As people left the crowded cities, the population of the suburbs doubled. The suburbs offered inexpensive homes that people could buy with low-interest loans and money from income tax deductions. Many new homeowners and others started families between 1945 and 1961. This period is called the **baby boom,** and more than 65 million children were born.

Fewer **blue-collar workers,** or laborers, were needed to work on farms or in factories. More Americans took **white-collar jobs,** or office jobs, in large corporations. Many corporations became **multinational corporations** by moving overseas, often near important resources. **Franchises** also sprung up across the nation. In a franchise, a person owns and runs one of several stores of a chain operation.

Notes | Read to Learn

Scientific Advances *(page 802)*

Making Generalizations

Read the summary and then complete the statement below.

Advances in electronics and medicine helped to make people's lives ___________ and ___________.

The United States witnessed many advances in electronics and medicine after World War II. In 1947, American scientists developed a small tool called a transistor. This led to the invention of small portable radios and calculators. Scientists created one of the earliest computers in 1946. Soon after, newer models were being used by businesses. The computers and other changes helped people work quickly and efficiently. Americans began to enjoy more free time for leisure activities.

Advances in medicine ended or reduced the threat of many diseases. New treatments for cancer and heart disease, such as chemotherapy and CPR, helped patients survive. New antibiotics cured deadly diseases. Polio, however, was still a large problem. The disease attacked the young and caused death. Then Jonas Salk and later Albert Sabin created a vaccine. The threat of polio almost disappeared in the years that followed.

The New Mass Media *(page 804)*

Problems and Solutions

The rise of television led to problems in other industries. Read the summary. Write the letter P next to the sentences that describe these problems. Write the letter S next to the sentences that describe the solutions.

Televisions were popular household fixtures by the end of the 1950s. Approximately 40 million television sets were in use by 1957. Television programs included comedy, action and adventure, and variety shows. In 1953, Lucille Ball starred in the popular show *I Love Lucy.* Americans enjoyed the action show The *Lone Ranger* and the police show *Dragnet.* Television news became an important source of information. Variety shows, quiz shows, and televised sports were also popular. However, as people watched more television, they stopped watching movies.

One-fifth of the nation's movie theaters had closed by 1960. Hollywood tried to make films more exciting. They tried contests, prizes, and even 3-D films. These plans did not bring people back to the theaters. Full-colored movies shown on large, wide screens brought people back. These kinds of movies were expensive to make, but they drew in audiences and made large profits.

Television also took away radio listeners. The radio industry looked for new ways to draw listeners. Many radio stations began to broadcast music, news, and talk shows for people in their cars. Radio stations survived and the industry grew. The number of radio stations more than doubled to more than 3,600 between 1948 and 1957.

Notes

Read to Learn

New Music and Poetry *(page 805)*

Detecting Bias

Circle the group that may not have appreciated rock 'n' roll music. Explain why.

teens

beats

African Americans

In the 1950s, the sounds of African American rhythm and blues music was the basis for a new type of music called **rock 'n' roll.** American teens loved the music and its themes. They rushed to buy records from Buddy Holly, Elvis Presley, and other artists. Many parents thought rock 'n' roll was loud, mindless, and dangerous. This music, along with new types of clothing and literature, united teens. The result was a **generation gap,** or a cultural separation between children and their parents.

During the 1950s, white artists who called themselves **beats** criticized American life. The beats used poetry and literature to attack American popular culture and values. African American artists looked for acceptance in the nation. Instead, they were mostly rejected by television and mass media while finding some acceptance through their music.

Section Wrap-up

Answer these questions to check your understanding of the entire section.

1. What led to the growth of suburbs?

2. What types of programs did television show in the 1950s?

Descriptive Writing

In the space provided write a short poem about the economy or society of the United States in the 1950s. You might write your poem from a beat's perspective.

The Other Side of American Life

Big Idea

As you read pages 810–815 in your textbook, complete the outline using the major headings of the section.

The Other Side of American Life

I. Poverty Amidst Prosperity
   A. ______
   B. ______
   C. ______
   D. ______
   E. ______
II. ______

Notes

Read to Learn

Poverty Amidst Prosperity *(page 810)*

Formulating Questions

Place an X next to the question best answered by the passage.

____ ***What were urban renewal projects?***

____ ***What groups of Americans suffered from poverty in the 1950s?***

Many Americans prospered during the 1950s. However, more than 30 million Americans lived below the **poverty line,** the lowest income needed to support a family. Many were African Americans, some of the approximately 3 million who had moved north after 1940. They came to find work and better lives but found racial discrimination, few jobs, and low pay. The cities failed to offer adequate housing, schools, or medical care. Government **urban renewal** programs built new public housing but often increased crime and poverty and destroyed more homes than they built.

Hispanics in the United States also faced poverty. Nearly 5 million Mexicans came to work on farms and ranches during the 1950s and 1960s. Called braceros, these people worked long hours for low pay. Native Americans were the poorest group in the nation. The government's **termination policy** forced many to move off of reservations and into cities and made them subject to the same laws and conditions as other Americans. Many white families in Appalachia also faced difficulties. Work, doctors, and nutritious foods were all scarce there.

Notes

Read to Learn

Juvenile Delinquency *(page 815)*

Distinguishing Fact from Opinion

Read the second paragraph of the passage. Circle three sentences that describe opinions.

Drawing Conclusions

Write a conclusion you can draw based on the passage.

Another problem facing the nation was **juvenile delinquency,** or the antisocial and criminal behavior of young people. Juvenile crime rose by 45 percent between 1948 and 1953. A 1954 book titled *1,000,000 Delinquents* claimed that by 1955 one million young people would get into trouble. The book was correct. Americans searched for the causes.

Experts blamed juvenile delinquency on several causes. They blamed it on a lack of religion and discipline. Others claimed that television, movies, and comic books were the causes. A number of experts pointed the finger at the rising divorce rate and fears of the military draft. Some critics said that young people were just acting out against tradition. Bishop Fulton J. Sheen stated that Americans were raising bored children. He claimed children were looking for new ways to have fun. Many tried to link delinquency with poverty. However, delinquency involved children from all classes and races in American society. Most teens were not involved in crime or drugs, but the public came to think of all young people as juvenile delinquents. Many parents thought that improving the nation's schools was the solution to delinquency.

In the 1950s, the baby boomers began entering the school system. The number of school children increased by 13 million. School districts struggled to pay for new schools and new teachers. Americans became even more concerned about education after 1957. In that year, the Soviet Union launched the world's first satellites. Americans were afraid of falling behind their Cold War enemy. They believed that schools lacked technical education. New efforts were made to improve math and science education in the schools.

Section Wrap-up

Answer these questions to check your understanding of the entire section.

1. What was the result of urban renewal programs?

2. What were some concerns about the educational system in the United States during the 1950s?

Expository Writing

Compare the experiences of African Americans in the inner cities with Hispanics and Native Americans. What did these groups have in common?

Chapter 24, Section 1 (Pages 824–829)

The New Frontier

Big Idea

As you read pages 824–829 in your textbook, complete the graphic organizer by listing some domestic successes and setbacks of Kennedy's administration.

Successes	Setbacks
1.	4.
2.	5.
3.	6.

Notes

Read to Learn

The Election of 1960 *(page 824)*

Making Inferences

Read the passage to answer the question below.

Americans saw Kennedy as youthful and optimistic. How do you think they viewed Nixon?

____

____

____

____

____

____

The presidential election of 1960 centered on the economy and the Cold War. Television played an important part in the election. The Democrats nominated John F. Kennedy, a Catholic from a wealthy Massachusetts family. The Republicans nominated Vice President Richard M. Nixon, a Quaker from California who had simple beginnings.

The candidates' opinions on the economy and the Cold War were similar. Kennedy believed that the Soviets were a serious threat. He was concerned about a **"missile gap."** He believed that the United States had fallen behind the Soviet Union in the number of weapons it had. Nixon felt that the Democrats' plans would boost inflation. He also believed that he had the foreign policy experience needed to lead the nation.

Kennedy's religion became an issue in the campaign. The United States had never had a Catholic president and many Protestants were concerned about Kennedy's loyalties. Kennedy emphasized his belief in the separation of church and state. Four televised presidential debates also influenced voters. Kennedy's youth and optimism made him popular. He narrowly won the popular vote and the Electoral College to become president.

Notes

Read to Learn

Kennedy Takes Office *(page 825)*

Identifying the Main Idea

Reread the passage. Fill in the missing words of the main idea.

Although __________ refused to pass many of Kennedy's programs, the president was able to enact legislation helping groups such as __________ and the disabled.

After Kennedy was elected, he sent his New Frontier legislation to Congress. Kennedy had little support in Congress and found it difficult to get his programs passed. The Democrats in Congress followed their own interests instead of the president's. Southern Democrats and Republicans also viewed the New Frontier as too expensive.

However, some of Kennedy's economic programs were passed. In the late 1950s, unemployment was high and the economic growth rate was low. Kennedy suggested deficit spending to boost the economy. He convinced Congress to spend more on defense and space exploration. This created more jobs and grew the economy. He also asked business leaders to keep prices and pay increases down. Kennedy pushed for tax cuts as well, but was unsuccessful. However, Kennedy increased the minimum wage and passed public works projects.

Many women held important positions in Kennedy's administration. He even issued an executive order to end gender discrimination in the federal civil service. In 1963, he signed the Equal Pay Act for women.

Warren Court Reforms *(page 828)*

Problems and Solutions

In the passage, underline the solution to the problem below.

Problem: By 1960 more people lived in urban areas, but rural districts had more representation.

In 1953 Earl Warren became the chief justice of the United States. The Warren Court issued several rulings that reshaped American society. It made important decisions about **reapportionment,** which is the way states drew up political districts based on changes in population. By 1960 more people lived in urban areas than rural areas. However, many states had not changed their electoral districts to match. The Court ruled that the system was unconstitutional. The ruling forced states to reapportion electoral districts. It gave people's votes equal weight.

The Supreme Court also began to use the Fourteenth Amendment to apply the Bill of Rights to the states. This amendment ruled that states could not deprive individuals of the right to **due process.** This meant that the law could not treat individuals unfairly or unreasonably. It also meant that the courts had to follow correct procedures and rules to try cases. Using due process applied the federal Bill of Rights to the states. In other rulings, the Court did not allow states to use evidence found illegally. It also stated that defendants had the right to lawyers and to be told they could stay silent before questioning. It also bolstered the separation of church and state.

Section Wrap-up

Answer these questions to check your understanding of the entire section.

1. Why was John F. Kennedy's religion an issue in the 1960 election, and how did Kennedy deal with this issue?

2. How did Kennedy help the economy of the United States in the early 1960s?

Descriptive Writing

You just watched one of the televised presidential debates between John F. Kennedy and Vice President Nixon. Write a summary for a friend who missed it. Describe the two men and their political views.

Chapter 24, Section 2 (Pages 830–835)

JFK and the Cold War

Big Idea

As you read pages 830–835 in your textbook, complete the time line to record some of the major events of the Cold War in the late 1950s and early 1960s.

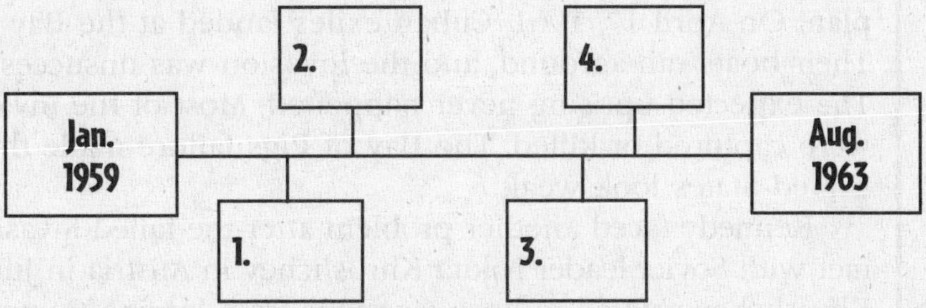

Notes

Read to Learn

Containing Communism (*page 830*)

Analyzing Information

Read the passage to answer the question below.

What two things did Kennedy do to help fight the spread of communism in Latin America?

1. ______________________

____

2. ______________________

____

Kennedy tried to reduce the threat of nuclear war and contain communism. He wanted the option of a **flexible response,** in which conventional troops and weapons could be used to contain communism. He expanded the Special Forces. This army unit used guerilla warfare in limited conflicts.

Kennedy also tried to improve relations with Latin America. Many governments there were controlled by the wealthy few. Most of the people lived in poverty. In some countries, leftist groups tried to overthrow their governments. To improve conditions in Latin America, Kennedy proposed an Alliance for Progress. This was a series of aid projects in which the United States promised $20 billion to help these countries. The projects set up better schools, housing, and health care.

The United States and the Soviet Union also competed in a **space race** in which both superpowers attempted to dominate space technology. In 1961 the Soviets launched the first person into space. A few weeks later, Kennedy made a speech in which he announced the goal of landing a man on the moon before the end of the decade. In 1969 the United States achieved this goal.

Notes

Read to Learn

Crises of the Cold War *(page 833)*

Drawing Conclusions

Review the summary. Circle the sentences that support the following conclusion.

The United States feared a Communist Cuba and tried to eliminate this threat by any means.

Distinguishing Fact from Opinion

Underline the sentence that describes Kennedy's opinion about Soviet missiles in Cuba.

President Kennedy faced several crises in the Cold War. The first one started when Fidel Castro seized power in Cuba in 1959. Castro established ties with the Soviet Union. He also took over American and other foreign-owned businesses located in Cuba. Americans believed that the Soviets wanted to use Cuba as a base to spread communism in the Western Hemisphere. Eisenhower authorized the CIA to arm Cuban exiles and train them to invade Cuba, hoping that the invasion would start an uprising. When he became president, Kennedy approved the plan. On April 17, 1961, Cuban exiles landed at the Bay of Pigs. Their boats ran aground, and the invasion was unsuccessful. The expected uprising never happened. Most of the invaders were captured or killed. The Bay of Pigs failure made the United States look weak.

Kennedy faced another problem after the failed invasion. He met with Soviet leader Nikita Khrushchev in Austria in June 1961. Khrushchev wanted to keep Germans from leaving Communist East Germany and fleeing to West Berlin. He demanded that Western powers leave Berlin. When Kennedy refused, the Soviets built the Berlin Wall. It was guarded by armed soldiers who shot at people attempting to escape. The wall separated East Berlin from West Berlin for nearly 30 years.

In 1962 the United States learned that Soviet workers and equipment had arrived in Cuba. On October 22, 1962, Kennedy told Americans that photos taken by spy planes showed that the Soviets had placed missiles in Cuba. He believed that the weapons threatened the United States. He then ordered a naval blockade to stop more missiles from being delivered to Cuba. However, the Soviets continued to work on the missile sites.

The leaders of the two countries began secret talks. Both nations reached an agreement on October 28. The United States publicly agreed not to attack Cuba and privately agreed to remove its own missiles from Turkey. The Soviet Union agreed to remove the missiles from Cuba. The Cuban missile crisis brought the world close to nuclear war. It made the Soviet Union and United States see the dangers of nuclear war. They agreed to a treaty that banned testing of nuclear weapons in the atmosphere.

On November 22, 1963, President Kennedy was shot and killed while visiting Dallas, Texas. Lee Harvey Oswald, the man accused of killing the president, was then shot and killed while in police custody. In 1964 a commission headed by Chief Justice Warren stated that Oswald acted alone. The United States and the world mourned the loss of President Kennedy.

Section Wrap-up

Answer these questions to check your understanding of the entire section.

1. How was Kennedy's military policy different from Eisenhower's?

2. What were the results of the Cuban missile crisis?

Persuasive Writing

Some people think that the Alliance for Progress is not a good use of money. Use a television ad to help change their minds. Write a script for a short television commercial that supports President Kennedy's program.

Chapter 24, Section 3 (Pages 838–843)

The Great Society

Big Idea

As you read pages 838–843 in your textbook, complete the graphic organizer to list some social and economic programs started during Johnson's administration.

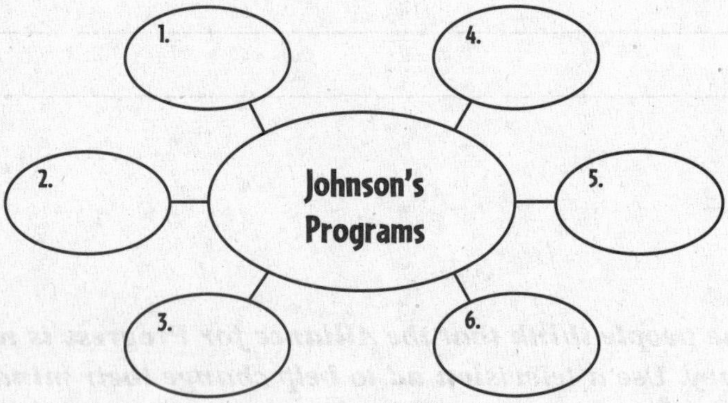

Notes

Read to Learn

Johnson Takes the Reins *(page 838)*

Formulating Questions

Write a question that might help you learn more about the "War on Poverty."

____

____

____

____

____

____

____

____

Vice President Lyndon Johnson was sworn in as president hours after Kennedy's death. Johnson had served in Congress for 26 years, developing a reputation as someone who got things done. Johnson always tried to build **consensus,** or general agreement. Unlike Kennedy, Johnson was not an elegant society man. His image was that of a plainspoken Texan.

Johnson wanted to push Kennedy's antipoverty and civil rights programs through Congress. He believed that governments should improve their citizens' lives. In his State of the Union address in 1964, Johnson declared a "War on Poverty in America." By the summer of 1964, he persuaded Congress to pass the Economic Opportunity Act. The act created new jobs. It established the Office of Economic Opportunity to coordinate new programs. Many of these programs were aimed at inner-city youth. The Neighborhood Youth Corps provided a work-study program. The Job Corps helped unemployed young people learn job skills. The VISTA program operated like a domestic Peace Corps for poor neighborhoods and rural areas. Johnson was reelected in 1964.

Notes

Read to Learn

The Great Society *(page 841)*

Synthesizing Information

Review the second and third paragraph of the summary. Place an X next to the sentence below that is true.

____ ***The Great Society targeted the health, education, and housing of the poor.***

____ ***The Great Society's main focus was on immigration reform.***

____ ***Medicare and Medicaid were the only successful Great Society programs.***

Determining Cause and Effect

Write the effect that goes with the cause below.

Cause: Money was needed for the war in Vietnam.

Effect:

____

____

____

____

____

President Johnson began his domestic programs soon after the election. He called them the "Great Society." The Civil Rights Act of 1964 was passed during his administration. This met many of the goals of the civil rights movement. The Voting Rights Act of 1965 also ensured that African Americans had the right to vote. Johnson's programs were passed for many reasons. The civil rights movement brought many of the problems of African Americans to light. Also, the economy was strong, so Americans thought that poverty could be reduced.

More than 60 of Johnson's programs were passed between 1965 and 1968. Among these were Medicare and Medicaid. Medicare is a health insurance program for the elderly. Medicaid provides health care for people on welfare. Other programs supported education. The Elementary and Secondary Education Act of 1965 gave millions of dollars to public and private schools. This paid for books and other educational materials. Project Head Start is an education program for poor preschool children. College preparation for low-income teenagers was offered through the Upward Bound program.

Johnson also urged Congress to pass laws that would help inner-city neighborhoods. One law created a new agency called the Department of Housing and Urban Development. It was led by Robert Weaver. He was the first African American to serve in a president's cabinet. Other laws gave federal funding to many city programs. These programs spent billions of dollars on transportation, healthcare, and housing.

One law changed the makeup of the American population. The Immigration Reform Act of 1965 continued to limit the number of immigrants allowed in the United States each year. However, it ended the national origin system. That system gave preference to immigrants from Northern Europe. The new law allowed immigration from all of Europe, Asia, and Africa.

The Great Society programs improved the lives of many Americans. However, people debated the programs' success. Many of these programs had been created quickly and did not work well. Some people believed that the federal government had become too involved in people's lives. The programs were also expensive. When money was needed for the war in Vietnam, the programs lost funding. However, some programs and agencies still exist today. They include Medicare, Medicaid, and Project Head Start. The Department of Housing and Urban Development and the Department of Transportation are two agencies that also exist today.

Section Wrap-up

Answer these questions to check your understanding of the entire section.

1. What was the purpose of the Office of Economic Opportunity?

2. What are Medicare and Medicaid?

Expository Writing

Suppose you are visiting the United States from another country. You want to share the benefits of the Great Society with people in your home country. Write a letter to a friend that lists the advantages of the Great Society's programs.

Chapter 25, Section 1 (Pages 850–857)

The Movement Begins

Big Idea

As you read pages 850–857 in your textbook, complete the graphic organizer by filling in the causes of the civil rights movement.

1.

2.

3.

Civil Right Movement

Notes

Read to Learn

The Origins of the Movement *(page 850)*

Determining Cause and Effect

List one effect of the* Brown *v.* Board of Education *decision.

The Supreme Court's 1896 decision in *Plessy* v. *Ferguson* set up a **separate but equal** policy. Laws that segregated African Americans were allowed as long as African Americans had equal places. Areas that did not have segregation laws often had **de facto segregation.** This was segregation by custom and tradition. In the 1940s members of the CORE organization began using **sit-ins,** a form of protest. CORE integrated many restaurants and public places in Northern cities.

In May 1954 the Supreme Court ruled in *Brown* v. *Board of Education* that segregation violated the Fourteenth Amendment. The ruling signaled to African Americans that it was time to challenge other forms of segregation. The *Brown* decision also upset many white Southerners. Many ignored the Supreme Court's ruling and kept schools segregated for years.

On December 1, 1955, Rosa Parks was arrested in Montgomery, Alabama, for refusing to give up her bus seat to a white person. She challenged bus segregation in court. African Americans in Montgomery quickly started a boycott of the bus system. In the next few years, boycotts and protests spread across the nation.

Notes | Read to Learn

The Civil Rights Movement Begins *(page 854)*

Making Generalizations

Read the passage above and then complete the statement below.

Martin Luther King, Jr., became an influential civil rights leader because

____

____

____

____

____

The Montgomery bus boycott marked the beginning of the civil rights movement among African Americans. The boycott was a success. Some African American leaders formed the Montgomery Improvement Association, which worked with city leaders to end segregation. The MIA chose the young minister Martin Luther King, Jr., to lead the group. King believed the way to end segregation was through nonviolent methods. This approach was based on the ideas of Mohandas Gandhi. A powerful speaker, King encouraged his listeners to disobey unjust laws. The Supreme Court decided Rosa Parks' case in 1956. It said that Alabama's bus segregation laws were unconstitutional.

African American churches and ministers played an important part in the success of the boycott. People met at churches to plan and organize protest meetings. African American ministers set up the Southern Christian Leadership Conference in 1957. King was the SCLC's first president. The SCLC set out to end segregation in America. It also pushed African Americans to register to vote. The group challenged segregation of public transportation and other public places.

Eisenhower Responds *(page 857)*

Making Inferences

Underline the parts of the summary that support the following inference:

Inference: President Eisenhower believed in putting the law above his personal beliefs.

____

____

____

____

____

____

President Eisenhower personally opposed segregation. But he disagreed with those who wanted to end it through protests and court rulings. He believed that segregation should end gradually. Eisenhower thought that the Supreme Court's decision in *Brown* v. *Board of Education* was wrong. However, he also thought that the federal government had the duty to uphold the decision.

In September 1957 the Little Rock, Arkansas, school board won a court order to admit nine African American students to Central High School. The governor of Arkansas ordered troops from the Arkansas National Guard to prevent the nine students from entering the school. Eisenhower ordered U.S. Army troops to Little Rock to protect the students and to uphold the law.

In the same year that the Little Rock crisis took place, Congress passed the Civil Rights Act of 1957. It was intended to protect African Americans' right to vote. The law created a civil rights division within the Department of Justice. It also created the United States Commission on Civil Rights to investigate instances in which the right to vote was denied.

Section Wrap-up

Answer these questions to check your understanding of the entire section.

1. How did the Southern Christian Leadership Conference originate?

2. Describe the role of the federal government in enforcing civil rights laws.

Persuasive Writing

In the space provided write a short poem about the nine African American students trying to attend Central High School in Little Rock, Arkansas. You might write your poem from the perspective of one of the students.

Chapter 25, Section 2 (Pages 858–867)

Challenging Segregation

Big Idea

As you read pages 858–867 in your textbook, complete the cause and effect chart.

Cause	Effect
Sit-In Movement	3.
Freedom Riders	4.
1.	African American support of Kennedy
2.	African American voter registration

Notes

Read to Learn

The Sit-In Movement *(page 858)*

Distinguishing Fact from Opinion

Read the first paragraph. Underline the sentences that express or explain a person's opinion.

In 1960 four college students in Greensboro, North Carolina, staged a sit-in that touched off a new mass movement for civil rights. By 1961 sit-ins had been held in more than 100 cities. Many African American college students joined the sit-in movement. Students like Jesse Jackson thought sit-ins were a way to take things into their own hands. At first, the leaders of the NAACP and the SCLC were concerned about the sit-ins. They feared that the students might fight back if attacked. The students remained peaceful, despite being punched, kicked, and beaten.

As the sit-ins spread, student leaders realized that they needed to create an organization of their own. Ella Baker, the executive director of the SCLC, invited student leaders to a convention in Raleigh, North Carolina, where she urged them to start their own organization instead of joining SCLC or the NAACP. The students established the Student Nonviolent Coordinating Committee (SNCC). SNCC was instrumental in desegregating public places in many communities. Members of SNCC began working in the rural areas of the Deep South.

Notes

Read to Learn

The Freedom Riders *(page 860)*

Synthesizing Information

How was the reaction of segregation supporters to the early sit-ins, the Freedom Rider turnouts, and demonstrations in Birmingham similar?

In 1961 civil rights volunteers began traveling to the South. They hoped to draw attention to the South's segregation of bus terminals. These groups became known as Freedom Riders. White mobs often attacked the Freedom Riders when they arrived in Southern cities. President John F. Kennedy decided he had to do something to stop the violence. At first Kennedy seemed as cautious as Eisenhower on civil rights. Kennedy needed the support of Southern senators to get his legislation passed. He did not want to challenge these senators on the subject of civil rights.

However, Kennedy did name about 40 African Americans to high-level government jobs. He also allowed the Justice Department to actively support the civil rights movement. In addition, he ordered the Interstate Commerce Commission to tighten regulations against segregated bus terminals.

Meanwhile, activists worked to integrate public schools. African American James Meredith applied to the University of Mississippi but was denied admittance. President Kennedy ordered army troops to protect Meredith.

To force Kennedy to support civil rights, Martin Luther King, Jr., ordered demonstrations in Birmingham, Alabama. The demonstrations turned violent and were broadcast on national television. Kennedy then prepared a new civil rights bill.

The Civil Rights Act of 1964 *(page 864)*

Problems and Solutions

What did Dr. King do to help get Kennedy's civil rights bill through Congress?

In June 1963, Alabama governor George Wallace stood in front of the University of Alabama's admissions office. He was trying to stop two African Americans from enrolling. Federal marshals ordered him to move. President Kennedy used this event to present his civil rights bill.

To build support for the bill, Martin Luther King, Jr., took part in a large march in Washington, D.C. On August 28, 1963, more than 200,000 demonstrators gathered peacefully at the nation's capital. Dr. King delivered his powerful "I Have a Dream" speech. The march built support for Kennedy's civil rights bill.

In November 1963, Kennedy was assassinated. Vice President Lyndon Johnson became president. The civil rights bill passed the House of Representatives in February 1964. In the Senate, Southern Democrats participated in a **filibuster.** This means that they kept speaking and refused to allow **cloture,** or ending debate. The bill finally passed. It was the largest civil rights law Congress had ever enacted. It gave the federal government broad power to prevent racial discrimination.

Notes

Read to Learn

The Struggle for Voting Rights *(page 867)*

Formulating Questions

Place an X next to the question best answered by the passage.

____ ***Where were literacy tests most common?***

____ ***What events led to the passing of the Voting Rights Act of 1965?***

To keep the pressure on the president and Congress to act on voting rights, Dr. King and others organized an Alabama march from Selma to Montgomery. It began on March 7, 1965. At one point in the march, state troopers and deputized citizens rushed the demonstrators. The attack left more than 70 African Americans hospitalized. The nation was shocked at the brutality it saw on television. President Johnson was furious. He went before Congress to present a new voting rights law.

In August 1965, Congress passed the Voting Rights Act of 1965. It ordered federal examiners to register qualified voters. It ended discriminatory practices such as literacy tests. The civil rights movement had achieved its two goals. Segregation had been outlawed, and laws were in place to protect voting rights.

Section Wrap-up

Answer these questions to check your understanding of the entire section.

1. Why was Kennedy cautious about supporting civil rights when he first took office?

____

2. By the end of 1965, what two major goals had the civil rights movement achieved?

____

____

Persuasive Writing

Suppose it is February of 1965 and Martin Luther King, Jr., has asked you whether he should organize a march from Selma to Montgomery. King is worried the march may turn violent. Write a letter to Dr. King giving your opinion.

____

____

____

____

____

____

Chapter 25, Section 3 (Pages 870–875)

New Civil Rights Issues

Big Idea

As you read pages 870–875 in your textbook, complete the chart by filling in three major violent events and their results.

Event	Result
1.	
2.	
3.	

Notes

Read to Learn

Urban Problems *(page 870)*

Identifying the Main Idea

Write the main idea of the passage.

In the 1960s, **racism**, discrimination toward someone because of his or her race, was still common. In 1965 about 70 percent of African Americans lived in large cities. They were often trapped by poverty in the inner city. They were aware of the gains made by the civil rights movement, but knew the gains did not address their social and economic problems. Their anger at the situation erupted into violence. Race riots broke out around the country. Thirty-four people were killed during a six-day riot in Watts, a neighborhood in Los Angeles. The worst riot occurred in Detroit in 1967. The U.S. Army was called in to control the situation.

President Johnson picked Otto Kerner to head a commission to look at the causes of the riots. It blamed racism for most of the problems in the inner city and recommended more jobs and housing for African Americans. In 1965 Dr. King decided to focus on improving the economic conditions of African Americans. He and his wife moved into a slum apartment in Chicago to call attention to the problems there. The Chicago Movement was largely unsuccessful in ending urban poverty.

Notes

Read to Learn

Black Power *(page 872)*

Comparing and Contrasting

How did Black Panthers' view of violence differ from that of Dr. Martin Luther King, Jr.?

____

____

____

____

____

____

____

____

____

Dr. King's failure in Chicago convinced some African Americans that nonviolence was not the solution to their problems. Many poor, young African Americans turned away from King's movement. They turned to more aggressive forms of protest. Many called for **black power.** A few believed that the term meant that self-defense and violence were acceptable when defending one's freedom. Others thought that black power meant that African Americans should control the social, political, and economic direction of their struggle for equality. Black power stressed pride in African American culture. It rejected the idea that African Americans should try to imitate white society. Black power was very popular in the poor urban neighborhoods where many African Americans lived.

By the early 1960s, Malcolm X had become the symbol of black power. He gained fame as part of the Nation of Islam, or the Black Muslims, but by 1964 he had broken with the group. He started to believe, unlike the Black Muslims, that an integrated society was possible. In February 1965 members of the Nation of Islam killed Malcolm X in New York. Malcolm X is remembered for encouraging African Americans to believe in their abilities to make their own way in the world.

Malcolm X's ideas affected a new generation of militant African American leaders. One group, the Black Panthers, preached black power, black nationalism, and economic self-sufficiency. The Black Panthers believed a revolution was necessary. They urged African Americans to arm themselves and confront white society to force whites to grant them equal rights.

Martin Luther King, Jr., Is Killed *(page 875)*

Determining Cause and Effect

Write one effect.
Cause: Dr. King is assassinated.

Effect: _______________

____

____

____

By the late 1960s, the civil rights movement was divided. Some African Americans called for violent action. This angered many white supporters of the civil rights movement.

In 1968 Dr. Martin Luther King, Jr., went to Memphis, Tennessee, to support a strike of African American sanitation workers. On April 4 he was shot to death as he stood on his hotel balcony. King's death touched off riots in more than 100 cities. After Dr. King's death, Congress passed the Civil Rights Act of 1968. The law banned discrimination in the sale and rental of housing. The civil rights movement continued, but it lacked the vision that Dr. King had given it. Still, the movement had created many new opportunities for African Americans in the 1950s and 1960s.

Section Wrap-up

Answer these questions to check your understanding of the entire section.

1. What division arose between Dr. King and the black power movement?

2. Why did the civil rights movement lose its focus after 1968?

Informative Writing

In the space provided write a brief history of the black power movement. Be sure to include any important dates, events, and key figures from the passages.

Chapter 26, Section 1 (Pages 882–889)

Going to War in Vietnam

Big Idea

As you read pages 882–889 in your textbook, complete the graphic organizer by providing reasons that the United States aided France in Vietnam.

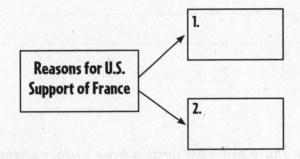

Reasons for U.S. Support of France

1.

2.

Notes

Read to Learn

American Involvement in Vietnam *(page 882)*

Making Inferences

Why do you think guerrilla troops try to look like civilians?

____

____

____

____

____

____

____

____

From the late 1800s, France ruled Vietnam. By the early 1900s, several political parties wanted independence from France. One of the leaders of the movement was Ho Chi Minh. In 1941, after Japan had taken control of Vietnam, Ho Chi Minh organized a group called the Vietminh to try to get rid of the Japanese. When Japan was defeated in 1945, it gave up control of Vietnam. France asked the United States to regain control of Vietnam. The United States did not want Vietnam to be communist, so it agreed. President Eisenhower continued to support the French because he believed in the **domino theory,** which said that if Vietnam fell to communism, other Southeast Asian nations would also.

The Vietminh used **guerrillas,** or irregular troops who look like civilians and are difficult to fight. In 1954 the Vietminh defeated the French at Dien Bien Phu. Negotiations to end the conflict took place in Geneva, Switzerland. Vietnam was divided into North Vietnam and South Vietnam. Ho Chi Minh and the Vietminh controlled North Vietnam. A pro-Western regime controlled South Vietnam.

Notes

Read to Learn

America Becomes Involved in Vietnam *(page 885)*

Analyzing Information

How did the Gulf of Tonkin Resolution benefit President Johnson?

Ho Chi Minh tried to reunify Vietnam by force. He started a new guerrilla army called the Vietcong. Eisenhower sent military advisers to help South Vietnam, but the Vietcong's power increased. President Kennedy continued to support South Vietnam. The United States believed that the Vietcong were popular because South Vietnam's government, led by Ngo Dinh Diem, was corrupt. Several Vietnamese generals overthrew Diem and executed him. After his death, the government became even more unstable. The United States became even more involved as it tried to support the weak South Vietnamese government. Shortly after Diem's death, Kennedy was assassinated. The conflict in Vietnam fell to President Johnson.

President Johnson was determined to stop Vietnam from becoming communist. Johnson asked Congress for authorization to use force to defend American forces. Congress passed the Gulf of Tonkin Resolution. It essentially handed over war powers to the president. Shortly afterward, the Vietcong began to attack American bases. Johnson ordered American aircraft to strike North Vietnam. In March 1965 Johnson began a bombing campaign against North Vietnam and ordered the first American combat troops into Vietnam.

A Bloody Stalemate *(page 888)*

Synthesizing Information

Reread the passage. Underline the reasons that American troops could not defeat the Vietcong.

The Vietcong used ambushes and booby traps. They blended into the civilian population and vanished. American troops tried to find the enemy and bomb their positions, destroy their supply lines, and force them into the open. To prevent the Vietcong from hiding in the jungles, American planes dropped **napalm,** a jellied gasoline that explodes on contact. They also used **Agent Orange,** a chemical that strips leaves from trees.

American military leaders believed that continuous bombing and the killing of many Vietcong would make them surrender. However, the guerrillas did not surrender. North Vietnam received supplies from the Soviet Union and China, and then sent supplies to South Vietnam through a network known as the Ho Chi Minh trail. President Johnson did not order an invasion of North Vietnam because he feared this would bring China into the war. Instead of conquering enemy territory, American troops tried to defeat the enemy by slowly wearing them down. As casualties on both sides mounted through 1967, the Vietcong still showed no sign of surrendering.

Section Wrap-up

Answer these questions to check your understanding of the entire section.

1. Why did Ho Chi Minh organize the Vietminh?

2. Why did the United States want to prevent Vietnam from becoming communist?

Expository Writing

In the space provided write a short essay describing the military tactics of the Vietcong and explain how American military forces tried to counter these tactics.

Chapter 26, Section 2 (Pages 892–897)

Vietnam Divides the Nation

Big Idea

As you read pages 892–897 in your textbook, complete the graphic organizer by listing the reasons for opposition to the war.

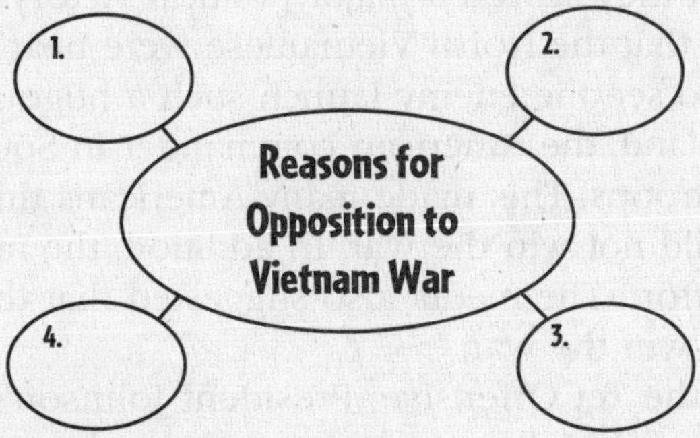

Notes

Read to Learn

An Antiwar Movement Emerges *(page 892)*

Determining Cause and Effect

Write the effect that goes with the cause.

Cause: People saw images of wounded and dead American soldiers in the media.

Effect:

____

____

____

____

____

Opposition to the Vietnam War grew in the late 1960s. Many Americans believed a **credibility gap** had developed. Images of wounded and dead American soldiers in the media made Americans doubt the government's truthfulness about the war. Many college students protested the war. Some held **teach-ins,** or informal discussions about the war.

People opposed the war for different reasons. Some believed it was a civil war that did not involve the United States. Others believed South Vietnam was a corrupt dictatorship, and supporting it was immoral. Some were against the draft system. At the beginning of the war, college students were able to postpone military service until after they graduated. Minorities and young people from low-income families were more likely to serve in the war because they could not afford college. In 1969 the government issued a lottery system for the draft. Despite the antiwar protests, a majority of people in early 1968 supported the war. Those who wanted to withdraw from Vietnam were called **doves.** Those who wanted to stay and fight were called **hawks.**

Notes

Read to Learn

1968: The Pivotal Year *(page 895)*

Predicting

Reread the passage. Underline the sentences that help you predict what Nixon will do as president.

Making Generalizations

Place an X next to the generalization that the passage supports.

___ ***1968 was a difficult year for the United States.***

___ ***In 1968, most Americans supported the Vietnam War.***

On January 30, 1968, the Vietcong and North Vietnamese launched a surprise attack during Tet, the Vietnamese New Year. It was called the Tet Offensive. Guerrillas attacked American airbases in South Vietnam and most of the South's major cities. After about a month of fighting, the American and South Vietnamese soldiers fended off the enemy troops.

In the Tet Offensive, the North Vietnamese suffered heavy losses, but they scored a major political victory. Americans had been told that the North Vietnamese were near defeat. They were shocked to see the enemy launch such a huge attack. General Westmoreland, the American commander in South Vietnam, called for more troops. This made many Americans think that the United States could not win the war. In addition, the media criticized the military effort. The media also suggested that the United States could not win the war.

After the Tet Offensive, President Johnson's approval rating fell. As a result, Johnson announced that he would not run for reelection in 1968. Even before his announcement, Democrats began looking for a different candidate. Eugene McCarthy, a dove, announced his candidacy in November 1967. Senator Robert Kennedy also declared that he would run.

In April 1968 Dr. Martin Luther King, Jr., was killed. This led to riots in several cities. In June 1968, Senator Robert Kennedy was shot and killed after winning California's Democratic primary. Violence continued in 1968 with a clash between police and protesters at the Democratic National Convention in Chicago. Protesters demanded that the Democrats adopt an antiwar platform.

The delegates to the convention chose Johnson's vice president, Hubert Humphrey, as their presidential nominee. At the same time, protesters and police began fighting near the convention hall. A riot broke out on the streets of downtown Chicago.

Richard Nixon was the Republican presidential candidate. He benefited from the violence associated with the Democratic Party. Nixon promised to restore law and order. He also announced that he had a plan to end the Vietnam War. Nixon defeated Humphrey.

Section Wrap-up

Answer these questions to check your understanding of the entire section.

1. Why did some Americans consider the draft system unfair?

2. What was the Tet Offensive, and how did it affect American perceptions of the war?

Descriptive Writing

In the space provided write about an antiwar demonstration in the late 1960s as if you were actually there. What position on the war would you take? What might you see and hear?

Chapter 26, Section 3 (Pages 898–903)

The War Winds Down

Big Idea

As you read pages 898–903 in your textbook, complete the graphic organizer by listing some steps that President Nixon took to end American involvement in Vietnam.

Steps Nixon Took
1.
2.
3.
4.

Notes

Read to Learn

Nixon Moves to End the War *(page 898)*

Problems and Solutions

In the passage, underline President Nixon's solution to the following problem:

Problem: After the 1972 election, peace talks with North Vietnam broke down.

President Nixon appointed Henry Kissinger to use diplomacy to end the war. Kissinger started a policy called **linkage,** in which the United States tried to persuade the Soviet Union and China to reduce aid to North Vietnam. Kissinger also began talks with a North Vietnamese negotiator. Nixon set up a plan called **Vietnamization,** which called for a gradual withdrawal of American troops. He still kept some troops in Vietnam to preserve America's strength during negotiations. In April 1970 Nixon announced that American troops had invaded Cambodia to destroy Vietcong bases there. Members of Congress were upset with the president for not notifying them of this plan and repealed the Gulf of Tonkin Resolution.

By 1971 most Americans wanted to end the war. In October 1972 Kissinger announced that peace was near. Nixon won the 1972 election. Soon after, peace talks broke down. Nixon began bombing raids to force North Vietnam to resume talks. In January 1973 an agreement was signed to end the war. The United States began to withdraw. In March 1975 North Vietnam invaded South Vietnam and reunited the country under communist rule.

Notes

Read to Learn

The Legacy of Vietnam *(page 902)*

Identifying the Main Idea

Reread the passage and circle details that support the following main idea:

Main idea: The Vietnam War left lasting effects on the United States.

Drawing Conclusions

Reread the second paragraph of the passage. What is one conclusion you can draw about veterans of the Vietnam War?

____

____

____

____

____

____

Americans hoped to put the Vietnam War behind them. Still, the war had lasting effects on the United States. It had cost more than $170 billion. It resulted in the deaths of about 58,000 Americans. More than 300,000 were injured. About one million North and South Vietnamese soldiers died. Countless Vietnamese civilians lost their lives as well.

The war had a psychological impact on American soldiers. Many Americans considered Vietnam a defeat. They wanted to forget the war. As a result, the sacrifices made by many veterans often went unrecognized. There were few welcome-home parades for American soldiers. The war continued for many American families whose relatives were prisoners of war (POWs) or missing in action (MIA). In spite of many official investigations, some families continued to believe that the government lied about its POW/MIA policies. In 1982 the Vietnam Veterans Memorial in Washington, D.C., was dedicated to help Americans come to terms with the war.

In 1973 Congress passed the War Powers Act. The Act attempted to set limits on the power of the president. The law required the president to inform Congress of any commitment of troops within 48 hours. It also required the president to withdraw troops in 60 to 90 days unless Congress approved the troop commitment. No president has ever recognized this law. However, presidents do ask Congress for authorization before sending troops into combat.

After the Vietnam War, many Americans became more reluctant to involve the United States in the affairs of other nations. The Vietnam War also made Americans more cynical about their government. Many believed that the government had misled them.

Section Wrap-up ***Answer these questions to check your understanding of the entire section.***

1. How did Henry Kissinger try to use diplomacy to end the Vietnam War?

2. How did the Vietnam War change many Americans' feelings about their government?

Informative Writing ***In the space provided write an essay detailing the experiences of veterans returning from the Vietnam War to American society.***

Chapter 27, Section 1 (Pages 910–913)

Students and the Counterculture

Big Idea

As you read pages 910–913 in your textbook, complete the outline using the major headings of the section.

Students and the Counterculture

I. The Rise of the Youth Movement
A. ______________________
B. ______________________
C. ______________________
II. ______________________
A. ______________________
B. ______________________

Notes | Read to Learn

The Rise of the Youth Movement (page 910)

Identifying the Main Idea

Write an X by the main idea of the passage.

1. ___ The youth protest movement was most active on college campuses.

2. ___ Young people challenged America's political and social systems during the 1960s.

The 1960s saw the rise of a youth movement that challenged American politics and society. Because of the baby boom, the number of young people attending college in the early 1960s increased. College life enabled them to bond and share feelings about society. This led to the youth protest movement, which began and peaked on college campuses across the country.

Young people concerned about the injustices they saw in the nation's political and social systems formed the "New Left." One famous group of activists was the Students for a Democratic Society (SDS). SDS wrote a declaration in 1962 that called for an end to apathy. It focused on protesting the Vietnam War as well as issues such as poverty and racism.

Other activists formed the Free Speech Movement at the University of California at Berkeley in 1964. They were reacting to a restriction of their rights on campus by the University administration. Arrests of 700 protesters led to even larger protests. The administration finally gave in. The Supreme Court upheld the students' rights to freedom of speech and assembly.

Notes

Read to Learn

The Counterculture *(page 912)*

Determining Cause and Effect

List two effects of the counterculture movement on mainstream America.

1. ______________

____

____

____

2. ______________

____

____

____

Making Generalizations

Write an X by the generalization you can make based on the passage.

___ ***Most members of the early counterculture movement were dissatisfied with traditional American values.***

___ ***Most members of the early counterculture movement became addicted to drugs.***

Many young people in the 1960s tried to create an alternative lifestyle based on flamboyant clothing, rock music, drug use, and communal living. They became known as the **counterculture** and were commonly called **"hippies."** The hippies rejected many traditional middle-class values. They wanted to create a utopian society that was free, close to nature, and based on love, empathy, tolerance, and cooperation. In part, their views were a reaction to the 1950s stereotype of the dull, colorless lives of white collar workers. As the counterculture movement grew, however, newcomers did not understand its original ideas. For them, what mattered most were the outward signs such as long hair, shabby jeans, and the use of drugs.

Some hippies left home and lived together with other young people in **communes.** These were group living arrangements in which members shared everything and worked together. Some hippies set up communes in rural areas, while others lived together in parks or in crowded apartments in cities. Thousands flocked to the Haight-Ashbury district in San Francisco, one of the most famous hippie destinations.

After a few years, the counterculture movement began to decline. Some hippie communities in cities became dangerous places in which to live. Drug use lost its appeal as some young people became addicted or died from overdoses. Others grew older and moved on from this lifestyle.

The counterculture did change aspects of American culture. Members often expressed themselves through clothes. By wearing recycled or patched clothing, they showed their rejection of consumerism and social classes. Ethnic clothing also became popular. Beads imitated Native American costumes. Tie-dyed shirts borrowed techniques from India and Africa. Hair became a powerful symbol of protest. Long hair, beards, and mustaches on young men represented defiance against conformity and the military. In time, longer hair on men and more individual clothes for both men and women became part of the mainstream.

Counterculture musicians expressed their views and feelings through folk music and rock and roll. Thousands celebrated the new protest music at rock festivals, such as Woodstock in New York and Altamont in California. Folk singers such as Bob Dylan, Joan Baez, and Pete Seeger became important voices of the movement. Major rock musicians included Jimi Hendrix, Janis Joplin, and The Who. They used electrically amplified instruments that changed the sound of rock music. These changes continue to influence musicians today.

Section Wrap-up

Answer these questions to check your understanding of the entire section.

1. What were the origins of the nation's youth movement?

2. What were the goals of the serious members of the counterculture?

Persuasive Writing

Imagine you're a young person living in the 1960s. Write a brief letter to an older relative explaining your decision to leave home to join a commune. Try to win them over to your way of thinking.

Chapter 27, Section 2 (Pages 914–919)

The Feminist Movement

Big Idea

As you read pages 914–919 in your textbook, complete the graphic organizer to compare the ideas of the two organizations that formed when the women's movement split.

Organization	Ideas
1.	2.
3.	4.

Notes

Read to Learn

A Renewed Women's Movement *(page 914)*

Formulating Questions

Write one question you have based on the passage.

The Feminist movement emerged in the 1960s. **Feminism** is the belief that men and women should be politically, economically, and socially equal. During World War II, many women joined the nation's workforce. After the war, many women returned to their roles as homemakers. However, more women took jobs outside the home during the 1950s. By the mid-1960s, almost half of American women worked outside the home, often in low-paying jobs. Women often faced employment discrimination, and their resentment grew.

In 1961, President Kennedy set up the Presidential Commission on the Status of Women. Its report helped create a network of feminist activists who lobbied Congress for women's laws. Congress passed the Equal Pay Act in 1963. It outlawed paying men more than women for the same job. Congress also added Title VII to the 1964 Civil Rights Act. It outlawed gender discrimination. In 1966 feminists formed the National Organization for Women (NOW). It focused on greater educational opportunities for women and on aiding women in the workplace.

Notes

Read to Learn

Successes and Failures (page 917)

Problems and Solutions

List one problem women faced in the early 1960s and 1970s. List one solution to it.

Problem:

____

____

____

Solution:

____

____

____

Distinguishing Fact from Opinion

Read the third paragraph. Underline one sentence that tells about an opinion on the issue of abortion.

In the late 1960s and early 1970s, the women's movement fought battles on many fronts. It had many successes but also faced strong opposition. In 1972 Congress passed the Equal Rights Amendment (ERA). If 38 states ratified this amendment, protection against gender discrimination would become part of the Constitution. By 1979, 35 states had done so. However, opposition to the ERA had begun to grow. Many people saw it as a threat to traditional values. Some feared it would take away the legal rights of wives and allow women to be drafted into the military. A vocal opponent of the ERA was Phyllis Schlafly. She organized the nationwide Stop-ERA campaign. By the end of 1979, four states had voted to rescind their approval. The ERA failed in 1982, unable to gain ratification by three-fourths of the states.

A major accomplishment of the women's movement was gaining greater equality for women in education. Leaders of the movement pushed lawmakers to pass federal laws banning discrimination in education. In 1972 Congress passed a collection of laws known as the Educational Amendments. One part of these laws was Title IX. It stopped federally funded schools from discriminating against females in nearly all areas, including admissions and sports.

Another important goal for many women was the repeal of laws against abortion. Until 1973, the right to regulate abortion was given to the states. This was in keeping with the original plan of the Constitution. In the mid-1800s, states also had passed laws prohibiting abortion except to save the mother's life. In the late 1960s, some states began adopting more liberal abortion laws. In 1973 the Supreme Court ruled in *Roe* v. *Wade* that state governments could not regulate abortion during the first three months of pregnancy. This was interpreted as being within a woman's constitutional right to privacy. The decision led to the rise of the right-to-life movement. Members of this movement considered abortion an absolute wrong and wanted it to be banned. The heated battle over abortion continues today.

The women's movement has greatly affected society. Many more women have pursued college degrees and careers outside of the home since the 1970s. Many employers now offer ways to help make work life more compatible with family life. Still, there remains a wide income gap between men and women. Most working women still hold lower paying jobs. In professional positions, however, women have made dramatic gains since the 1970s.

Section Wrap-up

Answer these questions to check your understanding of the entire section.

1. What led to the development of a new feminist movement in the 1960s?

2. What was the significance of Title IX?

Expository Writing

Write an article for your school newspaper. In it, explain the effects of the women's movement of the 1960s on students in your school today. How would their lives be different if the new women's movement had never occurred?

Latino Americans Organize

Big Idea

As you read pages 920–925 in your textbook, complete the time line by filling in some important events from the history of Latino Americans.

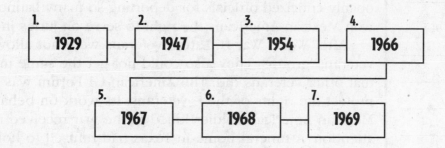

1. 1929
2. 1947
3. 1954
4. 1966
5. 1967
6. 1968
7. 1969

Notes

Read to Learn

Latinos Migrate North *(page 920)*

Drawing Conclusions

Place an X next to two sentences that support this conclusion: Discrimination had a major impact on the daily lives of Mexican Americans during the 1910s and 1920s.

Many people of Mexican descent lived in Texas, California, Arizona, New Mexico, and Colorado. These areas had once been part of Mexico. In the 1910s and 1920s, some Mexican Americans moved to cities in the Midwest and Northwest. They hoped to find jobs in factories. Most Mexican Americans in the Southwest lived in barrios, partly due to ethnic discrimination. Barrios are poor Hispanic and Latino neighborhoods. Discrimination in employment also kept Mexican Americans from finding well paying jobs. Many worked on farms.

Mexican Americans faced more discrimination during the Great Depression. Federal officials deported many Mexican immigrants in a program known as **"repatriation."** More than 3.7 million Mexicans were also deported while Eisenhower was president. Many of them were legal residents. Some had even been born in this country.

In the 1950s, other Latinos arrived in the country. They included large numbers of Puerto Ricans, and Cubans fleeing a revolution. By the late 1960s, more than 9 million Latinos lived in the United States.

Notes

Read to Learn

Latinos Organize *(page 923)*

Making Inferences

What other issues might the American GI Forum have addressed?

1. ____________________

____

____

____

2. ____________________

____

____

____

Latinos in the American Southwest were often treated as outsiders whether they were citizens or not. They began to organize to work for equal rights and fair treatment.

In 1929, several Mexican American groups created the League of United Latin American Citizens (LULAC). Its purpose was to fight discrimination against Latin Americans. LULAC helped end segregation in public places in Texas. It also ended the practice of segregating Mexican American children in schools. LULAC openly criticized officials for deporting so many Latinos. It also won Mexican Americans the right to serve on juries in Texas.

After World War II, Latino veterans were not allowed to join veterans' groups. They also could not get the same medical care that other veterans did. The American GI Forum was founded to protect the rights of these veterans. Its work on behalf of a Mexican American soldier killed in the war received national attention. A funeral home in Texas had refused to hold his funeral. With the help of President Johnson, the soldier was buried in Arlington National Cemetery.

Protests and Progress *(page 925)*

Predicting

Predict two possible outcomes of increased Latino voting.

1. ____________________

____

____

____

2. ____________________

____

____

____

Latino Americans still faced prejudice in the 1960s. They did not have the same rights to education, housing, and employment as other Americans. Latinos began campaigns to try to improve their economic status. They also wanted to end discrimination.

In the early 1960s, Latino leaders César Chávez and Dolores Huerta formed two groups to fight for farm workers' rights. The result was a strike against California growers in 1965. The workers demanded union recognition, higher wages, and better benefits. When that effort failed, Chávez organized a national boycott of table grapes. Around 17 million people stopped buying grapes. Profits tumbled. In 1966 Chávez and Huerta merged their two organizations to form the United Farm Workers (UFW). The boycott lasted until 1970. Grape growers agreed to raise wages and improve working conditions.

Latino youths also became involved in civil rights. The Mexican American Youth Organization led school walkouts and demonstrations. Its success led to a new political party, La Raza Unida, in 1969. La Raza worked for Latino causes and encouraged Latinos to vote. Many Mexican Americans began to fight prejudice and celebrate ethnic pride. Leaders began to promote **bilingualism,** or teaching immigrant students in their own language while they learn English.

Section Wrap-up

Answer these questions to check your understanding of the entire section.

1. Why did Latinos in the American Southwest need to organize?

2. How did Latino leaders help farm workers?

Informative Writing

In the space provided write an article about the ways Latinos experienced discrimination in this country. The article is for a Web site devoted to recording the experiences of immigrants.

Chapter 28, Section 1 (Pages 934–939)

The Nixon Administration

Big Idea

As you read pages 934–939 in your textbook, complete the graphic organizer by listing President Nixon's domestic and foreign policies.

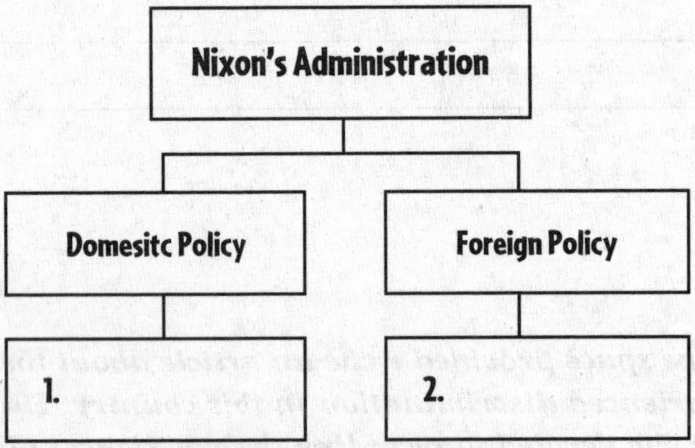

Notes

Read to Learn

Appealing to Middle America *(page 934)*

Making Inferences

Why do you think Nixon targeted antiwar protesters in his attempt to restore law and order?

____

____

____

____

____

____

____

Richard Nixon was the 1968 Republican presidential candidate. He promised peace in Vietnam, law and order, and a return to conservative values. He won. To restore law and order, Nixon targeted antiwar protesters and opposed Supreme Court rulings that expanded the rights of accused criminals.

Nixon's domestic policy became known as New Federalism. Nixon called for ending several federal programs and giving more control to state and local governments. Congress passed **revenue sharing** bills that gave federal money to state and local agencies. Because states came to depend on federal funds, the federal government could impose conditions on the states. Nixon also tried to increase the power of the executive branch by **impounding,** or refusing to release, funds to Congress for programs he opposed.

Many people argued that the nation's welfare system made it better for poor people to apply for benefits rather than take low-paying jobs. Nixon proposed a plan to give needy families $1,600 per year, which could be supplemented by outside earnings. The plan was defeated in the Senate.

Notes

Read to Learn

Nixon's Foreign Policy *(page 937)*

Synthesizing Information

Reread the passage. Underline two examples of Nixon's attempts at détente with the Soviet Union and China.

Identifying the Main Idea

Reread the fifth paragraph of the summary. What is the main idea of the paragraph?

Main idea:

____

____

____

____

____

____

____

____

President Nixon was more interested in foreign affairs than in domestic issues. He chose Henry Kissinger as his national security adviser. Kissinger was a former Harvard professor. He played a large part in helping Nixon shape his foreign policy.

Both Nixon and Kissinger wanted the United States to gradually withdraw from Vietnam. They wanted to continue to help train the South Vietnamese to defend themselves. This policy was called Vietnamization. Nixon believed that allies of the United States should be responsible for defending themselves. This policy became known as the Nixon Doctrine.

Nixon was an outspoken opponent of communism. However, he and Kissinger believed that the nation's policy against communism was too rigid. They believed the policy worked against the interests of the United States. Nixon and Kissinger wanted to contain communism, but they believed that negotiation was a better way for the United States to achieve its international goals.

Kissinger and Nixon developed an approach called **détente.** Détente was a relaxation of tensions between the United States and its Communist rivals, China and the Soviet Union. Nixon said that the United States had to build a better relationship with the two countries in the interest of world peace.

In February 1972 Nixon made a historic visit to China. He hoped to improve American-Chinese relations. Leaders of both nations agreed to set up more normal relations between their countries. Nixon believed that relaxing tensions with China would encourage the Soviet Union to pursue diplomacy.

Shortly after negotiations with China took place, the Soviets proposed a **summit** to be held between the United States and the Soviet Union in May 1972. A summit is a high-level diplomatic meeting. During the summit, the two countries signed the first Strategic Arms Limitation Treaty, or SALT I. This was a plan to limit nuclear arms. The two nations also agreed to increase trade and to exchange scientific information.

Section Wrap-up

Answer these questions to check your understanding of the entire section.

1. What was New Federalism?

2. What were Nixon's foreign policy achievements?

Persuasive Writing

In the space provided write a letter to a newspaper editor in support of or against Nixon's policy of détente with the Soviet Union and China.

Chapter 28, Section 2 (Pages 940–945)

The Watergate Scandal

Big Idea

As you read pages 940–945 in your textbook, complete the outline using the major headings of the section.

The Watergate Scandal

I. The Roots of Watergate
   A. ______________________________
   B. ______________________________
II. ______________________________
   A. ______________________________
   B. ______________________________
   C. ______________________________
   D. ______________________________

Notes | Read to Learn

The Roots of Watergate *(page 940)*

Distinguishing Fact from Opinion

Reread the first paragraph. Underline a sentence that describes an opinion.

Nixon became president when the nation was in turmoil. He viewed protesters as people out to bring down his administration. Nixon was expected to win re-election in 1972. His approval rating was high. However, the Vietnam War continued. Nixon and his advisers also remembered that he won in 1968 by a slim margin. As a result, his team tried to gain an advantage by any method. This included spying on the opposition, spreading rumors, and stealing information from the Democratic Party's headquarters. On June 17, 1972, a security guard at the Watergate complex discovered burglars. The police arrested the men.

One of the burglars, James McCord, was a member of the Committee for the Re-election of the President (CRP). Questions came up about the White House's connection to the burglary. To cover up any involvement, members of Nixon's administration destroyed documents and gave false testimony. The White House denied any involvement in the break-in. Most Americans believed the denial. Nixon was re-elected.

Notes

Read to Learn

The Cover-Up Unravels *(page 942)*

Detecting Bias

Give two reasons why Nixon may not have wanted the White House tapes released.

1. ______________________

____

____

____

2. ______________________

____

____

____

____

Formulating Questions

Underline the sentences that can help you answer the following question:

How did Watergate affect the way Americans viewed their government?

The Watergate burglars went on trial in 1973. James McCord agreed to testify before the grand jury and the Senate's Select Committee on Presidential Campaign Activities. Many people testified after McCord. John Dean, the counsel to the president, testified that former Attorney General John Mitchell had ordered the Watergate break-in and that Nixon had helped cover it up. The Nixon administration denied the charges. The committee then tried to find out who was telling the truth. White House aide Alexander Butterfield testified that Nixon had ordered a taping system installed in the White House to record conversations. The committee believed that the tapes would tell them what the president knew and when he knew it.

Everyone wanted the tapes. However, President Nixon refused to give them up, claiming **executive privilege.** This is the principle that White House conversations should remain confidential to protect national security. Nixon appointed Archibald Cox as a **special prosecutor,** or a lawyer from outside the government, to investigate the Watergate cases. Cox took Nixon to court to force him to give up the tapes. Nixon had Cox fired.

In the fall 1973 Vice President Spiro Agnew resigned because it was discovered that he had taken bribes. Gerald Ford, the Republican leader of the House of Representatives, became vice president.

President Nixon appointed a new special prosecutor, Leon Jaworski. He also wanted the president's tapes. In July the Supreme Court ruled that the president had to turn over the tapes. Nixon did so. A few days later the House Judiciary Committee voted to impeach Nixon, or officially charge him with misconduct. The committee charged that Nixon had obstructed justice in the Watergate cover-up. The next step was for the House of Representatives to vote whether or not to impeach the president. Investigators found evidence against the president. One of the tapes showed that Nixon had ordered the CIA to stop the FBI's investigation of the break-in. Nixon's impeachment and conviction now seemed certain. As a result, on August 9, 1974, Nixon resigned. Ford became president.

After Watergate, Congress passed laws to limit the power of the executive branch. The Federal Campaign Act Amendments limited campaign contributions. It also set up an independent agency to administer stricter election laws. The Ethics in Government Act required that high government officials provide financial disclosures. Watergate made many Americans distrust their public officials. Other Americans saw Watergate as proof that no one is above the law.

Section Wrap-up

Answer these questions to check your understanding of the entire section.

1. Describe Richard Nixon's character and the attitude of his administration.

2. After Watergate, what steps did Congress take to limit the power of the executive branch?

Informative Writing

In the space provided write an article explaining the Watergate crisis to someone who has never heard of it. In an objective and unemotional way, describe the time, place, people, and events of Watergate.

Ford and Carter

Big Idea

As you read pages 946–951 in your textbook, complete the graphic organizer by listing some causes of economic problems in the 1970s.

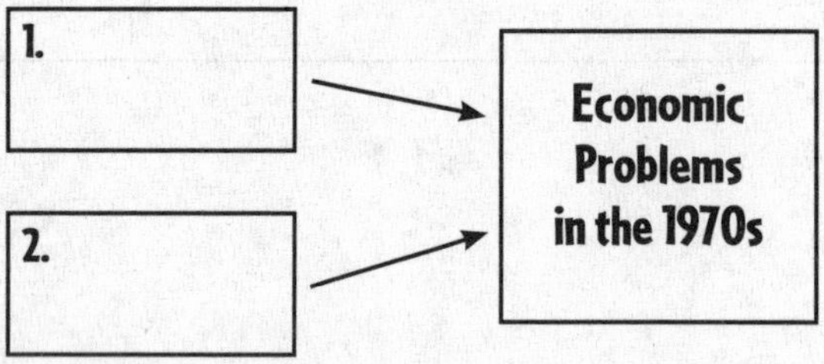

Notes

Read to Learn

The Economic Crisis of the 1970s *(page 946)*

Drawing Conclusions

Reread the passage and underline two ways Nixon tried to control inflation. Then draw a conclusion about Nixon's ability to help the economy.

____

____

____

____

____

____

Economic problems started in the mid-1960s under President Johnson. During the Vietnam War, he increased government spending. This led to **inflation,** or a rise in the cost of goods. The United States also had become dependent on oil imports. In the early 1970s, the Organization of Petroleum Exporting Countries (OPEC) began using oil as a political weapon. OPEC decided to **embargo,** or stop shipping, oil to countries that supported Israel. OPEC ended the embargo a few months after it began, but oil prices continued to rise. Americans had little money to spend on goods. This caused a recession.

By the 1970s U.S. manufacturers faced international competition. Factories closed and unemployment grew. Nixon faced **stagflation,** a combination of inflation and economic stagnation with high unemployment. He tried to control inflation. The government cut spending and raised taxes. However, people opposed the idea of a tax hike. Nixon then tried to get the Federal Reserve to raise interest rates. He hoped this would reduce consumer spending. This plan failed. Nixon then placed a freeze on all wages and prices. This plan also failed.

Notes | Read to Learn

Ford and Carter Battle the Economic Crisis *(page 948)*

Analyzing Information

How would deregulating the oil industry make the nation less dependent on foreign oil?

Inflation remained high after Nixon resigned. Ford began a plan called WIN—Whip Inflation Now. He urged Americans to use less oil and conserve energy. Ford then tried cutting government spending and raising interest rates. Both plans failed.

Ford continued Nixon's foreign policy. In 1975 Ford and the leaders of NATO and the Warsaw Pact signed the Helsinki Accords. They agreed to recognize the borders of Eastern Europe set up at the end of World War II. The Soviets promised to uphold basic human rights.

The 1976 presidential election pitted Ford against Democrat Jimmy Carter, who won. Carter dealt with the economy by increasing government spending and cutting taxes. When inflation rose in 1978, he tried reducing the money supply and raising interest rates. This was unsuccessful. To curb the nation's dependence on foreign oil, he proposed a program to conserve oil and to push for the use of coal and renewable energy sources. He also convinced Congress to create a Department of Energy. Many business leaders wanted Carter to end regulations on the oil industry that made it difficult for oil companies to make a profit, which they could use to invest in new oil wells at home. Carter agreed to deregulate, but he created a profit tax so that oil companies would not overcharge consumers. Because of this tax, however, oil companies did not have money for new wells.

Carter's Foreign Policy *(page 950)*

Making Generalizations

Reread the passage. Circle two examples that support the generalization that Carter had mixed success in his dealings with the Middle East.

Carter believed the United States should deal honestly with other nations. He agreed to turn over control of the Panama Canal to the Panamanians. He pointed to the Soviet Union as a violator of human rights. When the Soviet Union invaded Afghanistan in 1979, Carter placed an embargo on the Soviet Union and boycotted the Olympic Games in Moscow.

In 1978 Carter helped set up the Camp David Accords, a peace treaty between Israel and Egypt. A few months later, Carter faced conflict in Iran. The United States had supported Iran's ruler, the Shah, but he was unpopular with Iranians. In 1979 Iranian protesters forced the Shah to leave. The new government distrusted the United States. In November 1979 revolutionaries took 52 hostages at the American embassy in Tehran. Carter tried unsuccessfully to negotiate for their release. A rescue mission failed and resulted in the death of eight American servicemen. The hostages were released the day Carter left office.

Section Wrap-up

Answer these questions to check your understanding of the entire section.

1. Why did the United States face economic troubles in the 1970s?

2. How did Carter try to combat the nation's dependence on foreign oil?

Expository Writing

In the space provided write a journal entry as if you were Jimmy Carter on the last day of your presidency. Cite at least one of your successes and one of your failures.

Chapter 28, Section 4 (Pages 952–957)

New Approaches to Civil Rights

Big Idea

As you read pages 952–957 in your textbook, complete the time line to record new groups and their actions.

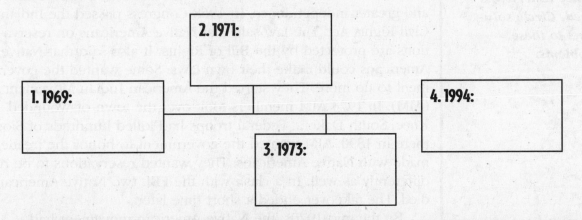

1. 1969:

2. 1971:

3. 1973:

4. 1994:

Notes

Read to Learn

African Americans Seek Greater Opportunity *(page 952)*

Determining Cause and Effect

Write the cause.

Cause:

____

____

____

____

____

Effect: Local governments began busing.

In the 1970s, African Americans began to push for equal access to education. Many schools were segregated because children went to neighborhood schools. A segregated neighborhood had segregated schools. Local governments started **busing.** They transported children to schools outside their neighborhoods to gain racial balance. Many whites opposed busing.

Civil rights leaders advocated **affirmative action.** It called for companies, schools, and institutions to recruit African Americans. Supporters hoped this would give African Americans new opportunities. Critics called it "reverse discrimination." In 1974 a white man named Allan Bakke was denied admission to the University of California medical school, which had set aside slots for minorities. Bakke sued. The Supreme Court ruled in favor of Bakke, but said that schools could use racial criteria for admission as long as they did not use quotas.

African Americans found new political leaders. One leader was Jesse Jackson. He started People United to Save Humanity (PUSH). In 1984 and 1988, Jackson ran for president.

Notes | Read to Learn

Native Americans Raise Their Voices *(page 955)*

Problems and Solutions

Reread the passage and underline examples of problems the Native Americans faced. Circle solutions to these problems.

Native Americans faced many problems. Their unemployment rate was 10 times the national rate. Unemployment was especially high on reservations, where more than half of Native Americans lived. Life expectancy for Native Americans was almost seven years below the national average. In the 1960s and 1970s, many Native Americans began trying to improve these conditions.

Native Americans worked for better economic opportunities and greater independence. In 1968 Congress passed the Indian Civil Rights Act. The law said that Native Americans on reservations are protected by the Bill of Rights. It also said that Native Americans could make their own laws. Some wanted the government to do more. They started the American Indian Movement (AIM). In 1973 AIM members took over the town of Wounded Knee, South Dakota. Federal troops had killed hundreds of Sioux there in 1890. AIM wanted the government to honor the treaties it made with Native Americans. They wanted reservations to be run differently as well. In a clash with the FBI, two Native Americans died. The takeover ended a short time later.

By the mid-1970s, the Native American movement had made some progress. In 1975 Congress passed the Indian Self-Determination and Educational Assistance Act. The law increased funds for Native American education. Native Americans also won land and water rights.

The Disability Rights Movement *(page 957)*

Comparing and Contrasting

Compare and contrast two laws discussed in this passage.

1. ____________________

____

____

2. ____________________

____

____

During the 1960s and 1970s, many persons with disabilities looked to the federal government to protect their civil rights. They wanted the same access to buildings and jobs as others had. One victory was the 1968 passage of the Architectural Barriers Act. It required that persons with disabilities be able to access all new buildings built with federal money. The Rehabilitation Act of 1973 went further to protect the rights of persons with disabilities, but wasn't enforced at first. In 1977 one group staged protests across the nation to force authorities to enforce the act.

In 1966 Congress started an agency to give money to help educate children with disabilities. A 1975 law made sure that all students with disabilities received a free, appropriate education. One trend in schools at this time was to mainstream students with disabilities. This meant bringing them into the regular classroom. In 1990 Congress enacted the Americans with Disabilities Act. It banned discrimination in many areas.

Section Wrap-up

Answer these questions to check your understanding of the entire section.

1. What was the goal of affirmative action policies?

2. How did Congress help Native Americans meet some of their goals?

Expository Writing

Suppose you are a Native American living in the 1970s. Write an article for your local newspaper describing how your struggle for better opportunities is similar to and different from the struggle of African Americans in the same time period.

Chapter 28, Section 5 (Pages 958–961)

Environmentalism

Big Idea

As you read pages 958–961 in your textbook, complete the graphic organizer by including some of the actions taken to combat environmental problems in the 1960s and 1970s.

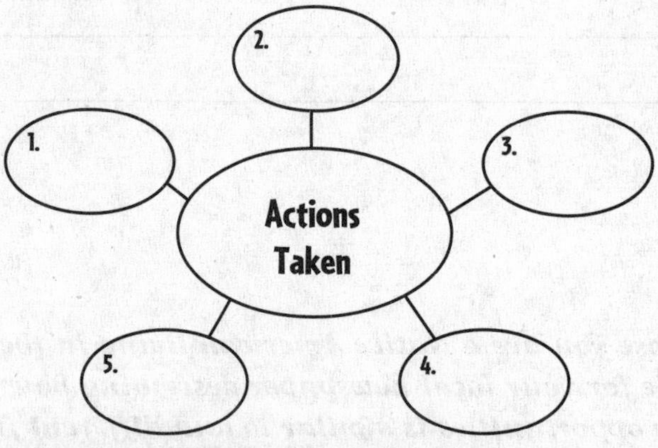

Notes

Read to Learn

The Origins of Environmentalism *(page 958)*

Determining Cause and Effect

What effect did Rachel Carson's book* Silent Spring *have on many Americans?

In 1966 a Long Island family discovered that the pesticide DDT was being used to control mosquitoes at a lake near their home. They feared that the pesticide might poison the lake and sued to stop its use. Scientists involved in the case established the Environmental Defense Fund to help stop the use of DDT throughout the country.

Rachel Carson helped start the new environmental movement. In her book *Silent Spring,* Carson wrote of the danger of the increasing use of pesticides. Many Americans took Carson's warnings seriously. They also saw that **smog,** or fog made heavier and darker by smoke and chemical fumes, covered many cities. Acres of forests were being cut down in the Northwest. Pollution and garbage had caused the death of nearly all the fish in Lake Erie. Many people believed it was time to take action.

In April 1970 the nation held the first Earth Day, a day devoted to environmental issues. Soon many people formed local environmental groups, such as the Sierra Club and the Wilderness Society. The Natural Resources Defense Council was made up of scientists, lawyers, and activists working on environmental issues.

Notes

Read to Learn

The Environmental Movement Blossoms *(page 960)*

Making Generalizations

Reread the passage. Underline examples that support this generalization.

In the 1970s, the U.S. government actively established laws to protect the environment.

Predicting

Make a prediction about the United States's use of nuclear energy after the Three Mile Island accident.

____

____

____

____

____

____

____

____

____

____

____

____

With the environmental movement gaining support, the federal government became involved with environmental issues. In 1970 the Environmental Protection Agency (EPA) was established. Its job was to set and enforce pollution standards. The agency also coordinated antipollution activities with state and local governments. The Clean Air Act set up air emissions standards for factories and automobiles. The Clean Water Act limited the amount of pollutants that could be released into the nation's lakes and rivers. The Endangered Species Act set up measures for saving threatened animal species. These laws eventually helped improve the nation's environment.

In the 1970s, people living in a housing development called Love Canal near Niagara Falls, New York, noticed a high rate of health problems in their community. The problems included nerve damage, blood diseases, and cancer. The people learned that their community was located on top of an old toxic waste dump. The hazardous materials in the dump had leaked into the ground. The people of Love Canal demanded that the government address the problem. After they made the problem known to the entire nation, the state relocated about 200 families. In 1980 President Carter declared Love Canal a federal disaster area. He moved the 600 remaining families to new locations. The Love Canal residents sued the company that created the dumpsite. They settled the case for $20 million. The site was cleaned up and homes above the dumping ground were burned.

During the 1970s, many Americans were concerned about the growth of nuclear power. Those who supported the use of nuclear power claimed it was a cleaner and less expensive alternative to **fossil fuels,** such as coal, oil, or natural gas. Those who opposed the use of nuclear power warned of the risks that nuclear energy posed, particularly if radiation was accidentally released into the air. On March 28, 1979, one of the reactors at the Three Mile Island nuclear facility outside Harrisburg, Pennsylvania, overheated. Two days later, low levels of radiation escaped from the reactor. Nearby residents were evacuated. Others left on their own. Citizens staged protests. The reactor was closed down and the leak was sealed. The Three Mile Island accident left many people doubtful about the safety of nuclear energy. The doubts continue today.

Section Wrap-up

Answer these questions to check your understanding of the entire section.

1. What were the origins of the environmental movement?

2. How did citizens outside of the government combat environmental problems?

Descriptive Writing

In the space provided write a newspaper article describing what you have done, or would like to do, to help preserve the environment.

Chapter 29, Section 1 (Pages 968–973)

The New Conservatism

Big Idea

As you read pages 968–973 in your textbook, complete the outline using the major headings of the section.

The New Conservatism

I. Conservatism and Liberalism
   A. ____________________
   B. ____________________
II. ____________________
   A. ____________________
   B. ____________________
   C. ____________________
   D. ____________________
   E. ____________________
   F. ____________________
   G. ____________________

Notes

Read to Learn

Liberalism and Conservatism *(page 968)*

Drawing Conclusions

Underline the statement in the passage that supports the following conclusion:

Liberals would not favor federal funding of religious schools.

Liberal politics dominated the United States for much of the 1960s. **Conservative** ideas gained strength during the 1970s. People who call themselves liberals believe that the government should regulate the economy. They also think it should help disadvantaged people. Liberals do not believe the government should try to control social behavior. They also oppose the government's support of religious beliefs in any way. Liberals believe that economic inequality is the cause of most social problems. They argue that high taxes on the wealthy makes society more equal.

Conservatives distrust the power of government. They believe that government control of the economy weakens the economy. Conservatives believe in free enterprise. They argue that when people are able to make their own economic decisions, there is more wealth for everyone. As a result, they oppose high taxes, believing they discourage people from working hard. Conservatives think that most social problems result from issues of morality. They believe that these issues are best solved through commitment to a religious faith.

Notes | Read to Learn

Conservatism Revives *(page 970)*

Determining Cause and Effect

List two causes of the shift to conservatism after World War II.

1. ______________

____

____

____

2. ______________

____

____

____

Evaluating Information

Why is the information about the population growth in the Sunbelt useful? Put an X next to the answer.

___ ***It helps to explain a change in voting patterns in the country.***

___ ***It helps to explain the problems in the Northeast.***

Conservative ideas gained support after World War II for two main reasons, both related to communism. One was that some Americans believed liberal economic ideas were leading the country toward communism. Secondly, Americans of deep religious faith embraced the struggle against communism. They saw it as a battle between good and evil. Communism rejected religion and stressed material things. Thus, many Americans turned away from liberalism, which focused on economic welfare. They turned toward conservatism.

In 1955 William Buckley founded a new magazine, the *National Review.* It helped to revive conservative ideas in the United States. In 1964 conservatives in the Republican Party displayed their power. They got Barry Goldwater, a conservative, nominated for president. Lyndon Johnson, however, defeated Goldwater in the election.

During and after World War II, many Americans moved to the South and West to get jobs in factories. This area was known as the Sunbelt. Its population began to view government differently than others did. Americans in the Northeast were battling high unemployment and pollution in cities. They looked to the government for help. People living in the Sunbelt were experiencing economic growth. They feared increased taxes and federal controls would stop growth in the region. For the first time since Reconstruction, many Southerners voted Republican. By 1980 the population of the Sunbelt was greater than the Northeast. This gave conservative regions of the country more electoral votes.

During the 1960s and 1970s, many Americans moved to the suburbs. They hoped to escape problems in the cities. However, rising inflation threatened their middle-class lifestyles. Many resented paying high taxes for social programs while their situations worsened. Antitax programs sprang up all over the country. Many middle-class Americans began to believe the conservatives were right—government had become too big.

Some Americans thought the country had abandoned its traditional values. They became conservatives for this reason. Religious conservatives included people from many faiths. The largest group were evangelical Protestants. Ministers known as **"televangelists"** reached large audiences through television. A new group called the "Moral Majority" backed conservative candidates. By 1980 the movement had formed a conservative bloc of voters.

Conservative voters were concerned about many issues, but they were united by a common belief. They thought American society had lost its way. Their spokesperson, Ronald Reagan, offered hope to a nation in distress.

Section Wrap-up

Answer these questions to check your understanding of the entire section.

1. How do liberal and conservative views differ regarding the government's role in the economy?

2. How did some Americans' views about communism influence them to become conservatives?

Expository Writing

Suppose you are working for a conservative politician's campaign in the 1970s. Write a profile of a typical conservative voter that your candidate might want to reach. Include data such as where the voter lives and what his or her values are.

Chapter 29, Section 2 (Pages 974–981)

The Reagan Years

Big Idea

As you read pages 974–981 in your textbook, complete the graphic organizer by filling in the major points of the supply-side theory of economics.

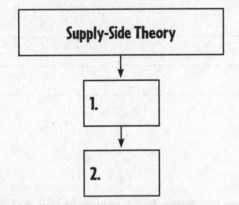

Supply-Side Theory

↓

1.

↓

2.

Notes

Read to Learn

The Road to the White House *(page 974)*

Identifying the Main Idea

What is the main idea of the passage?

Ronald Reagan started out as an actor. Over 25 years, he made more than 50 movies. In 1947 Reagan became president of the Screen Actors Guild, an actors' union. As the head of the union, he testified about communism in Hollywood before the House Un-American Activities Committee. In 1954 Reagan became the host of a television program called *General Electric Theater.* He was also a motivational speaker for the company. As he traveled across the country speaking to people, he became more politically conservative. He heard stories from Americans about high taxes. They described how government regulations made it impossible for them to get ahead in life.

In 1964 Barry Goldwater asked Reagan to speak on behalf of his presidential campaign. Reagan's speech impressed several wealthy people from California. They convinced Reagan to run for governor of California in 1966, and he won. In 1980 he was the Republican candidate for president. Reagan promised to cut taxes and increase defense spending. He called for a constitutional amendment banning abortion. His positions on issues won him the support of conservatives. Reagan won the election.

Notes | Read to Learn

Domestic Policies *(page 976)*

Problems and Solutions

Identify Reagan's solution.

Problem: The country was suffering from economic problems.

Solution:

____

____

____

____

____

____

Reagan's first priority was the nation's economy. One group of economists believed inflation was the biggest problem and raising interest rates was the solution. Another group supported **supply-side economics.** They believed high taxes weakened the economy and cutting taxes would allow businesses to grow and create more jobs. Reagan combined the two ideas. He urged the Federal Reserve to raise interest rates and asked Congress to cut taxes. Critics called this Reaganomics, or "trickle-down economics." Cutting tax rates would increase the government's **budget deficit,** the amount by which spending exceeds income. To control the deficit, Reagan proposed cuts for social programs such as welfare.

Reagan applied his conservative ideas to the judicial branch. He elevated a conservative Supreme Court justice to chief justice. Reagan also nominated Sandra Day O'Connor to be the first woman on the Court.

Reagan believed that government regulations also caused economic problems. He got rid of price controls for oil and gasoline, and energy prices fell. Other deregulations followed. The economy began to recover in 1983. This made Reagan very popular. He was reelected in 1984 in a landslide.

Reagan Oversees a Military Buildup *(page 979)*

Making Inferences

Write two inferences you can make based on the passage.

1. ______________________

____

____

____

2. ______________________

____

____

____

Reagan believed the United States had to show strength in dealing with the Soviet Union. He started a huge military buildup, which created new defense jobs. It pushed the annual budget deficit to $200 billion. Reagan also thought the United States should support guerrilla groups who fought to overthrow Communist or pro-Soviet governments. This policy became known as the Reagan Doctrine. In Nicaragua, the Reagan administration secretly armed guerrilla forces known as "contras." U.S. officials also secretly sold weapons to Iran and sent profits to the contras. This became known as the Iran-Contra affair.

Reagan disagreed with the military strategy known as nuclear deterrence, or **"mutual assured destruction."** It assumed that as long as both the United States and the Soviet Union could destroy each other with nuclear weapons, they would be afraid to use them. In 1983 Reagan proposed the Strategic Defense Initiative, nicknamed "Star Wars." It called for the development of weapons that could destroy incoming missiles. In 1985 Mikhail Gorbachev became the leader of the Soviet Union. The two leaders signed the Intermediate-Range Nuclear Forces (INF) Treaty. The treaty marked the beginning of the end of the Cold War.

Section Wrap-up

Answer these questions to check your understanding of the entire section.

1. What was "Reaganomics"?

2. Why did Reagan propose the Strategic Defense Initiative, or "Star Wars"?

Persuasive Writing

In the space provided write a short speech Reagan might have given in his campaign for reelection to the presidency.

Chapter 29, Section 3 (Pages 982–987)

Life in the 1980s

Big Idea

As you read pages 982–987 in your textbook, complete the graphic organizer by listing some of the social issues that the United States faced in this decade.

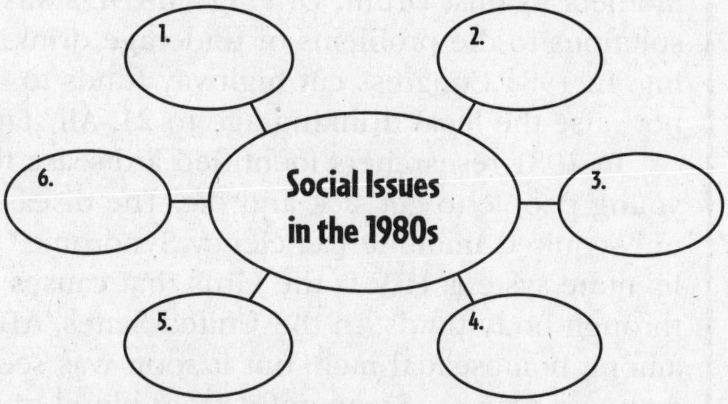

Notes

Read to Learn

A Booming Economy *(page 982)*

The American economy had revived by 1983. Many young brokers, speculators, and investors made multimillion-dollar deals buying and selling companies. The prices of real estate and stocks soared. Journalists referred to these young money-makers as **yuppies,** short for "young urban professionals."

By the 1980s, many baby boomers were focused on getting ahead in their jobs and acquiring goods. Due to their numbers, their concerns helped to shape the culture. The strong economic growth, however, mostly benefited middle- and upper-class Americans. Businesses also found a new way to sell goods to customers. It was called **discount retailing.** Discount retailers sell large quantities of goods at very low prices. They created millions of new jobs in the 1980s.

Technology changed news and entertainment. Cable television became available in homes across the country. In 1981 music and technology came together when Music Television (MTV) went on the air. A new style of music, called rap, became popular. Cassette tapes and the Sony Walkman made music portable. VCRs allowed people to watch movies at home.

Synthesizing Information

Circle the statement the author would most likely agree with.

Yuppies both fed and benefited from the country's economic growth.

Technological innovation was stagnant during the 1980s.

Notes

Read to Learn

New Social Activism *(page 986)*

Making Generalizations

Write an X by the generalization supported by the passage.

___ ***Activism in the 1980s addressed many different social issues.***

___ ***AIDS awareness was the biggest social issue of the 1980s.***

Predicting

Place an X next to the sentence in the passage that supports the following prediction.

Budget pressures on the federal government will continue to increase.

The United States dealt with many social problems during the 1980s. Drug abuse made many city neighborhoods violent and dangerous. Drug use also spread from cities to small towns and rural areas. Some schools even began searching student lockers and bags for hidden drugs. Alcohol abuse, particularly by teenagers, was another serious problem. Young people were involved in thousands of alcohol-related accidents. In 1980 Mothers Against Drunk Driving (MADD) was founded to find solutions to the problems of underage drinking and drunk driving. In 1984 Congress cut highway funds to any state that did not raise the legal drinking age to 21. All states complied.

In 1981 researchers identified a disease that caused healthy young people to get sick and die. The disease was called AIDS, or "Acquired Immune Deficiency Syndrome." It weakens the immune system. HIV is the virus that causes AIDS. It is spread through body fluids. In the United States, AIDS was first seen among homosexual men, but it soon was seen in heterosexual men and women. Some got it from blood transfusions. Some were drug users who shared needles with infected blood. Others were infected by sexual partners.

AIDS increased awareness of the gay and lesbian community in the United States. Some homosexuals had been involved in defending their civil rights since the 1960s. On June 27, 1969, New York City police raided the Stonewall Inn, a nightclub. The police had often raided the club because of its clients' sexuality. On this night, gays' and lesbians' frustration with the police actions peaked. They rioted. The Stonewall riot was the beginning of the Gay Liberation Movement. The movement tried to increase acceptance of homosexuality.

In the 1980s, many singers and other entertainers took up social causes. In 1984 Irish musician Bob Geldof organized musicians in England to put on benefit concerts to help starving people in Ethiopia. Country singer Willie Nelson organized benefit concerts to help American farmers going through hard times.

Senior citizens became activists in the 1980s. With new medical technology, more Americans were living to an older age. The birthrate had also declined. That meant younger people made up a smaller proportion of the population. More Americans were receiving Social Security payments, which created budget pressures for the government. Older Americans became more active in politics. They opposed cuts in Social Security or Medicare. Because they tend to vote in large numbers, they are an influential group. Their major organization is the American Association of Retired Persons (AARP), which was founded in 1958.

Section Wrap-up

Answer these questions to check your understanding of the entire section.

1. How were yuppies and baby boomers influential economically during the 1980s?

2. In what ways did social activism in the 1980s grow as a response to social issues?

Informative Writing

In the space provided write a news bulletin designed to increase awareness of one of the social problems mentioned in this section. Tell what the problem is, who it affects, how it can be addressed, and who can help.

Chapter 29, Section 4 (Pages 990–995)

The End of the Cold War

Big Idea

As you read pages 990–995 in your textbook, complete the chart by describing U.S. foreign policy in each of the places listed.

PLACE	Foreign Policy
Soviet Union	1.
China	2.
Panama	3.
Middle East	4.

Notes

Read to Learn

The Soviet Union Collapses *(page 990)*

Formulating Questions

Place an X next to the question that is answered in this passage.

___ ***What changes did Gorbachev make to try to save the Soviet Union?***

___ ***What were Reagan's policies with the Soviet Union?***

President Reagan left office in 1988, but most Americans wanted his domestic policies to continue. George H.W. Bush promised not to impose new taxes. Democrat Michael Dukakis promised to help working-class Americans, minorities, and the poor. Bush won.

President Bush continued Reagan's policies with the Soviets. Their leader Gorbachev instituted **perestroika,** or restructuring, to save the Soviet economy. He allowed some private businesses and profit-making. Gorbachev also encouraged **glasnost,** or openness. It allowed more freedom of speech and religion. Glasnost spread to Eastern Europe. Revolutions overthrew Communist leaders in Poland, Hungary, Romania, Czechoslovakia, and Bulgaria. In November 1989 the gates at the Berlin Wall were opened. Bulldozers leveled the wall, and East and West Germany reunited.

In August 1991 some Communist leaders tried to take over the Soviet government. Russian president Boris Yeltsin defied the attempt. Soon, all fifteen Soviet republics declared their independence. In December 1991 Gorbachev announced the end of the Soviet Union. The Cold War was over.

Notes | Read to Learn

A New World Order *(page 992)*

Comparing and Contrasting

Compare the United States's dealings with the two dictators.

Noriega:

___

___

___

___

Hussein:

___

___

___

___

After the Cold War, President Bush noted the arrival of a "new world order." His first crisis occurred in China. In May 1989 Chinese students and workers demonstrated for democracy. At protests in Beijing's Tiananmen Square, government forces killed many demonstrators. They arrested thousands more. Some received death sentences. The United States and other countries reduced their contacts with China.

A crisis also developed in Panama. The United States had agreed to hand over control of the Panama Canal, so it wanted to be sure Panama's government was stable and pro-American. The dictator, Manuel Noriega, would not cooperate with the United States. In late 1989, U.S. troops invaded Panama and arrested Noriega. He stood trial on drug charges in the United States. U.S. troops helped the Panamanians hold elections.

In August 1990 Iraq's dictator Saddam Hussein had troops invade Kuwait. President Bush persuaded other nations to join in a coalition to stop Hussein. On January 16, 1991, coalition forces launched Operation Desert Storm. After about six weeks of bombing and a brief ground attack, President Bush declared that Kuwait was liberated. Iraq accepted the coalition's cease-fire terms.

Domestic Challenges *(page 995)*

Analyzing Information

Place an X by the statement best supported by the passage.

___ ***President Bush's plan to cut the capital gains tax was misguided.***

___ ***Not all of the nation's problems were President Bush's fault.***

In addition to focusing on foreign affairs, President Bush had to address domestic issues. He faced a growing deficit and a recession. The recession was partly caused by an end to the Cold War. The United States began canceling orders for military equipment, resulting in the layoffs of thousands of defense workers. Many companies began **downsizing,** or laying off workers and managers to become more efficient. The federal government also faced a deficit, and had to pay interest on its debt.

Bush tried to improve the economy by suggesting a cut in the **capital gains tax.** This is a tax paid by businesses and investors when they sell stocks or real estate for a profit. He thought it would help businesses. Democrats defeated the idea. Bush finally had to break his campaign promise of "no new taxes." Many voters blamed him for increasing taxes.

Bush was the Republican nominee in the 1992 presidential election. The Democrats nominated Arkansas governor Bill Clinton, who promised to cut taxes and spending. H. Ross Perot ran as an independent candidate. A **grassroots movement,** in which groups of people organize at the local level, placed Perot on the ballot in all 50 states. Clinton won the election.

Section Wrap-up

Answer these questions to check your understanding of the entire section.

1. What events brought an end to the Cold War?

2. What domestic challenges did President George H.W. Bush's administration face?

Descriptive Writing

Write a diary entry describing your experience as a German citizen when the gates to the Berlin Wall were opened in November 1989. Your loved ones have lived on the other side of the wall for many years. What did you see, hear, smell, touch, and feel?

Chapter 30, Section 1 (Pages 1002–1005)

The Technological Revolution

Big Idea

As you read pages 1002–1005 in your textbook, complete the chart to describe products that revolutionized the computer industry.

	How It Revolutionized Computer Industry
Microprocessors	1.
Apple II	2.
Macintosh	3.
Windows	4.

Notes

Read to Learn

The Computer Changes Society *(page 1002)*

Analyzing Information

Complete the sentence.

Microprocessors making computers smaller and faster was important because

____

____

____

____

____

____

The first computer debuted in 1946 and weighed more than 30 tons. In 1959 Robert Noyce made the **integrated circuit**—a whole electronic circuit on a single silicon chip. In 1968 Noyce's company, Intel, put several integrated circuits on a single chip. These **microprocessors** made computers even smaller and faster. Stephan Wozniak and Steven Jobs founded Apple Computer in 1976, and they built the Apple II in 1977. In 1981 International Business Machines (IBM) introduced the "Personal Computer," or PC. Then Apple put out the Macintosh, which used on-screen symbols called icons.

Around the same time, IBM hired Microsoft, cofounded by Bill Gates, to make an operating system for its new PC. The system was called MS-DOS. Microsoft came out with the "Windows" operating system in 1985. Computers became essential in business. By the late 1990s, many workers were able to **telecommute,** or do their jobs from a computer at home.

In the l970s, the government began to deregulate telecommunications. The Telecommunications Act of 1996 led to the development of new technologies, such as cellular phones. Wireless digital technology also led to new products.

Notes

Read to Learn

The Rise of the Internet *(page 1004)*

Determining Cause and Effect

Reread the passage. Circle three sentences describing events that led to the development of the Internet.

Comparing and Contrasting

List one trait of the Internet and one of the World Wide Web.

Internet:

____

____

____

____

World Wide Web:

____

____

____

____

____

The U.S. Defense Department's Advanced Research Project Agency set up a computer networking system called ARPANET in 1969. This system linked computers at government agencies, defense contractors, and several universities. Doing so allowed them to communicate with one another. In 1986 the National Science Foundation built a network called NSFNet, which connected several supercomputer centers across the country. NSFNet was soon linked to ARPANET. As other computer networks were added, the system became known as the Internet. Computers on the Internet are physically connected by phone lines, cable lines, and wireless communications. As personal computers became cheaper, more people began connecting to the Internet.

In 1990 researchers at a physics laboratory in Switzerland developed the World Wide Web. It was a new way for computers on the Internet to present information. It used hypertext, or "links," and could be accessed with a Web browser. It allowed users to post information in the form of Web pages with links that enabled users to jump from Web site to Web site.

The World Wide Web started a "dot-com" economy. This name comes from the practice of using ".com" as part of the address of a business Web site. Many companies made millions of dollars for stock investors. Internet-related stocks helped fuel the economy of the 1990s, but the stocks of these companies fell in 2000. A few Web-based companies became major successes, including the bookseller Amazon.com and the search engine Google. Other companies made money using the World Wide Web by charging fees for advertising on their sites.

The World Wide Web has become more than a source of information. It has become a way to build communities. Many people have public diaries called **blogs,** short for Web logs. Web sites such as MySpace also allow users to share stories, comment on events, and post photos.

Section Wrap-up

Answer these questions to check your understanding of the entire section.

1. How did the computer evolve from a scientific tool to a household appliance?

2. How did the Internet change the way businesses operate?

Descriptive Writing

In the space provided write a diary entry that describes what a typical day would be like if there were no computers anywhere, including in your school and home.

Chapter 30, Section 2 (Pages 1008–1015)

The Clinton Years

Big Idea

As you read pages 1008–1015 in your textbook, complete the outline using the major headings of the section.

The Clinton Years

I. Clinton's Agenda
  A. ____________________
  B. ____________________
  C. ____________________
  D. ____________________
II. ____________________
  A. ____________________
  B. ____________________
  C. ____________________
III. ____________________
  A. ____________________
  B. ____________________
IV. ____________________
  A. ____________________
  B. ____________________
  C. ____________________

Notes

Read to Learn

Clinton's Agenda *(page 1008)*

Comparing and Contrasting

List one success and one failure of Clinton's domestic agenda.

Success:

____

____

____

Failure:

____

____

____

President Clinton believed the huge federal deficit was a problem. It forced the government to borrow money and drove up interest rates. Clinton wanted to lower interest rates to help businesses and consumers borrow money and spur economic growth. However, reducing government spending would involve cutting programs such as Social Security and Medicare. Clinton decided to raise taxes instead. This unpopular plan narrowly passed Congress.

Clinton created a task force led by his wife, Hillary Rodham Clinton, to create a plan that guaranteed health care to all Americans. The plan put too much of the burden of payment on employers. Small businesses, the insurance industry, and many members of Congress opposed it. It never came to a vote in Congress.

Clinton succeeded in having the Family Medical Leave Act passed. It gave workers time off for some family issues. Clinton also created the AmeriCorps program. It put students to work improving low-income housing, teaching children, and cleaning up the environment. Clinton also got Congress to pass a gun-control law and a bill that gave states money to build new prisons and hire more police officers.

Notes

Read to Learn

Republicans Gain Control of Congress (page 1010)

Problems and Solutions

Write the solution.

Problem: Congress and President Clinton clashed over the federal budget.

Solution:

Despite his successes, Clinton was unpopular by 1994. He had raised taxes and did not fix health care. Republicans in Congress created the Contract with America. It called for lower taxes, welfare reform, and a balanced budget. The Republicans won a majority in both houses in the 1994 elections. The House passed most of the Contract with America, but the Senate defeated parts of the contract, and Clinton vetoed others.

In 1995 Republicans in Congress clashed with Clinton over the new federal budget. Clinton vetoed several Republican budget proposals, claiming that they cut into social programs too much. The Republicans thought that if they stood firm, the president would finally approve the budget. Clinton did not budge, and the government shut down for lack of funds. Clinton regained much of the support he had lost. The Republicans realized they would have to work with the president. They eventually passed a budget as well as the Health Insurance Portability Act and the Welfare Reform Act.

In the 1996 presidential election, Clinton was very popular. The economy was good and crime rates and unemployment were down. Clinton won the election. Republicans kept control of Congress.

Clinton's Second Term (page 1012)

Identifying the Main Idea

Why was Clinton impeached?

During Clinton's second term, he and Congress continued to shrink the deficit. In 1997 Clinton presented a balanced budget to Congress. By 1998 the government collected more money than it spent. Clinton focused on the nation's children. He asked Congress to pass a $500 per child tax credit. He also signed the Children's Health Insurance Program, which provided health insurance to children whose parents could not afford it. Clinton also increased aid to students.

By 1998 Clinton became involved in a scandal. He was accused of setting up illegal loans for an Arkansas real estate company while he was governor of Arkansas. Kenneth Starr, a former federal judge, was appointed to investigate. A new scandal emerged involving a personal relationship between Clinton and a White House intern. Some evidence showed that Clinton had committed **perjury,** or lied under oath, about the relationship. Starr determined that Clinton had obstructed justice and committed perjury. The House began impeachment hearings and passed two articles of impeachment in December. The Senate voted that Clinton was not guilty, but Clinton's reputation had suffered.

Notes

Read to Learn

Clinton Foreign Policy *(page 1013)*

Predicting

Based on the passage, make a prediction about future U.S. relations with the Middle East.

Clinton faced many foreign policy challenges. In 1991 military leaders in Haiti overthrew the elected president. To restore democracy, Clinton urged the United Nations to set a trade embargo on Haiti and ordered an invasion of the country. Former president Jimmy Carter, however, convinced Haiti's rulers to step down. A civil war between Serbs, Croatians, and Bosnians began in Bosnia. Serbs began **ethnic cleansing,** the brutal removal of an ethnic group from an area. The United States convinced NATO to attack the Serbs and force them to negotiate. When another war broke out in Serbian Kosovo, NATO again used force to end it. In 1996 Iraq attacked the Kurds, an ethnic group in Iraq. The United States attacked Iraqi military posts. Clinton repeatedly failed to broker peace in the Middle East between Israel and the Palestinians.

Section Wrap-up

Answer these questions to check your understanding of the entire section.

1. Why was Clinton able to achieve reelection in 1996?

2. How was the nation involved in world affairs during the Clinton presidency?

Persuasive Writing

In the space provided write a newspaper editorial that presents your opinion on whether a president's personal life should be exposed to the American public.

Chapter 30, Section 3 (Pages 1016–1019)

A New Wave of Immigration

Big Idea

As you read pages 1016–1019 in your textbook, complete the graphic organizer by listing the effects of the Immigration Act of 1965.

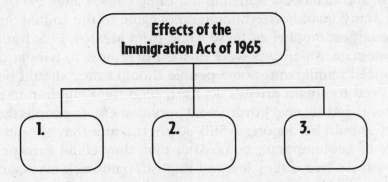

Effects of the Immigration Act of 1965

1.

2.

3.

Notes

Read to Learn

Changes in Immigration Law (page 1016)

Making Inferences

Put an X by the inference supported by the passage.

___ ***The 1986 Immigration Reform and Control Act was mostly successful.***

___ ***The 1986 Immigration Reform and Control Act did not stop illegal immigration.***

The Immigration Act of 1965 got rid of the national origins quota system and gave preference to people with close relatives who were U.S. citizens. This caused **migration chains.** As immigrants became citizens, they sent for relatives in their home countries. Immigration from non-European countries grew. Some newcomers were **refugees**—people who flee their country due to persecution based on race, religion, or political beliefs.

Congress passed the Immigration Reform and Control Act of 1986 to stop illegal immigration. It punished employers who hired illegal immigrants. It made border controls stronger. The law also gave **amnesty**—or a pardon—to people who had entered the country illegally before January 1, 1982. But illegal immigration was still a problem. In 1996 Congress passed a law that required families sponsoring an immigrant to have an income above the poverty level. It also strengthened border control and toughened laws against smuggling people into the country. The terrorist attacks of September 11, 2001, also led to changes in immigration laws. The USA Patriot Act made border control and customs inspections even stronger.

Notes

Read to Learn

Recent Immigration *(page 1018)*

Detecting Bias

Why would Latinos protest a bill allowing criminal prosecution of unauthorized aliens?

____

____

____

____

____

____

____

____

Formulating Questions

Write two questions you have after reading the passage.

1. ______________________

____

____

____

____

2. ______________________

____

____

____

More immigrants moved to some states than other states. In 1990 California, Texas, New York, Illinois, and Florida had the most immigrants. More than half of immigrants who arrived in the 1990s came from Latin America. Approximately one-fourth came from Asia. Many immigrants were refugees. These included Cubans coming to the United States after the 1959 Cuban Revolution. The Vietnam War also created refugees. Many people from Vietnam, Laos, and Cambodia settled in the United States after 1974.

Many unauthorized immigrants came to the United States. The largest number of these came from Mexico, El Salvador, and Guatemala. Americans were divided over how to handle unauthorized immigrants. Some people thought they should be allowed to obtain driver's licenses, send their children to public school, and receive government services. Other people thought they should be deported. Still others thought they should be able to get temporary visas. After that, they could earn permanent residence if they learned English, paid back taxes, and had no criminal record.

In 2006 President George W. Bush focused on immigration reform. Congress was split on how to solve the problem of undocumented aliens. Most senators wanted tougher enforcement of immigration laws. They also wanted some kind of earned citizenship for undocumented immigrants, or aliens. The House wanted to build a wall along the U.S.-Mexican border. Congress debated a bill that would allow criminal prosecution of unauthorized aliens. Latinos throughout the country protested this.

Other options were suggested. Some wanted to start a guest-worker program and find a way to legalize unauthorized immigrants that were already in the country. Many undocumented immigrants had lived in the United States for years. Many had raised families. Their children born in the United States were citizens and could not be deported. Deporting undocumented aliens would mean separating family members.

Section Wrap-up

Answer these questions to check your understanding of the entire section.

1. How did patterns of immigration into the United States change after 1965?

2. What was one way Congress tried to address the problem of unauthorized immigration?

Expository Writing

In the space provided write a short newspaper article that compares and contrasts two approaches to immigration reform.

Chapter 30, Section 4 (Pages 1022–1025)

An Interdependent World

Big Idea

As you read pages 1022–1025 in your textbook, complete the graphic organizer to chart the major political and economic problems facing the world at the turn of the century.

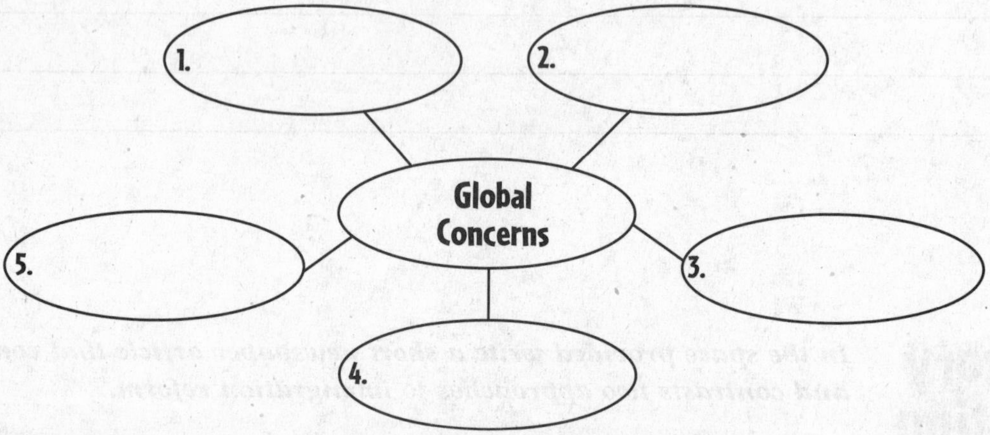

Notes

Read to Learn

The New Global Economy *(page 1022)*

Identifying the Main Idea

Why were regional trade pacts, such as NAFTA, created?

The idea that the world is becoming more linked and interdependent is called **globalism.** Americans who support international trade believe it helps U.S. businesses sell goods abroad. They also think importing low-cost goods keeps inflation and interest rates low. Others think the global economy causes manufacturing jobs to move to nations where wages are low.

In the 1990s, trade pacts increased international trade. The North American Free Trade Agreement (NAFTA) joined Canada, the United States, and Mexico in a free-trade zone. The European Union (EU) joined many European nations. It promoted economic and political cooperation. The EU set up the **euro,** common money used by member nations. The Asia Pacific Economic Cooperation (APEC) set up a Pacific trade community.

The World Trade Organization (WTO) promoted world trade. It helped form trade agreements and settled trade disputes. China played a big part in world trade. It was a huge market for American goods. In 2000 a U.S. bill gave China permanent normal trade relation status, despite concerns that inexpensive Chinese goods would flood the U.S. market.

Notes | Read to Learn

Global Environmentalism *(page 1025)*

Synthesizing Information

What two discoveries increased awareness of environmental issues?

1. ____________________

____

____

____

2. ____________________

____

____

____

Drawing Conclusions

Circle two sentences that support the following conclusion:

The Kyoto Protocol was not entirely successful.

With the rise of globalism, people realized that the environment is also a global system. In the 1980s, scientists found out that chemicals called chlorofluorocarbons (CFCs) could break down ozone in Earth's atmosphere. Ozone is a gas that protects life on Earth from the ultraviolet rays of the sun. CFCs were used in air conditioners and refrigerators. In the late 1980s, scientists found a large hole in the ozone layer above Antarctica. Many people wanted to stop the manufacture of CFCs. In 1987, the United States and other nations agreed to phase out the manufacture of CFCs and other chemicals that might be weakening the ozone layer.

In the early 1990s, scientists found evidence of **global warming.** This is an increase in average world temperatures over time. This rise in temperature could lead to more droughts and other types of extreme weather. Many experts believe that carbon dioxide emissions from factories and power plants cause global warming. Others disagree. The global warming issue is controversial because the cost of controlling emissions would fall on industries. These costs would eventually be passed on to consumers. Developing nations that are beginning to industrialize would be hurt the most.

In 1997 thirty-eight nations and the EU signed the Kyoto Protocol. The nations promised to reduce emissions, though very few nations put this into effect. President Clinton did not present the Kyoto Protocol to the Senate because most senators opposed it. In 2001 President George W. Bush withdrew the United States from the treaty. He believed that it had flaws.

Section Wrap-up

Answer these questions to check your understanding of the entire section.

1. Why do many people support international trade?

2. What environmental issues have become important internationally?

Informative Writing

In the space provided write a short magazine article about the ban on CFCs. Present facts in an objective way, explaining why CFCs were banned and who banned them.

Chapter 31, Section 1 (Pages 1032–1035)

America Enters a New Century

Big Idea

As you read pages 1032–1035 in your textbook, complete the graphic organizer by charting some key postelection events culminating in George W. Bush's victory.

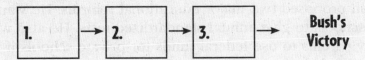

1. → 2. → 3. → Bush's Victory

Notes | Read to Learn

The Election of 2000 *(page 1032)*

Drawing Conclusions

Underline statements in the passage that support this conclusion:

The U.S. president is not always elected by a majority of voters.

In the 2000 presidential election, Democrat Al Gore ran against Republican George W. Bush. The election was one of the closest in American history. Gore won the popular vote. However, to win the presidency, candidates have to win a majority of the electoral votes. Both candidates needed Florida's 25 electoral votes to win. The vote in Florida was so close that state law required a recount using vote-counting machines. Thousands of ballots were tossed out, however, because the machines could not read the voting cards. Gore asked for a hand recount in strongly Democratic counties. A battle began over how to count a ballot when the **chad** was still attached. A chad is the piece of cardboard punched out on a voting card.

Florida law required election results be certified by a certain date. The Florida Supreme Court postponed the date, but some counties still could not meet the new deadline. On December 12, 2000, the United States Supreme Court ruled that there was not enough time for a manual recount before the electoral votes had to be cast. The ruling left Bush the winner.

Notes

Read to Learn

Bush Becomes President *(page 1035)*

Making Inferences

Write an X by the inference that can be made based on the last paragraph.

___ ***The United States was unprepared for an attack on its own soil.***

___ ***The United States was entering a war against terrorism.***

Predicting

Make a prediction about educational reforms based on the No Child Left Behind Act.

____

____

____

____

____

____

____

____

____

Bush became the forty-third president of the United States. His first priority was to cut taxes to boost the economy. During the campaign, the economy began to slow. The stock market dropped sharply, some companies went out of business, and unemployment began to rise. Congress passed a $1.35 trillion tax cut. Bush's plan introduced tax cuts over a 10-year period. However, it also gave taxpayers an immediate rebate. By mid-2001 Americans began receiving tax rebate checks. Bush hoped the rebates would put about $40 billion into the economy to prevent a recession.

Bush proposed two major educational reforms. He wanted public schools to give annual standardized tests. He also wanted to allow parents to use federal funds for private schools if their public schools were performing poorly. Congress did not support the idea of using federal funds for private schools. It did support the idea of states being required to annually test students' reading and math skills. This law became known as the No Child Left Behind Act.

Bush also focused on a Medicare reform bill that added prescription drug benefits to Medicare. The bill was controversial. Some opponents argued it would be too costly. Others believed the law did not go far enough. However, the bill was passed in November 2003.

Congress reacted to a number of corporate scandals. The most famous took place at a large energy trading company called Enron. The company's leaders cost investors and employees billions of dollars. The company eventually went bankrupt. Congress passed a new law—the Sarbanes-Oxley Act—that tightened accounting rules and created tougher penalties for dishonest executives.

Bush called for new military programs that would meet the needs of the post-Cold War era. He favored a program known as **strategic defense.** Its purpose was to develop missiles and other devices that can shoot down nuclear missiles. Bush argued that missile defense was needed because hostile nations were developing long-range missiles.

Debate about the nation's military programs continued during the summer of 2001. Then, a disastrous event changed everything. On September 11, 2001, terrorists attacked the World Trade Center in New York City and the Pentagon in Washington, D.C. A new war had begun.

Section Wrap-up

Answer these questions to check your understanding of the entire section.

1. What unusual circumstances surrounded the outcome of the 2000 presidential election?

2. Summarize the proposals Bush made early in his presidency.

Persuasive Writing

In the space provided write a letter to your representative in Congress voicing your support or opposition to a proposed constitutional amendment abolishing the electoral vote in presidential elections.

Chapter 31, Section 2 (Pages 1036–1041)

The War on Terrorism Begins

Big Idea

As you read pages 1036–1041 in your textbook, complete the graphic organizer to show the different reasons terrorists attack Americans.

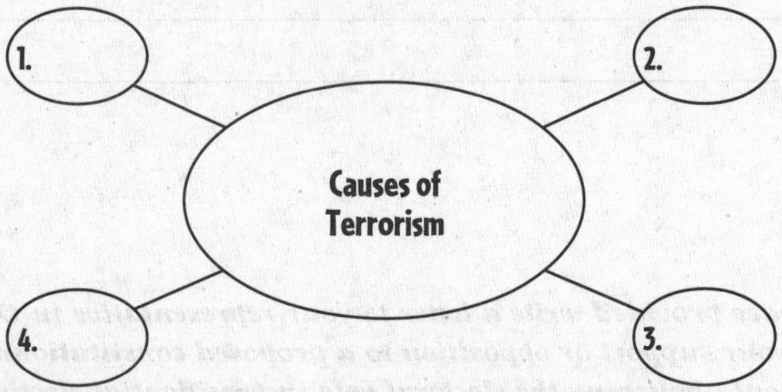

Notes

Read to Learn

September 11, 2001 *(page 1036)*

Formulating Questions

Write one question you have after reading the passage.

On September 11, 2001, hijackers crashed two passenger jets into the World Trade Center in New York City. Hijackers crashed a third jet into the Pentagon in Washington, D.C. A fourth plane crashed in Pennsylvania. Thousands of people were killed. President Bush declared a national emergency and put the armed forces on high alert. Intelligence sources and the FBI determined that the attacks were the work of Osama bin Laden and his group, al-Qaeda. The attacks were acts of **terrorism**—the use of violence by nongovernmental groups against civilians to achieve a political goal.

Fundamentalist militants wanted to topple pro-Western governments in the Middle East. They used terrorism to reach their goals. In the 1970s, several Middle Eastern nations began providing terrorist groups with money and weapons to fight the United States and Israel. When a government secretly supports terrorism, it is called **state-sponsored terrorism.** Bin Laden operated al-Qaeda from Afghanistan. Al-Qaeda attacked American embassies in Tanzania and Kenya and the USS *Cole* in 2000.

Notes

Read to Learn

A New War Begins *(page 1039)*

Identifying the Main Idea

Read the second paragraph. Write the main idea. Write one detail that supports it.

Main Idea:

___

___

___

Detail:

___

___

___

Distinguishing Fact from Opinion

Read the statements. Write* F *next to one that tells a fact. Write* O *next to the one that includes an opinion.

___ ***He warned that the war on terrorism would be a war like none other.***

___ ***Several occurrences of anthrax were found, but no suspects were arrested.***

President Bush demanded the Taliban—the rulers in Afghanistan—turn over bin Laden and his followers and close all terrorist camps. He declared that the war on terrorism would not end until every terrorist group had been defeated. Secretary of State Colin Powell worked to form an international coalition to support the United States. Secretary of Defense Donald Rumsfeld began sending American troops, aircraft, and warships to the Middle East. He warned that the war on terrorism would be a war like none other. President Bush announced that the United States would not tolerate countries that helped or harbored terrorists. He also warned Americans that the war would not end quickly.

There are several ways to fight terrorism. One major way is to cut off terrorists' funds. President Bush issued an order to hold the money of several individuals and organizations suspected of terrorism. He also asked other nations to help. Within weeks, about 80 other nations also held the money of individuals and groups suspected of terrorism. The president also created a new federal agency—the Office of Homeland Security. Its purpose is to coordinate the dozens of federal agencies and departments working to prevent terrorism.

Bush asked Congress to create a law to help agencies track down terrorist suspects. This took time. Congress had to make sure the law would protect Americans' Fourth Amendment rights. In October 2001 Bush signed a new antiterrorist law—the USA Patriot Act. The law permitted secret searches and allowed authorities to use a single nationwide search warrant. The law also made it easier to wiretap suspects.

The Office of Homeland Security struggled to manage all of the federal agencies now fighting terrorism. President Bush asked Congress to combine all of the agencies into the Department of Homeland Security.

Terrorists posed a new threat in October 2001 when they began to use the mail to spread anthrax. **Anthrax** is a type of bacteria that can become lethal if left untreated. The United States, Russia, and Iraq are among the nations that have used anthrax to create biological weapons. Several occurrences of anthrax were found, but no suspects were arrested.

On October 7, 2001, the United States began bombing al-Qaeda's camps and the Taliban's forces in Afghanistan. President Bush explained to the nation that Islam and the Afghan people were not the enemy. He said that the United States would send food, medicine, and other supplies to Afghan refugees. The attack on the Taliban was only the beginning of the war on terrorism.

Section Wrap-up

Answer these questions to check your understanding of the entire section.

1. What was the political goal of Middle East terrorists and how did they try to achieve it?

2. How did the United States respond to the terrorist attacks on the World Trade Center and the Pentagon?

Informative Writing

Write a front-page newspaper article covering the events of September 11, 2001. Tell the who, what, where, when, and how of the events. Include at least one quote from an "eyewitness," as well as a headline.

Chapter 31, Section 3 (Pages 1042–1047)

The Invasion of Iraq

Big Idea

As you read pages 1042–1047 in your textbook, complete the graphic organizer to show the different groups in Iraq.

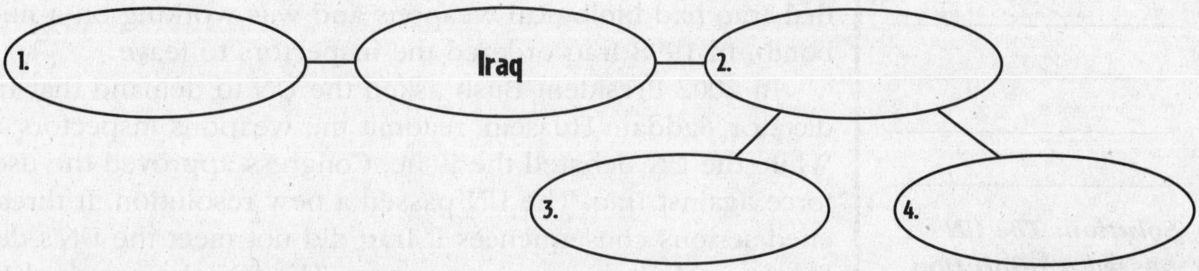

Notes

Read to Learn

The War on Terror Continues *(page 1042)*

Analyzing Information

Write an X by the statement the author would most likely agree with.

___ ***Afghanistan is on a slow road to recovery.***

___ ***Democracy probably will not work in Afghanistan.***

In October 2001 the United States launched a war in Afghanistan. The goal was to bring down the Taliban regime and capture Osama bin Laden. The United States also began sending military aid to the Northern Alliance, an Afghan group who had fought the Taliban for many years. In December 2001 the Taliban government collapsed. Afghanistan slowly began to recover from decades of war, but its people are still poor. In 2004 Afghanistan elected a president in its first national democratic election, but the country still suffers from violence.

American intelligence agencies believe Osama bin Laden entered Pakistan to hide out in its mountains. Pakistan has not officially allowed American troops to enter its country to search for bin Laden. Some news reports, however, suggest that U.S. Special Forces may be operating in the region. Pakistan also has been searching for al-Qaeda and Taliban forces. However, Osama bin Laden has not been captured. The United States continues its worldwide hunt for al-Qaeda members. In 2003 Pakistan and the United States captured Khalid Shaikh Mohammed. He was suspected of planning the September 11 attacks.

Notes

Read to Learn

Iraq and Weapons of Mass Destruction *(page 1044)*

Problems and Solutions

Write the problem.

Problem:

____

____

____

____

____

____

Solution: The UN passed a resolution threatening serious consequences.

President Bush worried terrorists might acquire **weapons of mass destruction** (WMD), which can kill many people at once. Nuclear, chemical, and biological weapons are examples of weapons of mass destruction. The United States' old policy of deterrence would not work against state-sponsored terrorism.

In 2002 President Bush warned the nation about an "axis of evil" made up of Iraq, Iran, and North Korea. He considered Iraq an immediate threat because it had used chemical weapons before. After the Gulf War, UN inspectors had found evidence that Iraq had biological weapons and was working on a nuclear bomb. In 1998 Iraq ordered the inspectors to leave.

In 2002 President Bush asked the UN to demand that Iraq's dictator, Saddam Hussein, readmit the weapons inspectors. While the UN debated the issue, Congress approved the use of force against Iraq. The UN passed a new resolution. It threatened serious consequences if Iraq did not meet the UN's deadline to readmit weapons inspectors. The UN also required Iraq to declare its weapons of mass destruction.

Confronting Iraq *(page 1046)*

Formulating Questions

Place an X by the question answered in the passage.

___ ***How and why would the new Iraqi government train its own forces?***

___ ***In what ways did fighting continue after Bush declared an end to major combat in Iraq?***

Iraq agreed to readmit weapons inspectors, but denied it had weapons of mass destruction. The Bush administration thought Iraq was lying and pushed for a war resolution in the UN Security Council. Although France and Russia refused to back it, the United States and Britain prepared for war. World opinion divided between those supporting the United States and those against the attack. Antiwar protests erupted around the world.

On March 20, 2003, U.S.-led coalition forces attacked Iraq and quickly seized control. On May 1, President Bush declared that major combat was over, but bombings, sniper attacks, and battles continued to plague American troops. Some groups carrying out attacks were linked to al-Qaeda. Other attacks were by ethnic or religious militias. Between 2003 and 2006, insurgents killed more than 3,000 American soldiers.

The United States was now trying to prevent a civil war while setting up a new Iraqi government. As the fighting dragged on, and no weapons of mass destruction were found, domestic support for the war began to decline. The Bush administration believed the best solution would be to set up a democratic Iraqi government that could train its own forces. Iraqi's first free elections were held in 2005. Voters also approved a new constitution.

Section Wrap-up

Answer these questions to check your understanding of the entire section.

1. Why did the United States launch a war in Afghanistan?

2. Who were the supporters of the Iraq War? Who opposed it?

Expository Writing

In the space provided write a brief speech explaining the important connection between weapons of mass destruction and Middle East terrorism today. Assume you will give the speech at your school's Current Events Club's monthly meeting.

Chapter 31, Section 4 (Pages 1048–1055)

A Time of Challenges

Big Idea

As you read pages 1048–1055 in your textbook, complete the outline using major headings from the section.

A Time of Challenges

I. The Election of 2004

II. Security vs. Liberty

   A. ______

   B. ______

   C. ______

III. ______

   A. ______

   B. ______

   C. ______

   D. ______

   E. ______

Notes

Read to Learn

The Election of 2004 *(page 1048)*

Evaluating Information

Why is it important to know about high voter turnout in the 2004 election?

______

______

______

______

______

______

______

______

As the war in Iraq dragged on, President Bush's popularity with Americans sank. Osama bin Laden had not been captured. Inspectors had not found weapons of mass destruction in Iraq. Many Americans were also upset by the abuse of Iraqi prisoners by American guards at Abu Ghraib prison. The war on terror and the war in Iraq took over the 2004 presidential election. Republicans renominated President Bush. Democrats nominated John Kerry, a Vietnam veteran who turned against the war after his return. His opponents used his actions from the 1970s against him in the 2004 election.

The candidates offered the country two distinct choices. President Bush promised to continue cutting taxes while building a strong national defense. Kerry pledged to focus on domestic issues such as health care and Social Security. He also promised to continue the war on terror. The candidates took opposite stands on most social issues. Nearly 61% of eligible voters went to the polls on Election Day—the highest turnout since 1968. The election was decided in Ohio in a very close vote. Despite the war in Iraq, voters felt it was safer to reelect President Bush.

Notes | Read to Learn

Security vs. Liberty (page 1050)

Comparing and Contrasting

List two ways the courts and the Bush administration differed in their views about civil liberties.

1. ________________

____

____

2. ________________

____

____

The war on terror increased tension in the United States between national security and civil liberties. Questions arose about what to do with al-Qaeda prisoners. President Bush decided to hold them indefinitely at Guantanamo Bay, an American military base in Cuba. Some people questioned this. They argued that the prisoners should have the same rights as Americans in custody. The administration claimed the prisoners were illegal enemy combatants—not suspects charged with crimes.

The Supreme Court disagreed. It ruled that prisoners should have their cases heard in court. The Bush administration reacted by creating military tribunals to hear the cases. The Court ruled against that too. The president then asked Congress to pass laws setting up tribunals that were acceptable to the Court. In doing this, Congress gave the prisoners some rights. However, it allowed tribunals to hold prisoners indefinitely without trial.

The National Security Agency expanded its use of wiretapping to include calls made to suspected terrorists overseas. Civil rights groups feared this violated Americans' free speech and privacy rights. A federal judge declared the practice unconstitutional.

A Stormy Second Term (page 1051)

Making Generalizations

Circle the generalization that can be made based on the passage.

Many Americans lost confidence in Bush during his second term.

Bush was responsible for the Gulf Coast damage in 2005.

President Bush began his second term with an effort to reform the Social Security system. The plan failed, but Congress did enact Bush's prescription drug program.

President Bush was able to move the Supreme Court in a more conservative direction. He nominated federal judge John G. Roberts, Jr., to replace Chief Justice William Rehnquist, who had died. He also nominated Samuel Alito, Jr., to replace Justice Sandra Day O'Connor, who had retired.

On August 29, 2005, Hurricane Katrina smashed into the Gulf Coast. Thousands of people became homeless. At least 1,200 died. Floodwaters breached the levees around low-lying areas in New Orleans, Louisiana. Many people were forced onto roofs to await rescue. Thousands more found shelter in the convention center and Superdome, where there was little food or water. The government was unprepared in its response.

Confidence in the Bush administration dropped sharply. Congress suffered several scandals. Federal spending rose rapidly, partly because of earmarks added to spending bills. **Earmarks** specify money for particular projects, such as building a bridge, usually in a Congressperson's own state. In the 2006 election, Democrats gained control of the House and the Senate.

Section Wrap-up

Answer these questions to check your understanding of the entire section.

1. How did the war on terror also threaten Americans' civil liberties?

2. What challenges did President Bush face in his second term?

Descriptive Writing

In the space provided write three entries in your diary for August 29–31, 2005. You live in New Orleans. Describe the events of those days as you experience them. Be as vivid as possible in your description, using all five senses in your writing.